Where Are They Now?

Former Aston Villa Players

Dear Dad,
Happy Christmas
lots of love
Caitlyn
xxx

Jamie Spoor

Where
are they
now

www.where-are-they-now.co.uk/aston-villa

First published in 2019 by
Media House Books

© Media House Books 2019

ISBN 978-1-912027-58-3

Original cover design by Marten Sealby

Introduction

Aston Villa Football Club, one of the Football League's founding fathers and an iconic symbol of the English game.

Twenty one major honours and one of only five English clubs to be crowned champions of Europe, the Villa sit right up there with United, Liverpool and Arsenal in the upper echelons of the sport. Undoubtedly the pride of the Midlands, Villa regained their rightful place in the Premier League for 2019/20 after being led to play-off glory by one of their own, Dean Smith. I believe they're back where they truly belong.

It was on my second visit to Villa Park - under the floodlights in a midweek game - that I first got the feel of just why this is a special club in the hearts of so many. I could sense the history, the passion and the love the Villa faithful had for the club.

In this book, we take a look at the colourful, the controversial and the charismatic as we take you on a magical mystery ride through Villa's history featuring some of the greatest players ever to wear the famous claret and blue. You may think that most former players take the well trodden path of becoming a manager, coach or agent and whilst that may be true, often it is a tale of the unexpected. For example, have you heard the one about the former Villa star who became a taekwando champion at the age of 65? What about the former European Cup winning keeper who continues to always deliver as a courier? It's all here.

From "Mr Aston Villa" Charles Aitken to journeyman Willie Young and just about everyone in between, this fascinating insight is a must have for any died-in-the-wool claret and blue. It tells the story of the famous, historic club's exploits through the eyes of those to have represented them - some with brilliant distinction, others considerably less so! It's the perfect gift you've all been waiting for.

We hope you enjoy reading the book as much as we've enjoyed writing it. UTV!

Thank you to everyone that has helped to put this together.

Jamie

AITKEN, Charlie
Defender
Born: *Edinburgh, Scotland*
Playing career: *Gorebridge Juniors, Edinburgh Thistle, Aston Villa, New York Cosmos (1959-1977)*
Widely considered to be Villa's greatest ever player, Charlie Aitken's appearance record is almost certain never to be beaten. The Scottish defender turned out 660 times in claret and blue during his 17 years with the club. He played in three separate divisions, as well as the League Cup, FA Cup and UEFA Cup—and the Charity Shield, too. Having singed from Edinburgh Thistle in 1959, the Scotsman had to bide his time before eventually making his Villa debut almost a full year after joining. From there, however, he established himself at left-back, making the spot his for years to come. Synonymous with the club's glory days, upon retirement he opened a jewellery and antiques shop in Birmingham after a short spell in the USA with New York Cosmos.

ADAM, Jimmy
Midfielder
Born: *Blantyre, Scotland*
Playing career: *Blantyre Celtic, Aldershot, Spennymoor United, Luton Town, Aston Villa, Stoke City, Falkirk, South Melbourne Hellas (1950-1964)*
Adam began his career in the lower leagues with Aldershot and Spennymoor, and then made 138 appearances for Luton. He moved to Villa Park after the Hatters relegation, and spent two seasons in the Midlands before moving on again to Stoke. He later migrated to Australia where he had a spell as player-manager of South Melbourne Hellas. Now aged 88, Adam still lives north of the border.

AGATHE, Didier
Wing-back
Born: *Saint-Pierre, France*
Playing career: *Montpellier, Raith Rovers, Hibernian, Celtic, Aston Villa, JS Saint-Pierroise (1992-2007)*
Agathe began his career at Montpellier in his native France, before moving to Scotland where he played for Raith Rovers and then Hibernian. A string of impressive performances earned him a move to Celtic, where he enjoyed the most successful spell of his career, winning three league titles and the UEFA Cup. After six years in Glasgow, he re-signed for former boss Martin O'Neill on a short term deal at Villa Park. He had an underwhelming spell in the Midlands, making six substitute appearances without starting a single game. Since retiring, he returned to his homeland to set up a football Academy.

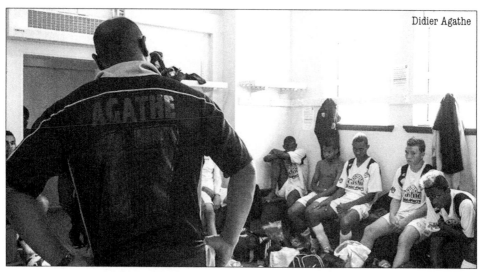

Didier Agathe

ALDIS, Peter
Defender
Born: *Kings Heath*
Playing career: *Hay Green, Aston Villa (1948-1960)*
Birmingham-born Aldis played 294 games for Villa in league and cup, having joined from local club Hay Green. In the early post-war years, he moved to Hinckley Athletic and then on to Villa in 1949. An integral part of the Midlands club 1957 FA Cup win under Eric Houghton's management, his headed goal against Sunderland was not only his solitary goal for Villa - but also a 35-yard header! Now aged 81, he had a spell as player/manager of non league Alvechurch before drifting out of the game.

ALDRIDGE, Albert
Full-back
Born: *Walsall*
Died: 1891
Playing career: *Walsall Swifts, West Bromwich Albion, Walsall Town Swifts, Aston Villa (1889-1890)*
Twice capped by England in the fledgling days of the professional game, Aldridge began his career at hometown club Walsall Swifts where he spent six seasons. Moving to West Bromwich Albion, Aldridge won the trophy with the Baggies in 1888, then moved back to Walsall Swifts before a move to Villa followed in 1889. He made 14 appearances as they finished runner ups in the First Division that year. Aldridge tragically died at only 27 years of age due to illness, at his home in Walsall in June 1891.

ALLBACK, Marcus
Striker
Born: *Gothenburg, Sweden*
Playing career: *Lyngby Boldklub, Bari, Heerenveen, Aston Villa, Hansa Rostock, Copenhagen (1992-2011)*
A much travelled Swedish international, Allback arrived at Aston Villa in 2002, but became third choice forward, behind Juan Pablo Angel and Darius Vassell, throughout his two year stay in the Midlands. At the end of his contract, he joined Hansa Rostock and then moved on to Copenhagen before he rejoined his first professional club Orgryte. He played in five major tournaments for Sweden and later became assistant manager of the national team. Since stepping down from this role after Euro 2016, he has done some coaching and commentary work back in his homeland.

ALLEN, Jimmy
Defender
Born: *Poole*
Died: 1995
Playing career: *Portsmouth, Aston Villa (1932-1944)*
Allen played 132 times for Pompey, scoring once and earning an FA Cup runners up medal. Villa smashed the British transfer record when they signed Allen in 1934 for a fee of £10,775. He played in 147 league matches for Villa, scoring two goals and captained the side to the Second Division title in 1938. He was in his prime when his career was disrupted by the outbreak of war. Forced to retire through injury, he had a five year tenure as manager of Colchester United before going on to run a pub in Portsmouth. Allen died in a Southsea nursing home in 1995 at the age of 85.

ALLEN, Malcolm
Striker
Born: *Deiniolen, Gwynedd, Wales*
Playing career: *Watford, Aston Villa, Norwich City, Newcastle United (1985-1995)*
No relation to namesake Jimmy, Welsh-speaking Allen began his career with Watford, scoring in an FA Cup semi final for the Hornets.

Marcus Allback

He was loaned to Aston Villa by new Watford boss Dave Bassett but made only four league appearances during his brief spell in the Midlands. Allen retired through injury in 1995 and returned to Wales where he became a coach at Aberystwyth and a television pundit for Welsh Channels S4C's Sgorio and Radio Cymru's Camp Lawn. In 2006 he appeared in court in Watford for assault charges and in 2008 he was handed a suspended sentence for drink driving offences. Allen played 14 times for Wales and scored three goals. Origianally from Deiniolen, Malcolm Allen released his autobiography in 2009. See: https://www.ylolfa.com/authors/702/malcolm-allen

Malcolm Allen

AMOO, Ryan
Midfielder or right-back
Born: *Leicester*
Playing career: *Aston Villa, Northampton Town (loan), Northampton Town, Highfield Rangers, Lincoln City, Barwell, Solihull Moors, Thurnby Nirvana (2000-2011)*
Amoo started his career at Villa and featured in the Youth-Cup winning side of 2002. He never made a senior appearance though in two years at Villa Park and moved on to Northampton in 2004. A succession of lower and non-league clubs followed, notably at Lincoln City where he played over 70 times for the Imps. Amoo, still only 35, continues to ply his trade in the lower echelons of league football for his hometown side Leicester Nirvana of the United Counties Premier Division.

ANDERSON, Willie
Winger
Born: *Liverpool*
Playing career: *Manchester United, Aston Villa, Cardiff City, Portland Timbers (loan), Portland Timbers, Wichita Wings (indoor), Portland Timbers (indoor) (1962-1982)*
An FA Youth Cup winner in 1963-1964 with Manchester United having joined them straight from school. Made his league debut as a 16 year old on the opposite wing to another rookie, George Best. He found that his chances were limited even though he played in a FA Cup and European Cup semi-finals and was sold to Aston Villa in January 1967 for £20,000. Moved to Oregon, USA to work as an executive with a local radio station. Anderson also coached BSC Portland and covered Portland Timbers matches for US TV network KPTV.

ANGEL, Juan Pablo
Forward
Born: *Medellin, Colombia*
Playing career: *Atletico Nacional, River Plate, Villa, New York Red Bulls, LA Galaxy, Chivas (1993-2014)*
The Colombian international striker is fondly remembered as a cult hero at Villa Park. He joined the club as a record signing, for £9.5 million in 2001 from River Plate and quickly became a fans' favourite.

During his time in claret and blue, Angel hit 62 goals in 205 games in all competitions - only Dwight Yorke and Gabriel Agbonlahor have scored more in the Premier League era for the club. Angel only retired from playing in his native Colombia three years ago, and has enrolled on the UEFA B Licence Course as he looks to return to the game in a coaching capacity. Now lives in Medellin, Columbia and acts as an ambassador for Mercedes Benz. Twitter: https://twitter.com/JUANPABLOANGEL

ANSELL, Barry
Defender
Born: *Birmingham* **Died:** 2018
Playing career: *Aston Villa (1967-1968)*
A Birmingham-born centre back who played a solitary match for Villa. Ansell can claim to have played alongside Claret and Blue legend Peter Withe - but only after he had moved on to South African second tier side Arcadia Shepherds. His one and only match for Villa came in a 3-0 defeat at Cardiff on Boxing Day 1967 - long before Withe arrived. After moving to South Africa, Ansell worked as a property developer and flew back for a reunion at Villa Park in 2013. He died in March 2018 at the age of 70.

ANSTEY, Brendel
Goalkeeper
Born: *Bristol* **Died:** 1933
Playing career: *Hanham Athletic, Bristol Rovers, Aston Villa, Leicester City (1911-1919)*
Born in Bristol. Anstey was a goalkeeper who played for Bristol Rovers before signing for Aston Villa in February 1911. He made 55 appearances for them across four seasons until the outbreak of World War One. When football resumed after the war, he moved on to Leicester City before he moved on to non league football with Mid Rhondda and Wednesbury Athletic where he later became a coach. He died in Wednesbury in December 1933 aged 46.

ARMSTRONG, Bill
Defender
Born: *Throckley* **Died:** 1995
Playing career: *Rochdale, Aston Villa, Swindon Town, Gillingham (1931-1938)*
Armstrong played over 130 times in the Football League and moved to Villa from Rochdale in 1933. After two seasons at Villa Park, he dropped down a division to move to Swindon, then on to Gillingham. Upon retirement as a player, he ran a shop. He suffered ill health in later life and died in his native north east in 1995, aged 82.

Juan Pablo Angel

Brookwood Memorial

ARMSTRONG, Matthew
Wing-half
Born: *High Spen*
Died: 1941
Playing career: *Darlington, Aston Villa (1936-1939)*
Armstrong - no relation to namesake Bill - began his career in Division Three (North) with Darlington in 1936 and made 38 appearances *The Quakers*, scoring twice. He joined Aston Villa in 1939 but never played a senior match before the league was abandoned due to the outbreak of World War Two. Armstrong died on active service in July 1941, aged 22, while serving in the Middle East as a private with 149 Field Ambulance, Royal Army Medical Corps. He is commemorated on the Brookwood Memorial.

ASHE, Norman
Winger
Born: *Walsall*
Playing career: *Aston Villa, Rotherham United, Nuneaton Borough (1959-1963)*
The Walsall-born winger rose through the ranks from apprentice to senior team at Villa, making his first team debut in 1959 during the side's Second Division title-winning season. He made only five league appearances for the club, and moved on to Rotherham in 1962. After an expansive lower league career, where he plied his trade for numerous clubs in the south west, Ashe retired in 1985 to bring an end his 26 year playing career. He was part of the Falmouth Town side to reach the FA Cup first round proper in 1970 and later had a stint coaching the Cornish side before moving on to the club's board. Ashe later returned to the Midlands, where he still lives aged 75.

ASHFIELD, George
Full-back
Born: *Manchester*
Died: 1985
Playing career: *Stockport County, Aston Villa, Chester, Rhyl (1949-1959)*
Ashfield began his career with Stockport County, without making a senior appearance, before going on to play nine league games for top flight Villa in 1954. After a brief stint with Fourth Division Chester, he dropped into Non-league football with Welsh club Rhyl. He saw out the rest of his ten year career there, before retiring and drifting out the game. Went on to run a sports shop in Stockport. Ashfield died aged only 50 in March 1985

ASHMORE, Walter
Goalkeeper
Born: *Smethwick*
Died: 1940
Playing career: *Aston Villa, Aston Unity (1888-1889)*
Goalkeeper Ashmore first rose to prominence when he signed for the club that would later become West Bromwich Albion in 1886. He spent a couple of seasons there and then moved to Villa as back up keeper to Jimmy Warner. He would only make one single appearance in claret-and-blue, against Everton in in first ever Football League season (1888-89). Ashmore left Villa in 1889 and went on to play for Aston Unity. According to the Football League archives, it is believed that he may have gone on to play both football and cricket for the latter. Ashmore died in 1940 in Oldham.

ASHTON, Derek
Defender
Born: *Worksop*
Died: 1997
Playing career: *Wolverhampton Wanderers, Aston Villa, Wellington Town (1945-1949)*
Ashton was on the books at Wolves without appearing in senior league football, so he moved to Villa as football formalities re-commenced after the war in 1946. He played eight times across the following five years for the club before moving on to Telford based non league side Wellington in 1951. He later became their player/manager and then worked locally as a player scout. Ashton died, aged 74, in 1997.

ASPINALL, Warren
Midfielder/forward
Born: *Wigan*
Playing career: *Wigan Athletic, Everton, Aston Villa, Portsmouth, Bournemouth, Swansea City, Carlisle United, Brentford, Colchester United, Brighton & Hove Albion (1980-2000)*

A much travelled, versatile and controversial figure, Aspinall moved to Villa for a then club record fee of £300,000 from Everton in 1987. Aspinall finished as joint top scorer in his second season to help Villa back to the top flight at the first attempt. A series of ill-disciplined incidents saw him sold to Portsmouth, before he was forced to retire through a long-term ankle injury. After leaving the game, Aspinall turned to drink and gambling but has happily now recovered. Worked in a Sainsbury's distribution centre and then as a scout for Port Vale. He has remained involved in football and now works as a BBC Sussex radio commentator for Brighton & Hove Albion matches.

ASTLEY, Dai
Striker
Born: *Dowlais, Wales* **Died:** 1989
Playing career: *Charlton Athletic, Aston Villa, Derby County, Blackpool, FC Metz (1927-1947)*

A prolific inside forward for club and country, Astley scored a remarkable 92 goals for Villa in 165 matches. After spells at Derby County and Blackpool, he moved to France and FC Metz after the war. Capped 13 times by Wales, he consistently plundered goals for the national side, scoring 12 goals during a seven year international career. Upon retirement, Astley took up a career as a manager, coaching in Italy with Inter Milan and Genoa, and then in Sweden where he took charge of Djurgardens and then Sandvikens IF. He died at 80 in 1989.

ASTON, Charlie
Full-back
Born: *Bilston* **Died:** 1931
Playing career: *Bilston United, Walsall, Aston Villa, QPR, Burton United, Gresley Rovers, Burton United, Watford, Leyton (1895-1908)*

Aston joined First Division Villa in 1898 and played 13 games in his first season as they won the league. Villa retained the title the next season, before Aston moved on to pastures new. He had one season spells at QPR, Burton United, Gresley Rovers and Burton United for a second time. Upon retirement, he remained in London and worked as a PE teacher at a local college. He was only 56 when he died in 1931.

ATHERSMITH, Charlie
Outside-right
Born: *Bloxwich* **Died:** 1910
Playing career: *Aston Villa, Small Heath (1887-1905)*

Athersmith was a key man in Aston Villa's Victorian-era dominance of the English domestic game. He won five league titles and two FA Cups between 1894 and 1900 and played twelve times for England scoring three goals. Before becoming a professional football, Athersmith was a clerk in Birmingham. Having left Villa in 1901, he moved on to local rivals Small Heath (now known as Birmingham City). After he retired, he became a pub landlord at the Vine Inn, and then spent two years as a coach at Grimsby Town. He returned to Redditch to take up ownership of another pub - the Royal George - and died soon afterwards at only 38 years of age.

ATKINS, Bill
Forward
Born: *Solihull*
Playing career: *Aston Villa, Swindon Town, Halifax Town, Stockport County , Portsmouth, Halifax Town, Rochdale, Darlington (1959-1975)*

Solihull born Atkins never made a senior appearance in his two seasons at Villa Park. He played in the Football League for six different clubs, including over 200 games for Halifax Town. A tall, rangy forward, he spent nine months at Fratton Park with Portsmouth but scored only twice in this time. Atkins later returned to Birmingham to buy a baker's and confectionary store which he ran for 30 years. Now retired, he is 80 and lives in west Yorkshire.

ATKINSON, Dalian
Striker
Born: *Telford, Shropshire* **Died:** 2006
Playing career: *Ipswich Town, Sheffield Wednesday, Real Sociedad, Aston Villa, Fenerbahce, Metz, Manchester City, Al-Ittihad, Daejeon Citizen, Jeonbuk Hyundai Motors (1985-2001)*

After finishing the latter stages of his career in the middle east and Asia, Atkinson returned to England to run sports consultancy "Players Come First" - an agency for clubs, players and agents. His time at Villa Park is often remembered for Atkinson's penchant for the spectacular - notably his goal in the 1994 League Cup final win over Manchester United and a stunning solo finish against Wimbledon in the first Premier League season. It was a goal later named as Match of the Day's best of the campaign. Atkinson played for many teams abroad, and retired as a player in 2001. Having suffered with heart and kidney problems, Atkinson died at the age of 48 after he went into cardiac arrest having been tasered by the police at his home in 2016.

ATKINSON, Ron
Wing-half
Born: *Liverpool*
Playing career: *Aston Villa, Oxford United, Kettering Town, Cambridge United, West Bromwich Albion, Manchester United, Atletico Madrid, Sheffield Wed, Coventry City, Nottingham Forest (1956-1999)*

Affectionately known as "Big Ron", Atkinson remains one of British football's most colourful and well known characters. He did not achieve great heights in his playing career, after moving to Villa in 1956. He never played a first team match before moving on to Oxford where he spent the rest of his playing days, making over 400 appearances. As a manager, he won the FA Cup with Manchester United in 1983 and 1985 and the League Cup with Sheffield Wednesday.

He returned to Villa Park as boss in 1991, winning the League Cup again three years later and taking the team to second place in the first ever Premier League season. Went on to manage Coventry City, Atletico Madrid, Wednesday again and Nottingham Forest. His later career as a TV pundit was cut short when he was forced to resign after controversial on-air comments.

BACHE, Joseph
Inside-forward
Born: *Stourbridge* **Died:** 1960
Playing career: *Aston Villa, Mid Rhondda, Grimsby Town (1900-1920)*

Fourth on the list of Aston Villa's all-time appearance makers, England international Bache spent 14 years in the Midlands. During that time he played 474 times for the club, finding the net on 185 occasions. He was one of Villa's all-time greatest forwards, winning the FA Cup in 1905 and 1913, as well as the league Championship in 1910. Bache went on to serve on the Western Front during the First World War. Despite being involved in a number of actions, Bache survived the war and returned home to resume his playing career. He moved on to Mid-Rhondda in Wales and later Grimsby where he also became player/coach. He died in 1960 aged 80.

RON ATKINSON
THE MANAGER

BAIRD, John

Full-back

Born: *Alexandria, West Dunbartonshire, Scotland*
Died: 1905
Playing career: *Vale Athletic, Vale of Leven, Aston Villa, Kidderminster Olympic, Kidderminster Harriers, Leicester Fosse, Clyde, Vale of Leven (1888-1896)*

Defender Baird played for Villa briefly in 1889, before he returned two years later and made 60 appearances in the First Division across four seasons in the Midlands. Baird also turned our for Kidderminster Harriers and played 13 league games for Leicester Fosse before he returned to his homeland where he played for Clyde and then signed for amateur side Vale of Leven FC. He had a spell as their player/coach. He died in his native Scotland from a heart attack in 1905 aged 34.

BAKER, Alan

Forward

Born: *Tipton, Staffordshire*
Playing career: *Aston Villa, Walsall. (1960-1970)*

Striker Baker played for several Football League clubs, most notably Walsall and Aston Villa, where he spent the last five years of his playing career. He joined Villa as a schoolboy and went on to play 109 times for the club (92 league games and 17 cup appearances), scoring 17 times. He was a runner up in the League Cup final of 1963 as the side lost the two legged tie to fierce local rivals Birmingham City. He also represented England Schoolboys. Upon retirement, Baker went into the Leather trade in Walsall where he worked as a Castings Inspector.

BAKKE, Eirik

Midfielder

Born: *Sogndal, Norway*
Playing career: *Leeds United, Aston Villa (loan), Brann, Sogndal (1993-2012)*

Bakke was signed by Leeds in 1999 from Songdal in his native Norway for £1.75 million. He hit the ground running, but injuries and poor forms meant he never became a mainstay at Elland Road. He joined David O'Leary's Aston Villa on loan for the 2005-06 season. The loan however was ended early after Leeds told Villa that they would only let Bakke go permanently, not on loan and Doug Ellis decided that it was not worth permanently acquiring his services. In total, he played 14 times for the claret and blue during his brief loan spell. He earned 27 caps for Norway, where he now lives again and coaches one of Sogndal's youth sides.

Erik Bakke

Bosko Balaban

BALABAN, Bosko
Striker
Born: *Rijeka, SFR Yugoslavia*
Playing career: *Rijeka, Dinamo Zagreb, Aston Villa, Dinamo Zagreb (loan), Club Brugge K.V., Panionios, Selangor FA (1995-2012)*

After impressive form for local club Rijeka and then Dinamo Zagreb in his homeland, the Croatian striker was signed by Villa for £5.8million in 2001 - a big price tag and even loftier expectations. Balaban failed to find any form for Aston Villa, making just nine appearances, seven as a substitute, in two and a half years and never found the net. He was loaned back to Dinamo Zagreb for the 2002–03 season, scoring 15 times in 24 appearances. In December 2003, Aston Villa released Balaban from his contract and he signed for Club Brugge on a free transfer. He played in Greece and Malaysia and got 35 caps for Croatia between 2000 and 2007. Having returned home to Zagreb, Balaban started a business called BB Sport Management & Consulting.

Centre-half Ball, who played 77 times for Villa across three seasons, remains the first - and to date only - active Football League player to have been murdered. He made no first team appearances for Newcastle before moving to the Midlands to join First Division Aston Villa as cover for Frank Barson. After Barson left, Ball became first choice centre half and continued to perform well, being tipped for an England call up. On the evening of 11 November 1923, Ball was shot dead in the garden of his home by his neighbour and landlord, ex policeman George Stagg.

Tommy Ball's Grave

BALL, Tommy
Centre-half
Born: *Chester-le-Street*
Died: 1923
Playing career: *Usworth Central School, Wadley Colliery, , Felling Colliery, Newcastle United, Aston Villa (1919-1923)*

BANKS, Herbert
Inside-left
Born: *Coventry*
Died: 1947
Playing career: *72nd Seaforth Highlanders, Everton, St Mirren, Third Lanark, Millwall Athletic, Aston Villa, Bristol City, Watford, Coventry City, Stafford Rangers, Veritys A (1896-1906)*

Began his League career with Everton and moved on to Villa in 1901, shortly before winning his only cap for England. He made five league appearances for Villa, then signed for Bristol City, Watford and Coventry, scoring over 50 goals for these three clubs. After leaving football, he worked for a Birmingham engineering firm and also saw active service with the Royal Garrison Artillery during World War One. Banks died in 1947.

BARDSLEY, Phil
Defender
Born: Salford
Playing career: *Manchester United, Royal Antwerp (loan), Burnley (loan), Rangers (loan), Aston Villa (loan), Sheffield United (loan), Sunderland, Stoke City, Burnley (2003 -)*

Having grown up near Manchester United's old training ground, The Cliff, Bardsley rose through the ranks to make ten first team appearances at Old Trafford. A succession of brief loan spells followed his departure from United, and he joined Villa in January 2007 until the end of the season. Under Martin O'Neill, he played 13 times before moving on again to Sheffield United, Sunderland and Stoke. As of 2019, Bardsley continues to ply his trade in the Premier League for Sean Dyche's Burnley and he's also earned 13 caps for the Scotland national team, who he qualifies for through his Glasgow-born father.

BARBER, Tommy
Half-back/Inside-left
Born: *West Stanley* **Died:** 1925
Playing career: *Shankhouse, West Stanley, Hamsterley, Bolton Wanderers, Aston Villa, Belfast Celtic (guest), Celtic (guest), Partick Thistle (guest), Linfield (guest), Distillery (guest), Stalybridge Celtic, Crystal Palace, Merthyr Town, Ton Pentre, Pontypridd, Walsall, Darlaston, Hinckley United, Barwell United (1908-1921)*

A much traveled veteran of the lower league scene, Barber played at the top level for Bolton and Aston Villa, whom he joined in 1912. He scored the winning goal in the club's 1913 FA Cup final win over Sunderland, playing 65 times in total for the Midlands side across two seasons. Made a handful of wartime guest appearances in Ireland and also for Celtic. Barber served as a private for the 17th Battalion of the Middlesex Regiment in France during the war. He suffered gunshot wounds and was evacuated to Britain. He was later transferred to the Labour Corps and also worked in a munitions factory in Glasgow. He died of tuberculosis in 1925 aged 39.

BARKER, Jeff
Defender
Born: *Scunthorpe* **Died:** 1985
Playing career: *Lindsey United, Aston Villa, Huddersfield Town, Scunthorpe United (1935-1952)*

After his first season playing in the Midland League, Barker was scouted and signed by Villa for £400 in 1936. He remained at Villa for a decade but only managed three league appearances, before the interruption of World War Two. He continued to play for the club in wartime, He was in charge of Scunthope for three games as interim manager in 1974 and died in the town eleven years later.

Statue of William McGregor, former Villa director and founder of the Football League.

Milan Baros

BARLOW, Ray

Midfielder

Born: Swindon
Died: 2012
Playing career: *West Bromwich Albion....and I think Aston Villa*

Having made over 400 games for Villa's Midlands rivals West Bromwich Albion, Barlow won the FA Cup with the Baggies under Vic Buckingham in 1954. After a stellar 16 year career at the Hawthorns, Barlow moved on to Birmingham where he played five games and ended up at Aston Villa for one season in 1962 after a brief spell at Stourbridge. He played once for England and then, upon retirement, remained in the area to run first a tobacconist's and sweet shop and then a post office. He died in 2012 aged 85.

BAROS, Milan

Striker

Born: Czechoslovakia
Playing career: *Banik Ostrava, Liverpool, Aston Villa, Lyon, Portsmouth (loan), Galatasaray (1998-date)*

Baros moved to Villa from Liverpool for £6.5 million in 2005 on a four year deal, but struggled to ever really recapture the form that persuaded Martin O'Neill to sign him. He scored 12 times in 51 games for Villa during his two season stay at the club. His 41 goals for Czech Republic is second only to Jan Koller. He moved to Lyon and then Portsmouth on loan where he played a key role in their 2008 FA Cup win despite never scoring for the club. He had two years in Turkey with Galatasaray and Antalyspor before he returned to his first club, Banik Ostrava, in his homeland 2017. Now aged 37, he continues to play for the club. Baros was capped 93 times for his country, winning the Golden Boot at Euro 2004.

BARRETT, Earl

Defender

Born: Rochdale
Playing career: *Manchester City, Chester City, Oldham Athletic, Aston Villa, Everton, Sheffield United and Sheffield Wednesday 1995-2000*

Barrett began his career at Manchester City, then moved on to Oldham Athletic via a brief loan spell at Chester. He own the first of his three England caps whilst with the Latics, then moved on to Villa where he enjoyed his greatest success as a player.

The team became runners up in the Premier League during his first few months at Villa Park and then won the League Cup in 1993/94, beating Man United 3-1 in the final. The following year he moved on again to Everton, then played for both Sheffield clubs and hung up his boots in 2000. He had a spell as youth coach at both Stoke City and Oldham, and currently is in charge of the US Soccer Development Academy Program at Houston Express (HESC).

BARRETT, Ken

Forward

Born: Bromsgrove   **Died:** 2015
Playing career: *Aston Villa, Lincoln City (1958-1968)*

Barrett was spotted by Villa as a 15-year-old and invited for a trial which saw him rise through the ranks to a senior debut in 1958. He scored three times in five games before moving on to Lincoln City. His national service saw him in the Army as a Physical Training Instructor, and he represented the army football team. Following the completion of his duties, he returned to Lincoln but found opportunities with the Imps limited. He linked up with non league side Stourbridge in 1963/64 and scored 74 goals in 200 games before retiring. Upon finishing his playing career, Barrett worked as a bookmaker and then on the committee of his local golf club in Bromsgrove. He died at the age of 77 in 2015.

BARRY, Gareth
Midfielder
Born: *Hastings*
Playing career: *Brighton & Hove Albion, Aston Villa, Manchester City, Everton (loan), Everton (1995-2014)*

A Premier League stalwart synonymous with longevity, Barry has played 653 times in the Premier League, the highest number of appearances by any player in the competition's history. 365 of these came for Villa across an 11 year career, and he also won 53 caps for England under five different managers. Eighth on the list of all time appearance makers for the Villa Park side, Sussex-born Barry still lives in the Midlands, and, at the age of 38, is playing for his old side's local rivals West Bromwich Albion in the Championship. His nephew, Bradley Barry is also a professional footballer for National League side Barrow.

BARTELT, Gustavo
Striker
Born: *Buenos Aires, Argentina*
Playing career: *All Boys, Lanus, Roma, Aston Villa (loan), Rayo (loan), Gimnasia La Plata, Talleres, Gimnasia de Jujuy (1993-2011)*

One of the more obscure names to be on the books at Villa in recent times, Bartelt spent virtually all of his career in his native Argentina. Bartelt started playing for All Boys in 1993. Whilst at Villa, he never got along with then manager John Gregory and only ever played for the reserves.

While at Roma, both Bartelt and Cafu were accused of using false documents to gain Italian passports. Bartelt was banned for one year and Cafu was acquitted. He never played for Roma again and was released by the club in 2003. In 2006 he was finally acquitted by the court for the fake documents charge. He ended his career where it began back at All Boys in Argentina.

Gareth Barry

Barson, Frank

Midfielder

Born: *Burngreave, Sheffield*

Died: 1968

Playing career: *Barnsley, Aston Villa, Manchester United, Watford, Hartlepool United (1911-1930)*

Notorious for his fiery temper and penchant to lose control, Barton is believed to have been sent off 12 times during his career. One challenge in a game against Fulham resulted in a seven match ban. He picked up many lengthy suspensions including one following the 1926 FA Cup Final against Manchester City, when he fouled Sam Cowan who was knocked out. He was popular throughout his six years at Old Trafford and helped the club win promotion in 1925. Was given a free transfer at the age of 37, three years later. A blacksmith by trade, he was promised a pub if he captained United to promotion and when he did, he took over a hotel in Ardwick Green but walked out after 15 minutes after getting fed up of admirers. He joined the Aston Villa coaching staff in 1935 before moving to Swansea Town 12 years later. He stayed in South Wales until 1954 when he returned to Birmingham working for Lye Town until his retirement. He died in September 1968. Barton played once for England in 1920.

BAXTER, Bill

Wing-half

Born: *Methil, Fife, Scotland*

Died: 2002

Playing career: *Wolverhampton Wanderers, Aston Villa, Wellington Town (1939-1957)*

Baxter joined Wolves as an apprentice in 1939. After guesting for Leicester City, Mansfield and Notts County during wartime, he signed professionally at Molineux and went on to play 43 times for Wolverhampton until 1953. Although never a regular starter for Wolves, he made five appearances in 1953-54 as the club won their first championship. Lacking playing time, he moved to Midlands neighbours Villa in 1953. Baxter made over 100 appearances for Villa before retiring in Summer 1957. He stayed with the club to serve them as coach and assistant manager until 1967. He then moved back to his native Scotland where he had short spells as a manager in charge of both East Fife and Raith Rovers. Baxter died in Leven in 2002 at the age of 78.

BEARD, Malcolm

Wing-half

Born: *Cannock*

Playing career: *Birmingham City, Aston Villa, Atherstone Town (1957-1974)*

Beard made more than 350 appearances in the Football League and spent most of his career at Birmingham, for whom he made over 400 appearances. He earned runners up medals in both the Inter-Cities Fairs Cup (1960/61) and the League Cup (1962/63) before he moved to Villa in 1971. He made six appearances for Villa and also turned out in non-league football for Atherstone Town. After retirement, he went on to coach in England and abroad, and was employed as chief scout by Leicester City and Villa. He was capped for England at youth level but never got a senior call-up.

BEATON, Bill

Goalkeeper

Born: *Kincardine, Scotland*

Playing career: *Thornton Hibs, Dunfermline Athletic, Aston Villa, Airdrieonians, Alloa Athletic, Sauchie Juniors (1956-1963)*

Goalkeeper Beaton played a solitary game for Aston Villa, and it was one he'd rather forget. During the 1958-59 season, Beaton deputised for the unavailable Nigel Sims in a match at Leicester in November 1958. The Scottish stopper let in six goals, his side lost 6-3 and his 90-minute Villa career was over before it had even really begun. He then joined Airdrie in his native Scotland and moved on to Alloa, finishing his career with Scottish non league side Sauchie. He worked as a coach in Scotland and now resides in Glasgow.

BEINLICH, Stefan
Midfielder
Born: *East Berlin, East Germany*
Playing career: *Berliner FC Dynamo, SG Bergmann-Borsig, Aston Villa, Hansa Rostock, Bayer Leverkusen, Hertha BSC, Hamburger SV (1978-2008)*

German international Beinlich was one of the first players from his country to play in the Premier League, albeit during an underwhelming three year stint at Villa. He spent almost his entire career in Germany, punctuated by the move to the Midlands in 1991. Beinlich's only goal for Villa came in a 5–1 defeat to Newcastle United in April 1994. He then returned to his homeland with Hansa Rostock, Bayer Leverkusen and Hertha Berlin. Beinlich retired in in 2008 after two seasons at former side Hansa. He had to retire due to knee problems, having played 398 career games. He also earned five caps for his country in a two year international career but missed out a call up for the Euro 2000 championships.

BELFORD, Dale
Goalkeeper
Born: *Burton upon Trent*
Playing career: *Aston Villa, Sutton Coldfield Town, Notts County, VS Rugby, Nuneaton Borough, Tamworth, Hinckley United, Atherstone United, Gresley Rovers, Hinckley United (loan), Shepshed Dynamo, Coalville Town, Atherstone Town, Atherstone Town, Nuneaton Griff (loan) (1985-2015)*

Belford started his career as an apprentice at Aston Villa, before signing a professional contract in 1985. However, having failed to secure a first team slot, he moved on to Sutton Coldfield Town less than a year later.

Darren Bent

He had three spells at that club, and after moving on again, Belford became a veteran, well-travelled non league keeper. Upon retirement, he became a player/goalkeeping coach at Tamworth, and had three spells as the Lambs caretaker boss. Belford then had a season in charge at Rugby Town in 2015-16 before a brief tenure at Hinckley. As of 2019, the former stopper now works as assistant manager alongside Jimmy Ginnelly at National League North side Nuneaton Borough.

BENNETT, Tom
Midfielder
Born: *Boness, Falkirk, Scotland*
Playing career: *Aston Villa, Wolves, Stockport County, Walsall (loan), Walsall, Boston United, Kidderminster H, Hamilton Academical (1984-2005)*

Having joined Villa as a schoolboy aged 14, Bennett was given a professional contract but became another player to never play a senior game for the club. He left for Midlands rivals Wolves in 1988 and went on to make over 100 appearances at Molineux. Spells at Stockport, Walsall (twice) and Kidderminster. He returned to his native Scotland with Hamilton Academical, but played only three times before a knee injury prematurely ended his career. Since leaving football, the former midfielder has swapped one stage for another to join Stockport-based rock band "Cold Fracture" as lead vocalist.

BENT, Darren
Striker
Born: *Tooting*
Playing career: *Ipswich Town, Charlton Athletic, Tottenham Hotspur, Sunderland, Aston Villa, Fulham (loan), Brighton (loan), Derby County (1998-2015)*

Bent retired earlier this year having plied his trade at the top level of the game for the past 17 years. He rose through the ranks at Ipswich before joining Charlton for £2.5m in 2005. He was the Addicks top scorer for two consecutive seasons, and then moved again to Tottenham and Sunderland. He signed for Villa for a club record £24m in 2011 and went on to notch his 100th Premier League goal whilst at the club. He kept Villa up with 21 goals in 65 league games. Bent had loan spells at Brighton, Fulham, Derby and Burton Albion. Bent retired in July 2019 and also earned 13 caps for England, scoring four goals for his country.

Patrik Berger

BERESFORD, Joseph

Inside - right
Born: Shuttlewood, Derbyshire
Died: 1978
Playing career: *Aston Villa, Mansfield Town, Preston North End (1927-1935)*
An inside forward who signed for Aston Villa from Mansfield in 1926. After 224 appearances and 66 goals, he left the Midlands to join Preston and ended his career with a two season stint at Stourbridge of the Birmingham & District League. He won one cap for England and got an FA Cup runners up medal whilst with Preston. After retiring he worked at Bentley Colliery coal mine and later ran a fish shop in Doncaster. He died aged 72 in Derbyshire in 1978.

BERGER, Patrik

Left winger/attacking midfielder
Born: *Prague, Czechoslovakia*
Playing career: *Slavia Prague, Borussia Dortmund, Liverpool, Portsmouth, Aston Villa, Stoke City, Sparta Prague (1991-2010)*
Best known for his seven years at Anfield in which he won the FA Cup and the UEFA Cup, Czech winger Berger struggled to become a Villa regular due to injury. He signed there for David O'Leary, but only played twice in his second season under O'Leary's successor Martin O'Neill. He also played for Portsmouth as part of their rise to Premier League prominence. He played 42 times for the Czech national team, and scored in the final against Germany at Euro 1996, albeit in a losing cause. He retired in January 2010 due to persistent injury. At the age of 40 Berger was still playing on an amateur basis for Dolni Chabry in his native Czech Republic.

BERRY, Trevor

Midfielder
Born: *Haslemere*
Playing career: *Bournemouth, Aston Villa, Rotherham United (loan), Rotherham United, Scunthorpe United (loan), Waterford (1991-2003)*
Berry never made a senior appearance for either AFC Bournemouth or Villa despite three years in the Midlands. It was not until he moved to Rotherham United in 1995 that his career took off. He played 141 games for the Millers, scoring 22 goals. Berry was part of the Rotherham team to win the Football League Trophy in 1996.

Had a brief loan spell at Scunthorpe and later returned to Rotherham where he worked as a scout and in player recruitment. He retired in 2003 after a season in Ireland with Waterford. He has done some punditry and radio work, and is still involved at Rotherham United as an after-dinner speaker and matchday host.

BERSON, Mathieu

Midfielder
Born: *Vannes, France*
Playing career: *Nantes, Aston Villa, Auxerre (loan), Levante, Toulouse, Vannes (1997-2013)*
A player whom, apart from his two seasons at Villa between 2004 and 2006, spent the entirety of his professional career in his native France. Berson began his career with Nantes and won the French league during his debut season. Having featured for the club consistently over a four-year period, he was transferred to Premier League club Aston Villa in the summer of 2004. In January 2005, Villa signed Eric Djemba-Djemba in an attempt to replicate the successful partnership they had formed at Nantes, where they played 50 games together. However, six months later, Berson was back in France, having joined Auxerre on a season-long loan. Later played in Italy and for Toulouse who released him in the summer of 2010 due to budget cuts, Berson remained without a club until signing a two-year contract with third tier Vannes in June 2011

BETTS, Tony
Forward
Born: *Derby*
Playing career: *Aston Villa, Southport (loan), Portland Timbers, Port Vale, Boldmere St. Michael's, Minnesota Kicks (1974-1982)*

Betts started his career at Aston Villa and played for claret and blue in the 1972 Youth Cup final loss to Liverpool. A first team debut followed, and he played four times for the senior side in the Second Division under Ron Saunders. Betts represented England at youth and amateur level whilst at Villa. He was loaned out to Southport and then crossed the pond to link up with the Portland Timbers. He had brief loan spells with Port Vale and Bolder St Michael's before returning Stateside. His career ended in unusual fashion when he was signed by indoor professional side Buffalo Stallions. After retiring he settled in the Portland area and founded the West Villa Soccer Club. At the turn of the millennium he was working as an independent sales rep, selling sports shoes.

BEWERS, Jon
Defender/midfielder
Born: *Kettering*
Playing career: *FA National School of Excellence, Aston Villa, Notts County, Walsall, (1996-2009)*

Bewers came through the Football Association's National School of Excellence at Lilleshall, and began his club career as a schoolboy with Aston Villa. He turned professional in 1999, captained the club's reserve team as a 17-year-old, and made his first-team debut as a late substitute in the Premier League game against Tottenham Hotspur at White Hart Lane in April 2000. Villa won the game 4–2. It proved to be his only appearance for the Villa first team. He was on the bench as Aston Villa won the 2001 UEFA Intertoto Cup. After brief spells at Notts County and Walsall, he signed for Southern League side Aylesbury United in 2005. He then played for a succession of non league sides before retirement in 2010. He opened a convenience store in Aylesbury after hanging up his boots.

BEYE, Habib
Right-back
Born: *Suresnes, France*
Playing career: *Paris Saint-Germain, Strasbourg, Marseille, Newcastle United, Aston Villa, Doncaster Rovers (loan), Doncaster Rovers (1997-2012)*

French born Senegalese international defender Beye became a key man for Marseille as they reached the 2004 UEFA Cup final, where his impressive performance against Newcastle persuaded Sir Bobby Robson to sign him for the Toon. Beye became a cult hero at SJP, winning the club's Player of the Year award and established a chant with his name to the tune of Happy Mondays. However, having moved to Villa in 2009, he suffered contrasting fortunes in the Midlands, where he played only nine times across two and a half years.

He was sent on loan to Doncaster and retired after his contract expired in 2013. He played 35 times for Senegal (one goal) in a seven year international career from 2001 to 2008.

Habib Beye

BIDDLESTONE, Fred

Goalkeeper
Born: *Pensnett*
Died: 1982
Playing career: *Aston Villa, Walsall, Mansfield Town*

Biddlestone turned out for a number of local amateur sides before making the move to Aston Villa in 1930 for £1,750 from Walsall. He played 160 times for the Midlands side in five seasons at Villa Park in league and cup. He was sold to Mansfield in 1939 and then retired in the early 1950s with his career disrupted by the outbreak of World War Two. Having hung up his boots, Biddlestone stayed in the Midlands area but drifted out of the game and went into factory work. He died in 1982 aged 75. One of the first Villa goalkeepers to be inducted into the club's Hall of Fame.

BIRCH, James

Forward
Born: *Blackwell, Derbyshire*
Died: 1940
Playing career: *Stourbridge, Aston Villa, QPR, Brentford (1911-1926)*

Birch was best known for his 14 year career at QPR, where he played 363 games in all competitions for the west London club. Had World War Two not intervened, Birch would surely have added to his total. Birch was signed by QPR manager James Cowan from former side Aston Villa, where Birch played three times and scored twice. He had been prolific for Villa's youth teams but was only a peripheral first-team face, prompting the move to the capital. In 1926 he was transferred to Brentford. The Blackwell-born forward died in 1940 aged 51. He remains as QPR's third highest goalscorer of all time.

BIRCH, Paul

Midfielder
Born: *West Bromwich*
Died: 2009
Playing career: *Aston Villa, Wolverhampton Wanderers, Preston North End (loan), Doncaster Rovers, Exeter City, Halesowen Town (1980-2000)*

No relation to either of his other two namesakes on this list, Birch was a mainstay of the Villa midfield throughout the 1980s and early 90s. He began his career as a Villa schoolboy, and made his first team debut in the European Super Cup victory over Barcelona in 1983. He did not feature in the club's title win of two years previously or their European Cup triumph in 1982. He became a Holte End favourite and went on to play almost 200 games at Villa Park. Having fallen out of favour under Jozef Venglos, he moved on to Wolves, then finished his career with a solitary season at both Doncaster Rovers and Exeter City. Having retired from the professional game, he turned out for Halesowen Town and briefly worked as a postman. He joined the coaching staff at Forest Green Rovers in 2001, then two years later took up a role coaching the youth teams at Birmingham. He suffered bone cancer and died at the young age of 46 in 2009 in Sutton Coldfield.

BIRCH, Trevor
Wing-half
Born: *West Bromwich*
Playing career: *Accles & Pollock, Aston Villa, Stockport County, Nuneaton Borough (1954-1962)*
Birch's career was a relatively short one, spanning six seasons at Villa and another two at Stockport County. Not much is known about Birch's post-football career. He had a spell as player/coach of Nuneaton Borough and then worked as a coach for Stockport. Birch died aged 79 in May 2013.

BLACKBURN, Ernest
Full-back
Born: *Crawshawbooth*
Died: 1964
Playing career: *Lovelough, Manchester Youth Club, The Army, Aston Villa, Bradford City (1919-1924)*
For Aston Villa, Blackburn made 32 appearances in the Football League and also played once in the FA Cup. He played as a full-back and turned out for The Army and Manchester City Youth Club along with several other representative sides before his move to Villa in 1919. After retiring as a player (1925), Blackburn remained in the game as a coach and trainer. He worked on the coaching staff at Accrington Stanley, and later went on to manage Wrexham, Hull City and had a nine-year tenure as boss of Tranmere Rovers. He died in 1964 aged 71 in a Birkenhead nursing home.

BLACKBURN, George
Outside-left
Born: *Halifax*
Died: 1957
Playing career: *Aston Villa, Cardiff City, Mansfield Town, Cheltenham Town (1920-1932)*
No relation to namesake Ernest, George made over 250 appearances in the Football League during the early years of the professional game in England. At Villa he played 145 times, including their 1924 FA Cup final defeat to Newcastle United, scoring twice in his time at the club. He earned a solitary England cap and later went on to play for Cardiff and Mansfield Town.After retirement, he had a stint as player/manager of Cheltenham Town a before joining his former side's local rivals Birmingham City as a coach during World War Two. Blackburn was later appointed as the Blues interim boss for a four game spell.

BLAIR, Andy
Midfielder
Born: *Kirkcaldy, Scotland*
Playing career: *Coventry City, Aston Villa, Wolverhampton Wanderers, Sheffield Wednesday, Aston Villa, Barnsley, Northampton T. (1977-1988).*
Scottish full-back Blair moved to Aston Villa from Coventry City. He was an unused sub in the '82 European Cup final. Capped five times by Scotland at youth level, he later returned for a second spell at Villa Park after playing for Wolves on loan and Sheffield Wednesday. Whilst at the latter, he became the first player to ever score a hat-trick of penalties. He also appeared for Barnsley and Northampton Town, before a knee injury ended his professional career in 1989, at the age of 30. He is currently working as a scout for Stoke City. After retirement, he opened the first of a small chain of shops across Coventry, selling sports clothing, shoes and sports goods. He also owned a play school.

BLAIR, Danny
Wing-half/full-back
Born: *Parkhead, Scotland*
Died: 1985
Playing career: *Providence Clamdiggers, Parkhead Juniors, Clyde, Aston Villa, Blackpool (1924-1939)*
Blair began his career in Canada then, after spells with Toronto Scottish and Willys Overland MW, he signed for the wonderfully named Toronto Clamdiggers in 1924. After one season, he returned to his native Scotland and Clyde in 1925. He signed for Villa for £7,000 and played 138 League and Cup games for the club. Having left the Midlands, he moved on to Blackpool and also earned eight caps for the Scotland national side. He returned to Clyde in a coaching capacity after retirement as a player in in 1939. He died in the Lancashire seaside town where he had served as a player, aged 80 in 1985.

BLAKE, Mark
Midfielder
Born: *Nottingham*
Playing career: *Aston Villa, Wolverhampton Wanderers, Portsmouth, Leicester City, Walsall, Mansfield Town, Kidderminster Harriers (1989-2002)*
A much travelled midfielder, he started out at Villa and went on to make 31 appearances for the club's first team in four years, scoring twice. A £400,000 move to Portsmouth came his way in 1993, before he returned to the Midlands with Leicester and later Walsall. Also played twice for Wolves in a brief loan spell at Molineux. Played 83 times for Mansfield and finished his career at Kidderminster Harriers. He was forced to retire in 2002 through injury. He won nine caps for England at Under 21 level but never received a senior call up.

BLAKE, Noel
Defender
Born: *Kingston, Jamaica*
Playing career: *Sutton Coldfield Town, Aston Villa, Shrewsbury Town, Birmingham City, Portsmouth, Leeds United, Stoke City, Bradford City, Dundee, Exeter City (1978-2001)*
Born in Kingston, Jamaica, his 6ft 2in frame provided an intimidating challenge for opposing strikers He played four times for Villa between 1979 and 1982. After 168 appearances in a Pompey shirt he moved on to Leeds United in 1988. It was at his last club, Exeter City, where he made his first management step when he was appointed player-manager in 2000.

He has since made a name for himself as a successful youth coach, managing England's Under 19s side between 2009 and 2014, leading the side the to UEFA European U-19 Championship semi finals in 2010 and 2012. Having left his position as one of the Football Association's National Coaches, Blake had a stroke in 2015. Fully recovered, two years later the former defender set up his own football consultancy business to support players, coaches and agents.

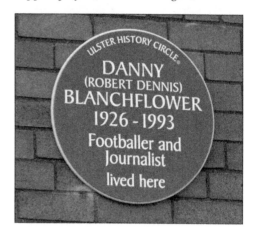

BLANCHFLOWER, Danny
Midfielder
Born: *Belfast, Northern Ireland*
Died: 1993
Playing career: *Barnsley, Villa, Spurs. (1948-1963) .*
Elder brother of Jackie, Danny played almost 700 games and was best known for his ten years at White Hart Lane. He captained Spurs to their unforgettable Double winning season of 1960-61 (becoming the first side to do so since Villa in 1897) and played 337 times for the club under legendary manager Bill Nicholson. He had moved to north London after a successful three seasons in the Midlands with Villa, where he made 55 senior appearances, scoring ten goals. Spurs signed him for £30,000 in 1954. He also represented Toronto City in Canada and Durban in South Africa and earned 56 caps for Northern Ireland, going on to manage the national side. He missed out on becoming Spurs boss and instead had a 15-game spell as boss of Chelsea. He also did some commentary work. After battling both Alzheimer's and Parkinson's disease, he died of pneumonia in a Staines nursing home aged 67 in 1993.

BLOOMFIELD, Ray
Striker
Born: *London*
Playing career: *Kensington Boys, Arsenal, Aston Villa, Atlanta Chiefs, Dallas Tornado (1964-1973)*

Striker Bloomfield rose through the ranks at Arsenal but never made a senior appearance for the Gunners. He signed for Villa in 1964 but only played three times before crossing the pond to join Atlanta Chiefs. He won two NASL titles in the newly professional league and a second with Dallas Tornado in 1971 after which he then ended his playing career. He later became a scout and player agent, involved in bringing several Croatian international players to England. He represented England at age group level alongside Ron "Chopper" Harris, David Pleast and Barry Fry.

BLORE, Vincent
Goalkeeper
Born: *Uttoxeter*
Died: 1997
Playing career: *Uttoxeter Amateurs, Burton Town, Aston Villa, Derby County, West Ham United, Crystal Palace, Exeter City (1932-1938)*

Blore played for Uttoxeter Amateurs, Burton Town and Aston Villa before moving to Derby County in August 1933. We say 'played', but the keeper never actually made a senior appearance in claret and blue. He moved on to Derby having only ever played for the Villa youth teams.

He donned claret again when he joined West Ham in 1935. Latterly of Crystal Palace and Exeter, he became a goalkeeping coach at Palace after he retired. Blore died in his home town of Uttoxeter in 1997 at the age of 90.

Boateng
GEORGE

BOATENG, George
Defensive midfielder
Born: *Nkawkaw, Ghana*
Playing career: *Excelsior, Feyenoord, Coventry City, Aston Villa, Middlesbrough, Hull City, Skoda Xanthi, Nottingham Forest, T-Team (1994-2013)*

Having joined Villa for £4.5 million from Coventry, the Ghanaian born Dutchman went on to play 131 times for the club, including a 2-0 defeat to Chelsea in the FA Cup final of 2000. He fell out with manager Graham Taylor and was sold to Middlesbrough. Also represented Hull, Skoda Xanthi in Greece, and Nottingham Forest. He played for the Netherlands at full international level, earning four caps. He went on to carve out a career in management, with a one season stint in charge of Malaysian side Kelantan. In 2018-19, the rangy formed midfielder worked for Blackburn Rovers as head coach of their Academy before returning to the club he served with distinction as a player. Boateng currently serves as manager of the Villa Under 18 side.

BODEN, Chris

Defender

Born: *Wolverhampton*
Playing career: *Aston Villa, Barnsley (loan), Derby County, Shrewsbury Town (loan), Hereford United (1991-1999)*

Boden was a trainee at Aston Villa, where he made just one senior appearance despite being at the club between 1991 and 1995. He also briefly played for Barnsley, Derby County, Shrewsbury Town and Hereford United during a short eight year career. Wolverhampton born Boden retired from professional football in 2001 after suffering a knee injury. Still based in the Midlands, he has now taken up a new career as a teacher.

BODEN, John

Defender/half-back/centre forward

Born: *Northwich*
Died: 1946
Playing career: *Glossop, Clapton Orient, Aston Villa, Northwich Victoria, Reading, Croydon Common, Plymouth Argyle, New Brompton (1902-1913)*

A defender or half-back, diminutive Boden (no relation to namesake Chris) played in the Football League for Glossop, Clapton Orient and Aston Villa. He featured 17 times for the latter and scored twice as they finished fifth in the First Division in the 1906-07 season. He then moved into the Southern League to play for Reading, Croydon Common, Plymouth and New Brompton. Despite starting out as a defender by trade, Boden was known for his versatility, being equally adept is as many as six different positions. Later worked as a coach and was assistant manager at Argyle. Boden died in his native Northwich in Cheshire in 1946 aged 64.

BOSNICH, Mark

Goalkeeper

Born: *Liverpool, Australia*
Playing career: *Sydney United, Manchester United, Aston Villa, Chelsea, Central Coast Mariners, Sydney Olympic (1988-2009)*

Bosnich played for Sydney as a youth player before he moved to England and signed for Manchester United at 17. There, he played 23 times before briefly returning to Australia. He moved back to the Premier League and signed for Villa on a free transfer in 1992. He picked up a League Cup winners medal in 1994 and went on to feature 227 times in all competitions across seven and a half seasons at Villa Park. He went back to United, then had a brief spell at Chelsea before he returned to his native Australia, for whom he earned 17 international caps. Bosnich holds the rare distinction of scoring as a goalkeeper for his country, a late penalty in a 13-0 World Cup qualifying win. Whilst at Villa in 1996, he was fined £1,000 and found guilty of misconduct after giving a Nazi salute during a match against Spurs (a club with a large Jewish following). Bosnich is now a football analyst and commentator for Fox Sports football programmes. He also works as a players' agent.

BOULDING, Michael

Forward/winger

Born: *Sheffield*
Playing career: *Hallam, Mansfield Town, Grimsby Town, Aston Villa, Sheffield United (loan), Grimsby Town (loan), Barnsley, Cardiff City (loan), Rotherham United, Mansfield Town, Bradford City, Barnsley, Derby County (1998-2011)*

Had he not been a footballer, Boulding could have plied his trade as a professional tennis player. He was ranked as the British number three with a ranking high of 960, and played at junior Wimbledon and the qualifying rounds of all four major tournaments. Having chosen football, he played for a number of Football League clubs (most notably Mansfield Town and Bradford City). Boulding turned out for Villa in the Intertoto Cup of 2002. He never played in the Premier League for the club, however. Since retiring in 2012, he has run his family's property business along with his brother Rory, who was also a professional footballer.

Mark Bosnich

BOUMA, Wilfred

Left-back/centre-back
Born: *Helmond, Netherlands*
Playing career: *PSV, MVV (loan), Fortuna Sittard (loan), Aston Villa, (1994-2013)*
The Netherlands international signed for Aston Villa for £3.5m in 2005 under Martin O'Neill. Despite an injury ravaged start to his claret and blue career, he quickly became an established cult hero and went on to play 90 times for the club across five seasons, scoring one goal. Bouma was known for his hard-working nature, his intelligent reading of the game and tenacious approach. A dislocated ankle saw him ruled out for over a year and that spelt the end of his time at Villa Park. He had two spells at PSV, and also featured for MVV and Fortuna Sittard in his native homeland, both on loan. The pacy, powerful left-back represented his country at every level, from Under 15 to the full senior Dutch side, playing in two major tournaments, the Euros of 2004 and 2008. Since hanging up his boots Bouma has set foot on the coaching ladder and has been teaching children at PSV's academy. The 40-year-old was recently promoted to PSV under-17s coach.

BOWDEN, James

Centre-half
Born: *Wolverhampton*
Died: 1951
Playing career: *Yardley Methodists, Erdington, Aston Villa, West Bromwich Albion, Southampton, Grimsby Town, Hyde, Stourbridge (1903-1916)*
Bowden was born in Wolverhampton and joined Aston Villa on amateur terms in January 1903. He failed to make the grade at Villa and never appeared in the first team, before moving to local rivals West Bromwich Albion in June 1904.

He also featured for Southampton and Grimsby, then dropped down into non league football with Hyde and Stourbridge of the Birmingham&District League. Having retired in 1918, he drifted out the game and became a post war railway worker in Birmingham. Bowden died in 1951 at the age of 70 in Wolverhampton having lived in the Midlands all his life.

BOWEN, Teddy

Full-back
Born: *Hednesford*
Died: 1981
Playing career: *Aston Villa*
Bowen played over 200 games for Villa in the early days of the professional game in England. The full-back was scouted by Villa's first secretary/manager, George Ramsay, after playing for hometown team Hednesford Town. The claret and blue reached the FA Cup final that year, but Bowen did not play in the defeat to Newcastle. After 203 appearances, the full-back was sold to Norwich in 1934. He died in Stafford aged 78 in 1981.

BOWMAN, Tommy

Half-back
Born: *Tarbolton, Scotland*
Died: 1958
Playing career: *Annbank, Blackpool, Aston Villa, Southampton, Portsmouth, Eastleigh Athletic (1891-1912)*
Having played in Blackpool's first ever Football League fixture, centre half Bowman joined Aston Villa in 1897 and went on to play over 100 games for the club. In his four years at Villa, he was part of the team that won consecutive First Division titles in 1898/99 and 1899/00, becoming the English game's early powerhouses. Bowman moved to Southampton and played in the 1902 FA Cup final before he joined fierce rivals Portsmouth. He finished his playing career with works side Eastleigh Athletic in 1912. Although Bowman never received international recognition, he represented the Anglo-Scots in 1902 and 1903. After retirement from football, he resumed his original employment as a boiler scaler, where he worked on the docks at Southampton for many years. He remained on the south coast until his death in Southampton in 1958 aged 84.

BOYNE, Reginald

Inside-forward
Born: *Leeds*
Died: 1963
Playing career: *Aston Villa, Notts County (guest), Leicester Fosse (guest), Loughborough Brush, Brentford (1913-1921)*

Leeds-born Boyne moved to New Zealand at a young age and began his career in junior football there with Everton, named after the English club of the same name. After playing at junior level in the Yorkshire leagues, Boyne earned a pro contract by First Division Aston Villa in 1913 and went on to play 13 times in the next six years. The suspension of competitive football due to World War One ultimately hindered his career, but he continued to play for the club in wartime before departing in 1919. During the First World War, Boyne appeared as a guest for Notts County, Leicester Fosse and Loughborough Brush. He made 23 appearances and scored two goals in the Football League Midland Section for Leicester. He retired in 1921 and drifted out of the game to return to his native New Zealand, where he helped to run his family's farm. One of his brothers was killed in action on the Western Front in 1917. The ex inside forward died in Auckland in 1963, aged 71.

BRADLEY, Darren

Midfielder
Born: *Kings Norton*
Playing career: *Aston Villa, West Bromwich Albion, Walsall (1983-1997)*

Having signed for 'The Villains' as an apprentice in 1983, he went on to make 20 appearances in two years in claret and blue. He moved to West Brom in 1986 and will always be remembered for his long range screamer against Wolves in a 1993 Black Country derby. After being released by Wolves manager Alan Buckley, he remained in the Midlands for two further years with Walsall. Since hanging up his boots, he has played for Aston Villa Old Stars in charity and testimonial matches. Bradley has since become involved in launching Intergarage in 2000, a business designing and manufacturing underground garages, where he is currently a Sales Director.

Aston Villa All Stars

BRADLEY, Keith
Born: *Ellesmere Port, Cheshire*
Playing career: *Aston Villa, Everton (1971-1986)*
Bradley moved to the blue half of
Merseyside at the age of 16. He then began
his decade long association at the Villa
having been scouted and signed by the
claret-and-blue's then boss Joe Mercer.
A pacy and powerful full-back, Bradley
played in the 1971 League Cup final for
Villa at Wembley as they lost 2-0 to Spurs.
After leaving Villa, he moved to the Posh
of Peterborough for a further four years
until he retired from playing. He linked up
with another former Villa manager, Ron
Saunders, across the city at Birmingham,
where he coached the youth team. He left in
1986 and then opened and ran his successful
restaurant Badgers in Mojacar (Spain),
remaining there until 2011 when he retired
and handed it over to his son Lewis.

BRAWN, Billy
Outside-right
Born: *Wellingborough*
Died: 1932
Playing career: *Wellingborough Town, Northampton
Town, Sheffield United, Aston Villa, Middlesbrough,
Chelsea, Brentford, Tottenham Hotspur (1894-1918)*
At Villa Park, Wellingborough born winger
Brawn made 107 appearances and scored
20 goals in a five year spell at the club.
A winger, Brawn was in the Villa team
that won the FA Cup in 1905, cementing
their status as the pre-eminent force in
English football's Victorian era. He was
capped twice by England. Spent two years
at Middlesbrough before finishing his
career with Chelsea, Brentford and Spurs.

He retired in 1913. While with Brentford,
Brawn ran the Kings Arms Hotel in the town
and combined that role with an advisory
position on the board at Brentford FC
between 1919 and 1921. Brawn died in 1932
at the age of 54.

BREITKREUTZ, Matthias
Midfielder
Born: *Crivitz, East Germany*
Playing career: *SG Bergmann-Borsig, Aston Villa,
Hansa Rostock, Arminia Bielefeld, 1. FC Saarbr ucken,
VfB Leipzig, FC Augsburg (1988-2003)*
Breitkreuts spent his entire career in his
native homeland, save for his three years
in England with Villa, for whom he made
21 appearances, although only five of these
came in the top division. The midfielder
played in the early days of the newly formed
Premier League but failed to shine at Villa
Park and returned to Germany with Hansa
Rostock in 1994. Moved to Bielefeld and
then returned to Hansa for a second time.
Finished his career with Augsburg in 2003
and then returned to Hansa Rostock to take
up a position coaching their youth sides.

BREMNER, Des
Midfielder
Born: *Aberchirder, Banffshire, Scotland*
Playing career: *Deveronvale, Hibernian, Aston Villa,
Birmingham City, Fulham, Walsall, Stafford Rangers,
Sutton Town (1971-1994)*
A midfielder, Bremner started out in his
native Scotland with Highland League side
Deveronvale before he moved to Hibernian
and played over 200 games. Moving south
of the border to the Midlands, he signed
for Villa in 1979 for a fee of £275,000. A
promising athlete and full-back in his
younger days, Bremner brought speed as
well as skill to his game. Committed and
uncompromising, he was a determined ball-
winning midfield player who was equally
as good breaking up attacks or starting
them. An ever present in his second season
at the club, he won League Championship,
European Cup and UEFA Super Cup
medals during his time in claret and blue
before joining Birmingham City in 1984.
After retiring as a player he worked for
the Professional Footballers' Association,
subsequently becoming the managing
director of the financial division of the
organisation.

BRETT, Frank

Born: *Derby*
Died: 1988
Playing career: *Manchester United, Aston Villa, Northampton Town, Brighton & Hove Albion (1921-1930).*

Brett was only cleared to play for United by the FA after it emerged he had signed amateur forms with Villa. He started his only season as full back but lost his place after six games to Charlie Retford and left, ironically, for Villa Park at the end of his only season at the club. He never made a senior appearance for the claret and blue. He settled in Sussex running a coal merchants business in Hove before opening a bookmakers with his former Brighton team mate, Ernie Wilson, He lived in Chichester in retirement and died in July 1988, aged 89.

BRIGGS, Frank

Left-half
Born: *Salford, Greater Manchester*
Died: 1984
Playing career: *Port Vale, Aston Villa, Wrexham (1937-1938)*

A left-half, Briggs (no relation to Wilson), joined Port Vale at the age of 20 but played only eight games in the Third Division North before moving on. Briggs later joined Aston Villa and Wrexham, but never made a senior first team appearance for either club. He also guested for Watford during the Second World War. After retirement as a player he drifted out of the the game, working in retail and as a warehouse assistant. Briggs died in 1984 in Bury at the age of 67.

Des Bremner

BRIGGS, Wilson
Defender
Born: *Gorebridge, Scotland*
Died: 2005
Playing career: *Arniston Rangers, Aston Villa, Falkirk, East Fife, Raith Rovers (1961-1971)*
Wilson Briggs spent most of his career in his native Scotland with Arniston Rangers, until he moved to Aston Villa in 1961. The defender made two first team appearances under manager Joe Mercer as Villa finished seventh in the First Division. He was then without a club for five years until he returned to his homeland to sign for Falkirk. Brief stints at East Fife and Raith Rovers followed before he took up a job as a gardener, staying in Scotland, after retiring as a player in 1971. He died at the age of 62 in February 2005 in Birmingham.

BRITTLETON, John
Defender
Born: *Winsford*
Died: 1982
Playing career: *Aston Villa (1927-1930)*
Brittleton followed in his father Tom's footsteps by becoming a professional footballer although - unlike his Dad - he was never capped at international level. Defender Brittleton Jr. only ever played for the claret and blue, making ten appearances across three seasons in the 1920s between the wars. The club finished eighth in the top division during his debut season, then third and fourth in the following two campaigns. Became a labourer at a saltworks after he hung up his boots. He died in Winsford, Cheshire in 1982 (aged 76).

BROADBENT, Peter
Midfielder
Born: *Elvington, Kent*
Died: 2013
Playing career: *Dover Athletic, Brentford, Wolverhampton Wanderers, Shrewsbury Town, Aston Villa, Stockport County, Bromsgrove Rovers (1949-1971)*
An inside forward, he played in the Football League between 1950-1970. He played for Wolverhampton Wanderers between 1951-65 making 452 appearances in the Football League scoring 127 goals. During this time he won three league titles with them and the F.A.Cup. He won seven caps for England between 1958-60.

After his playing career finished he opened a shop in Halesowen with his wife which was called Babyland. He was a keen golfer. After a long battle with Alzheimers disease he died in a care home near Wolverhampton on 1st October 2013 aged 80.

BROCK, Stuart
Goalkeeper
Born: *West Bromwich*
Playing career: *Aston Villa, Northampton Town, Solihull Borough, Kidderminster Harriers, Halesowen Town, AFC Telford United, Hull City (loan), Bromsgrove Rovers, Willenhall Town, Hednesford Town, Stourbridge, (1995-2009)*
A trainee on schoolboy forms at Villa, goalkeeper Brock spent three years as a professional in claret and blue but never made a first team appearance. He went on to turn out for many different lower and non league clubs including Halesowen, Telford Bromsgrove and Hednesford across two spells. A superb shot-stopper at 6ft 1, he stayed on at the Staffordshire club as a goalkeeping coach after he retired. He continues to live in West Bromwich and has worked as a delivery driver.

BROCKLEBANK, Bob
Inside right
Born: *Finchley, London*
Died: 1981
Playing career: *Aston Villa, Burnley (1930-1939)*
North London born Brocklebank came to the attention of Aston Villa's scouts in 1929 while playing with London amateurs Finchley. Seven years at Villa Park were spent almost exclusively in the reserves before he was transferred to Burnley at the age of 28 in 1936. Brocklebank became a Turf Moor regular, making 121 League appearances and scoring 33 goals for the Clarets. He earned the nickname The Toff because of his gentlemanly approach to life and football. Brocklebank continued to play for Burnley throughout the Second World War but began to put out feelers for a post-playing career in the game. He began his managerial career at Chesterfield and later took charge of Birmingham City, Hull City and Bradford. He did not seek full-time employment in football again having resigned at Valley Parade, and eventually retired to Brixham, in Devon, where he died in 1981 at the age of 73.

WILLS'S CIGARETTES

F. H. BROOME (ASTON VILLA)

BROOME, Frank

Forward
Born: *Berkhamsted*
Died: 1994
Playing career: *Boxmoor United, Berkhamsted Town, Aston Villa, Derby County, Notts County, Brentford, Crewe Alexandra, Shelbourne (1934-1955)*

Hertfordshire born winger Frank Broomesigned for Aston Villa in November 1934, establishing himself as a regular from March the following year. He scored 29 goals in the 1936-37 campaign with hat-tricks against both Blackpool and Blackburn Rovers in March 1937 and scored another 26 goals in 1937-38 as Aston Villa won the Second Division Championship. A prolific goalscorer, he earned seven caps for the senior England team, even though his career with the national team was cut short by the Second World War. He guested for Nottingham Forest and Wolves during the War playing for them in their 1942 Wartime Cup Final victory. He returned to Villa Park after the War but then moved to Derby.

A spell in the League of Ireland followed before a career in management followed. He served Notts County as both caretaker boss and assistant, and went on to take charge of Exeter City and Southend. Broome also coached in Australia. Died in 1994

BROWN, Albert

Striker
Born: *Austrey, Warwickshire*
Died: 1955
Playing career: *Atherstone Star, Tamworth, Aston Villa, Southampton, QPR , Preston North End, Blackpool (1898-1906)*

Older sibling of Arthur Brown (below), he was in the Villa team that won the FA Cup in 1887, beating local rivals West Bromwich Albion 2-0 in the final, Also holds the distinction of being one of the eleven men to play in Villa's first ever professional league match. He went on to play every match for the club that season, the inaugral campaign of the Football League. In all he played 86 games for Villa, scoring 37 times as a winger/striker. He retired from the game through injury in 1909 and died in 1930.

BROWN, Arthur

Forward
Born: *Aston, Birmingham*
Died: 1909
Playing career: *Aston Cross, Aston Unity, Aston Comrades, Aston Villa, Mitchell St George's, Birchfield Trinity, Birmingham Excelsior, (1878-1886)*

Younger brother of Albert (above) and known as "Digger", his club career came before the inception of the Football League. All of his appearances came in friendlies and in the FA Cup. He played 22 matches and scored 15 times in the latter competition. Brown began his career playing for local junior sides including Aston Cross, Aston Unity and Aston Comrades before joining the region's major club Aston Villa in 1878. His time there only lasted a few weeks though before he left to join Mitchell St George's. By 1886, ill-health had forced Brown to retire and he therefore missed out on appearing in the inaugural Football League season. He also represented England on three occasions, all in the space of 23 days in 1882, scoring four times. He died in 1909, aged 50.

BROWN, George

Striker
Born: *Mickley*
Died: 1948
Playing career: *Mickley Colliery, Huddersfield Town, Aston Villa, Burnley, Leeds United, Darlington (1921-1938)*

A centre-forward, he was the highest ever goal-scorer for Huddersfield Town with 159 goals; 142 in the League in 213 appearances and 17 from 16 outings in the FA Cup. Signed straight from his pit team at Mickley in May 1921, he was eventually sold to Aston Villa in August 1929 for £5,000. During his career he scored 273 goals in 440 games, between 1921 and 1938, after which he retired to run a pub. He gained nine full England caps (five goals) and represented the Football League once. He also had a two year tenure as player/manager of Darlington in 1936.

BROWN, James

Midfielder
Born: *Bothwell, Scotland*
Playing career: *Aston Villa, Preston North End, Ethnikos, Portsmouth, Hibernian, Worcester City (1969-1981)*

In 1969, James'Jimmy' Brown became the youngest player ever to represent Villa in a first team competitive match. Villa lost 2-1 to Bolton but Brown created a piece of history that still stands to this day.

He was just 15 years and 349 days old when he made his debut, and went on to make 88 appearances for the club, scoring one goal. He won the FA Youth Cup at Villa Park and later moved on to play for Preston, Ethnikos in Greece and Portsmouth. Brown represented his native Scotland at youth level but never got capped for the senior squad. After retirement, he stayed in the area and took up a job in social services. Brown continues to live in Birmingham and now holds employment for the council on a play scheme in the Kitts Green area of the city.

BROWN, James

Wing-half
Born: *Birmingham*
Died: 1934
Playing career: *Aston Villa (1890-1893)*

Birmingham-born Brown played as a wing-half for Villa. He made over 50 appearances for the club in three years in the Midlands between 1890 and 1893, in the early days of competitive, professional league football in the country. He did not play for any other professional club but did go on to represent the Army and several works teams in the local area having left Aston Villa. He later worked as a stonemason and bricklayer upon retiring from the game in 1898. Brown died in 1934 aged 66.

BROWN, Sailor

Inside-forward

Born: *Great Yarmouth* Died: 2008
Playing career: *Great Yarmouth Town, Gorleston, Charlton A, Nottingham F, Aston Villa, (1934-1948)*

Recognised as one of the best forwards of his era, Brown's career was ultimately shattered by World War Two. Brown played alongside the likes of Stanley Matthews for England. He made his name with Charlton before he joined Villa for a then club record fee of £10,000 in 1947. Brown retired in 1956 and worked as a bookmaker and a timber merchant, while also scouting for Villa. He lived in Forres, Scotland in his later life and died in 2008, at the age of 93. Real name Bert, he was known as 'Sailor' - the nickname sticking after he was called Popeye because of his short, muscular build.

BROWNE, Paul

Central defender

Born: *Glasgow, Scotland*
Playing career: *Aston Villa, Raith Rovers, Arbroath (1993-2004)*

A commanding presence as a tall 6ft 1 defender, the Scot began his career in the Midlands. Despite his first team breakthrough, he was sold to Raith Rovers and went on to play 170 times for the Scottish club. In July 2003, Browne returned to Arbroath, after previous target Eddie Forrest left on the promise of full-time football at Raith Rovers. Arbroath manager John Brownlie signed Browne as a replacement for Forrest, then discovered that Forrest had been duped. A telephone call that Forrest had believed to be from Danny Smith, the Raith chairman, had been a hoax. Browne was sacked by Arbroath and fled the country although he was later re-signed. Browne was capped by Scotland under-21 during his time at Aston Villa. He later became a player agent upon retirement in 2005.

BUCKLEY, Chris

Centre-half

Born: *Urmston, Lancashire* Died: 1973
Playing career: *Brighton & Hove Albion, Aston Villa, Arsenal (1905-1921)*

The younger brother of the legendary Major Frank Buckley, centre half Chris Buckley was born in Urmston, Manchester, and had been an amateur at Manchester City as a teenager spending 1903-04 at Hyde Road without making their first eleven. His first professional contract came from Southern League Brighton & Hove Albion in 1905, and he was soon signed by Villa in 1906, However he suffered an early setback when he broke his ankle on the opening day of the following season against Manchester United, an injury that kept him out of the game for over a year. Fit again, he played 37 games as Aston Villa won the League Championship in 1909-10. After retiring, Buckley returned to Villa, joining the Club's Board of Directors in 1936, and serving as Chairman from 1955 to 1966. He stepped down as a director in 1967 and died in 1973 aged 86.

PROMINENT FOOTBALLERS.

C. L. BUCKLEY,

ASTON VILLA.

BUCKLEY, Major Frank
Defender
Born: Lancashire Died: 1964
Playing career: Aston Villa, Brighton, Manchester United, Manchester City, Birmingham City, Derby County, Bradford City, Norwich City (1902- 1920).
Having started his career at Villa, Frank Buckley spent one season at Old Trafford as understudy to Charlie Roberts and left after only making three appearances. He went on to rise to the rank of Major, serving in the Football Battalion during the Great War. Became a legendary manager with Wolves between 1927 and 1944 after cutting his teeth in management with Norwich City and Blackpool. Had worked as a salesman in between his first two jobs, he later had spells in charge of Notts County, Hull City, Leeds United and Walsall. After hanging up his boots, he was a progress section leader for Rolls Royce in Watford. Died in 1964.

BULCOCK, Joe
Right-back
Born: Burnley Died: 1918
Playing career: Brynn Central, Burnley, Aston Villa, Bury, Macclesfield, Exeter City, Crystal Palace, Swansea Town (1906-1915)
Corporal Joe Bulcock was best remembered for his five years at Crystal Palace where made over 150 appearances. After catching the eye in local football, he had a trial at Villa Park, and later twice had spells at Bury. Exeter City boss Arthur Chadwick persuaded him to move south in the close season of 1908. He ended up at Swansea Town, but was killed in action in France during World War One at the age of 39.

BULL, Nikki
Goalkeeper
Born: Hastings
Playing career: Aston Villa, QPR, Hayes (loan), Aldershot Town, Brentford, Wycombe Wanderers, Margate (1996-2014)
Sussex born Bull had a youth career at Villa and QPR, but never made the grade at that level. He moved on to a succession of lower league clubs, notably Aldershot where he scored a last minute penalty to secure their promotion in 2006. He earned four caps for England 'C' and went on to return to Margate, this time for a three season stint as their manager. He is currently player/boss of Isthmian League side Leatherhead.

BULLIVANT, Terry
Midfielder
Born: Lambeth
Playing career: Fulham, Aston Villa, Charlton Athletic, Reading, Brentford (1974-1986)
During his career, he was a tenacious, tough tackling, box to box midfielder. Bullivant enjoyed a successful playing career spent across spells with five clubs as he turned out for Fulham, Villa, Charlton, Reading and Brentford. He transferred to Aston Villa for £220,000 in November 1979. Since retiring, Bullivant has embarked on an extensive coaching and scouting having worked at Barnet, Reading, Brentford, Watford and Birmingham City amongst others. Bullivant is currently chief scout for Millwall.

BULLOCK, Norman
Winger
Born: Nuneaton Died: 2003
Playing career: Nuneaton Borough, Aston Villa, Chester-City, Rhyl (1949-1960)
A winger known his pace and trickery, who started out at Nuneaton Borough and then played for Villa for three seasons making 70 appearances. Moved on to Chester and then to Rhyl. He served in the Army, dropping into the Central League and then underwent National Service at Oswestry. In 1962 he joined Prestatyn Town in the Welsh league where he finished his playing days. He became a plumber and later a self employed house builder before his death in 2003 at 71.

BUNN, Mark
Goalkeeper
Born: Camden
Playing career: Tottenham Hotspur, Northampton Town, Kettering Town (loan), Blackburn Rovers, Leicester City (loan), Sheffield United (loan), Norwich City, Aston Villa (1998-2015)
A veteran and well-travelled custodian, Bunn has played for seven clubs across an 18 year career. He is currently a free agent having been released by Villa at the end of the last season. Bunn had a succession of permanent and loan spells with various clubs followed before being signed by Norwich from Blackburn Rovers as cover for John Ruddy, in time for the 2012–13 season. He then joined Aston Villa as a free transfer signing in 2015. Now 34, Bunn still plays as a goalkeeper in League Two for Cambridge United.

BURGESS, Richard
Forward
Born: *Stourport-on-Severn*
Playing career: *Aston Villa, Stoke City, Kidderminster Harriers (loan), Bromsgrove Rovers, Port Vale, Nuneaton Borough (1995-2002)*

Burgess started his career as a schoolboy at Villa Park, but left for Stoke City in 1997 without having played a first-team game for the "Villains." He helped Redditch to win the Southern League Division One West title in 2003–04. Having returned to the club in which he had four spells with during his playing career as a striker, Burgess is now a coach at Bromsgrove.

BURKE, Mark
Midfielder
Born: *Solihull*
Playing career: *Aston Villa, Middlesbrough, Darlington (loan), Wolverhampton Wanderers, Luton Town (loan), Port Vale, Fortuna Sittard, Omiya Ardija, Rapid Bucharest, IF Brommapojkarna, TOP Oss (1983-2002)*

A player known for his ball retention and distribution, Burke had a 15 year career for 11 different clubs in England, the Netherlands, Japan, Romania and Sweden. Burke joined Aston Villa as a youth team scholar in June 1985 and played for England at youth level, before signing as a full time pro in 1987. Burke managed only eight appearances for the club before joining fellow Second Division side Middlesbrough only ten months later. He played in 'Boro's' promotion winning side of but then fell out with manager Bruce Rioch and moved to Darlington on loan, then Wolves, before another loan foray at Luton. He then embarked on something of a world tour where he represented five different sides before retiring as a player in 2004. He became a children's author and is also multilingual being capable in English, Spanish and Dutch. The 50 year old Brummie now works as a scout for former club Middlesbrough.

BURRIDGE, John
Goalkeeper
Born: *Workington*
Playing career: *Workington, Blackpool, Aston Villa, Southend United, Crystal Palace, QPR, Wolves, Derby County, Sheffield United, Southampton, Newcastle United, Hibernian, Scarborough, Lincoln City, Enfield, Aberdeen, Dunfermline Athletic, Dumbarton, Falkirk, Manchester City, Notts County, Witton Albion, Darlington, Grimsby Town (1969-1997)*

In his senior career he played for 29 clubs in a career that lasted nearly 30 years. Overall, Burridge played 771 league games in the English and Scottish leagues, and several more at non-league level. Burridge (nicknamed Budgie), played for fifteen Football League teams, which is a still-existing record. He played 65 games for Villa under Ron Saunders, winning the League Cup before losing his place to Jimmy Rimmer. He signed for the club for £75,000 from Blackpool. He was the oldest player to appear in the Premier League aged 43 with Manchester City. He finished his playing career with a brief spell as player-manager at Blyth Spartans in 1997, following a similarly brief spell back at Newcastle United as goalkeeping coach. Since then, he has served in the same role with the Oman national side and currently works in India with Kerala Blasters as goalkeeping coach. He has also been involved in television punditry work.

John Burridge
@TheBudgieTweets

The greatest goalkeeper the world has never seen. I should still be playing.

BURROWS, Harry
Forward
Born: *Haydock*
Playing career: *Aston Villa, Stoke City, Cleveland Stokers (loan), Plymouth Argyle (1956-1975)*
Burrows could play in all forward positions but was most regularly played as an out and out winger. He was renowned for his pace and powerful left foot shot. He became an apprentice with the National Coal Board before being persuaded by Villa manager Joe Mercer to sign for them. Burrows was part of the Villa team to win the Second Division in his debut season and then played and scored in the final of the inaugural League Cup in 1961 as Villa beat Rotherham United 3–2. A highly prized asset at Villa Park, he went on to play over 150 times for the team before he transferred to Stoke for £27,000 in 1965. On his retirement Burrows returned to Staffordshire and ran a carpet business, a pub and a post office and occasionally turned out in charity matches. Burrows lived for a number of years in the Staffordshire village of Abbots Bromley where he is still the president of the local football club, the Abbots Bromley Stags.

BURTON, John
Defender
Born: *Birmingham* Died: 1914
Playing career: *Handsworth Victoria, Aston Park Unity, Aston Villa (1885-1893)*
Known as Jack, he signed for Villa in 1885 and stayed with them until 1893, playing for the club as they won the FA Cup in 1887. A wing - half, he made 28 appearances for the side across an eight year period, scoring once. A knee injury forced his retirement and he then became a welder. He died in Hockley, Birmingham, in 1914 at the age of 50. His career saw him play in Aston Villa's first ever match in the Football League.

BUTCHER, Fred
Left-back
Born: *Hemingfield* Died: 1996
Playing career: *Hoyland, Aston Villa, Blackpool, Swindon Town (1931-1939)*
Butcher started out as professional with Villa and made only two league appearances in claret and blue despite being at the club for five years. He moved on to Blackpool and became best known for his time at Swindon Town.

A tough-tackling left-back, Butcher made a total of 42 appearances for Town. A left-back, he went on to work in a munitions factory during World War Two and then lived in Swindon where he became a cab driver. He was 82 when he died in May 1996.

BUTLER, Lee
Goalkeeper
Born: *Sheffield*
Playing career: *Lincoln City, Barnsley, Wigan Athletic, Dunfermline Athletic, Halifax Town, Doncaster Rovers, Alfreton Town (1985-2008)*
His four-year stint at Aston Villa proved the zenith of the stopper's career, although he found first team opportunities limited as back up to Nigel Spink. He played eight times during his tenure in the Midlands (1987-1991). He went on to play more than 100 games for Barnsley, and also turned out for Scunthorpe, Wigan, Doncaster, Halifax and Dunfermline in Scotland. He retired as a player in 2009 and now works as goalkeeping coach at Bolton - a position he also filled at 'Donny' for three years between 2013 and 2016.

BUTTRESS, Mike
Defender
Born: *Peterborough*
Playing career: *Aston Villa, Gillingham, Telford United (1976-1978)*
Buttress only played three games for Villa, but his debut was a memorable one as he came off the bench in a 5-1 First Division thumping of all conquering Liverpool in 1976. A player who seems only a footnote in the annal of Villa's illustrious history featured in one of the team's greatest ever performances. He would only start one match for the club before moving on to Third Division Gillingham in 1976, where he played ten times. He then dropped into non league football with Telford, later becoming a coach at the club before working for a consultancy business.

"DID YOU KNOW?"

"The 128 goals during the 1930/31 season still stands as the record for the most top-flight goals scored in a single season."

BYFIELD, Darren

Forward

Born: *Sutton Coldfield*

Playing career: *Aston Villa, Preston North End (loan), Northampton Town (loan), Cambridge United (loan), Blackpool (loan), Walsall, Rotherham United (loan), Rotherham United, Sunderland, Gillingham, Millwall, Bristol City, Doncaster Rovers, Oldham Athletic (loan), Oldham Athletic, Solihull Moors, AFC Telford United, Tamworth, Solihull Moors (1997-2014)*

Byfield started his career at Aston Villa, and a rapid rise through the ranks led to a Premier League debut in 1997. Given his debut by outgoing boss Brian Little, he rarely featured under new "Villans" manager John Gregory. He made six further substitute appearances in 1997–98 and then moved on to three successive loan spells at Preston, Northampton and Cambridge. A journeyman player, he represented 18 clubs and also won six caps for Jamaica in 2003, scoring one goal. He was briefly married to pop star Jamelia, and after retiring he moved into management. He took over at Redditch United as player/manager, and also had a brief spell in charge of Stratford Town and Walsall Wood. As of 2019, he is currently boss of Southern League Premier Division side Alvechurch.

Colin Calderwood

CALDERWOOD, Colin

Defender

Born: *Stranraer, Scotland*

Playing career: *Mansfield Town, Swindon Town, Tottenham Hotspur, Aston Villa, Nottingham Forest, Notts County (1982-2001)*

Best known for his time at Swindon where he played over 300 times, he went on to Spurs - winning the League Cup - and then signed for Villa. Played 26 times for the Midlands club before he moved to Nottingham Forest and finished his career on loan at Notts County. He played 36 times for Scotland, scoring once and playing in two major tournaments for his country at Euro 96' and the 1998 World Cup. Upon retirement as a player, Calderwood became reserve team manager at Spurs. Later he was boss of Northampton Town, Nottingham Forest and Cambridge United. Best known for several stints as assistant manager, notably at Newcastle, Brighton and back at Villa. Calderwood is currently the head coach of League Two side Cambridge United.

Jamelia

CALLAGHAN, Ernie
Defender
Born: *Newtown* Died: 1972
Playing career: *Atherstone , Aston Villa (1930-1947)*
Birmingham born right back Callaghan. known as "Mush" played for non league Atherstone Town before signing for First Division Aston Villa in September 1930. He remained a fringe player at Villa making 13 appearances during their relegation season in 1935-36, but broke into the team on a regular basis from February 1937, missing only two games the following season as Villa won the Second Division Championship. During the Second World War he was also a constable in Birmingham City Police. Until it was overtaken by Brad Friedel, he previously held the Aston Villa club record for the oldest first team player, being 39 years and 257 days old when he played against Grimsby. After his retirement Callaghan became the groundskeeper for Aston Villa and lived in a house on site.

CALLAGHAN, Nigel
Right Wing
Born: *Singapore*
Playing career: *Watford, Derby County, Aston Villa, Stafford Rangers, Hellenic (1980-1994)*
A well travelled right winger, he played for Watford in the 1984 FA Cup final and also represented both the England Under 21s and the B team. He played 26 times for Villa (scoring once), securing First Division survival in his debut season, narrowly missing out on the title in his second. Having fallen out of favour he was loaned to Derby County. Also had brief spells at Watford, Huddersfield. He retired aged only 29 and continues to work as a DJ. He is also a bowel cancer survivor and continues to live in Stafford.

CAMPBELL, Archie
Right-half/Centre-half
Born: *Crook, County Durham* Died: 1980
Playing career: *Spennymoor United, Aston Villa, Lincoln City, Craghead United (1922-1927)*
He made over 50 appearances in the Football League during a six year career at two clubs, Villa and Lincoln. Equally as adept as either a right half or centre half, he was the nephew of Scotland international and Celtic and fellow Aston Villa player John Campbell. He made four appearances for Villa in two seasons having signed from Spennymoor United and was then sold to Lincoln in 1925, where he became a mainstay of the Imps defence. After retirement, he worked for the local council as a park warden in his native County Durham. He died there in 1980 aged 75.

CAMPBELL, Bobby
Striker
Born: *Belfast, Northern Ireland*
Playing career: *Aston Villa, Halifax Town (loan), Sheffield United, Vancouver Whitecaps, Huddersfield Town, Halifax Town, Brisbane City, Derby County, Bradford City, Wigan Athletic (1972-1988)*
His career at Villa will be remembered by many as merely a footnote, having become best known for his exploits in claret and amber of Bradford City. He made over 300 appearances for the Bantams, and became the club's all time leading goalscorer with 143. Campbell's record still stands today. He failed to establish himself in the Villa first team, making 10 league appearances for the club after joining in 1974. Twice capped by Northern Ireland, he was selected for the 1982 World Cup squad but didn't make an appearance. Upon retirement in 1988, he ran a working men's club in Huddersfield.

CAMPBELL, DJ
Forward
Born: *Hammersmith*
Playing career: *Aston Villa, Chesham United, Stevenage Borough, Brentford, Birmingham City, Leicester City, Derby County (loan), Blackburn Rovers, Millwall (loan), Maidenhead United (2000-2015)*
A much travelled striker who began his career at Villa as a trainee but was never offered a professional contract. He moved into non league football before returning to the Premier League with Birmingham City, Blackpool and latterly QPR.

Had several loan spells and then moved to National League South side Maidenhead, his most recent club, in 2014-15. Campbell has played twice for England C. Now aged 37, Campbell is without a club and has not taken up work elsewhere.

CAMPBELL, George

Half-back
Born: *Largs, Scotland* Died: 1898
Playing career: *Renton, Aston Villa, Dundee (1890-1893)*
Began and finished his career in his native Scotland, playing for Villa for three years in between. A half-back, he made 51 appearances for the club scoring twice, in the early years of professional league football. Despite Villa's early dominance in the English game, Campbell did not win a major honour at the club. Only five years after he last turned out for Villa in 1893, Campbell died at the young age of 27 in his hometown of Largs.

CAMPBELL, John

Forward
Born: *Glasgow, Scotland* Died: 1947
Playing career: *Celtic, Aston Villa, Celtic, Third Lanark (1890-1906)*
A wonderfully gifted and clever forward, Johnny Campbell signed for the Bhoys from Benburb in the spring of 1890 and made his debut in a Glasgow Cup tie at Parkhead in September that year. Coupling bravery and skill he originally played on the left wing and forged a memorable partnership on the flank with Sandy McMahon. Campbell was then surprisingly sold to Aston Villa in 1895 and he helped the Birmingham-based side claim a League and FA Cup double in season 1896-1897 (and was the first scorer of a goal at Villa Park) before gladly returning to Celtic Park that summer for his second spell with the Bhoys. It wasn't his only landmark in England. As well as scoring the first goal at Villa Park, he also scored the first goal at St James Park (Newcastle United's ground) in 1892. Campbell was capped 12 times by Scotland between 1893 and 1903. He scored four goals, including two against Ireland in March 1900. He retired in 1906 to become a coach at his last club Third Lanark and later worked as a scout for Celtic. He died in 1947 at the age of 76.

CAMPBELL, Lewis

Left-winger
Born: *Edinburgh, Scotland* Died: 1938
Playing career: *Aston Villa, Port Vale, Walsall Town Swifts, Burton Swifts (1893-1894)*
A pacy left-winger who was difficult to defend against, Campbell played for a plethora of clubs in his native Scotland. He moved south in 1889. At Villa he earned an FA Cup runner-up medal in 1892, playing in the final as the team suffered a defeat to local rivals West Brom. In August 1893, he joined Port Vale. He claimed 13 goals in 27 Second Division in the 1893–94 season, and became the first "Valiant" to score a hat-trick (he actually went one better and hit four) in the Football League in a 5–0 win over Walsall Town Swifts on 9 September. He moved on to that club on amateur terms and then Burton before retiring to work in a factory. He died in 1938 aged 74.

CANNING, Larry

Wing-half
Born: *Cowdenbeath, Scotland* Died: 2012
Playing career: *Broughty Amateurs, Paget Rangers, Aston Villa, Kettering Town, Northampton Town, Nuneaton Borough (1943-1957)*
He spent most of his career win the lower leagues, but played 39 times in the Football League for Villa, scoring three goals in eleven years at the club. He also had a brief spell at Division Three South side Northampton in 1956-57. Moved on to Nuneaton Borough and then retired in 1963 to return to Villa as a coach. He later served on the club's board and died aged 86 in 2012 after suffering with vascular dementia.

CAPALDI, John

Striker
Born: *Newarthill, Scotland*
Playing career: *Aston Villa, Motherwell, Pors Grenland (1975-1983)*
Capaldi played for the reserves and youth team from 1975–1979, before being sold to Motherwell in 1979 for £15,000. He played 11 times for the Scottish side before moving on to Pors Grenland in Norway where his son Tony - also a professional footballer - was born. Capaldi, a striker during his playing days, went on to manage non league side Bolehall Swifts during the 2002-03 season before he returned to Motherwell in his native Scotland as a scout and coach.

CAPEWELL, Len
Forward
Died: 1978
Playing career: *Aston Villa*

A free-scoring centre forward, Capewell signed for Aston Villa in January 1922, scoring on his debut. This was to be the first of exactly 100 goals for Aston Villa over the next seven years. He was a losing FA Cup Finalist in the 1924 Wembley defeat to Newcastle United in a season where he bagged 24 goals. He scored his 100th goal in his final Villa game but fell out of favour and in February 1930 he moved to Walsall. He drifted out of the game after retiring and went on to become a gardener and then a builder. Capewell died in 1978 aged 83. (Photo: His England v Scotland cap)

CARBONE, Benito
Forward
Born: *Bagnara Calabra, Italy*
Playing career: *Torino, Napoli, Internazionale, Sheffield Wednesday, Aston Villa, Bradford City, Como, Parma, Catanzaro, Vicenza, Pavia (1987-2010)*

A journeyman forward with a 22-year professional career, Carbone joined Villa for an undisclosed fee and had a season at Villa Park. He started the 2000 Cup final and earned a runners up medal. He moved on to Bradford and then had loan spells at Derby County and Middlesbrough before returning to his native Italy. He represented his country at Under 18 and Under 21 level. After retirement as a player, Carbone became a manager at Pavia, Varese, Vallee d'Aoste and most recently Terana in Italy's Serie C. He also briefly served in an advisory role at Leeds United.

CAREW, John
Striker
Born: *Lorenskog, Akershus, Norway*
Playing career: *Lorenskog, V,Äòlerenga, Rosenborg, Valencia, Roma (loan), Besiktas, Lyon,Aston Villa, Stoke City (loan), West Ham United (1995-2012)*

A cult hero at Villa Park, Carew scored 37 times in 117 games before he fell down the pecking order following Darren Bent's arrival. He spent four years at Villa then moved on Stoke and West Ham. He was capped 91 times for Norway (24 goals) as the first black player to play for his country, having been capped at every age group as well as senior level. He played at Euro 2000. Upon retirement he worked as coach at his first club, Lorenskog and then also had an acting career, starring in his first film 2014. In 2018 Carew starred in the Norwegian TV-series "Heimebane", playing an ageing star player for a small town Norwegian club.

CARR, Franz
Forward/Winger
Born: *Preston*
Playing career: *Blackburn Rovers, Nottingham Forest, Sheffield Wed, West Ham United, Newcastle United, Sheffield United, Leicester City, Aston Villa, Reggiana, Bolton Wanderers, West Bromwich Albion, Pittsburgh Bloodhounds, (1984-2000)*

After he burst on to the scenes in another area of the Midlands - at Forest - Carr earned a reputation as a hugely exciting and explosive winger who, at his peak, was known for his lightning pace. Carr began his career at Blackburn before he moved on to Forest for a then record £100,000 in 1984. He played only three games in two seasons at Villa Park but scored an FA Cup quarter final winner against old club Forest in that time. After retirement in 2000 following a spell in the Unitesd States playing for thwe wonderfully named Pittsburgh Bloodhounds, he moved into consultancy and most recently worked as a players' agent from his home in Derbyshire.

"DID YOU KNOW?"

"Archie Hunter became the first player to score in every round of the FA Cup in Villa's 1887 ccup winning campaign."

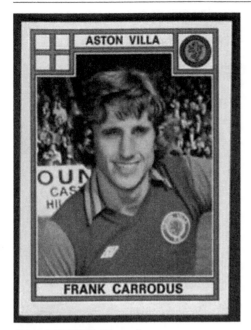

ASTON VILLA

FRANK CARRODUS

CARRODUS, Frank

Winger
Born: *Cheshire*
Playing career: *Man City, Aston Villa, Wrexham, Birmingham City, Bury, Altrincham (1964-1987)*
A winger best known for his time at Aston Villa he played in the Football League between 1969-84. He played over 150 games across six years at Villa Park. He continued playing non league football before getting a job in financial services which he did not like. He set up a Corporate Hospitality business in 1986 and was managing Director of the company Choice Events in Hale for 20 years. It dealt with hospitality at major sporting events. Alongside that, Carrodus became a very popular after dinner speaker for Aston Villa hospitality amongst others.

CARRUTHERS, Martin

Forward
Born: *Nottingham*
Playing career: *Aston Villa, Stoke City, Peterborough United, Darlington, Southend United, Scunthorpe United, Macclesfield Town, Lincoln City (1990-2005)*
In a long and distinguished playing career spanning 30 years, Carruthers turned out over 500 times for 12 different clubs, scoring 12 goals. 34 of those came in 86 games for Scunthorpe. He dropped into the non league game later on in his playing life, representing the likes of Grantham Town,

Ilkeston and Basford United, whom he also managed. Served as the club's player/ manager and the former striker also had a spell in charge of another of his ex clubs, Arnold Town. Carruthers worked at Education officer for Notts County before he was appointed as boss of United Counties League side Quorn AFC ahead of the 2019/20 season.

CARTLIDGE, Arthur

Goalkeeper
Born: *Stoke-upon-Trent*   Died: 1940
Playing career: *Penkell Victoria, Market Drayton Town, Bristol Rovers, Aston Villa, Stoke, South Shields (1899-1912)*
Stoke-on-Trent born goalkeeper Cartlidge was described as a "splendid specimen of an athlete" he won the Southern League Championship with Rovers in 1904-05 making 258 appearances for Rovers before transferring to Aston Villa in April 1908. He succeeded Billy George as Villa's first choice goalkeeper and playing 35 games as Aston Villa won the 1909-10 League Championship but lost his place that December and returned to Stoke, by now in The Southern League, in 1911 after 55 appearances for Villa. Retiring with the onset of World War One. He worked as coach at Bristol Rovers and then as a mechanic during the war.

CASCARINO, Tony

Striker
Born: *St Paul's Cray, Kent*
Playing career: *Gillingham, Millwall, Aston Villa, Celtic, Chelsea, Marseille, Red Star (1980-2000)*
A powerful, aggressive striker who join The Blues for £1.1m after only seven months with Celtic in Scotland. He was a regular for his two seasons at the club even though his goal return wasn't brilliant. Left for Marseille and he continued to play in France for seven years. Since hanging up his boots Cass has become a semi professional poker player and a media pundit. Has presented on Talksport, written for the Times and Hot Press and as well as making regular appearances on Sky Sports. Capped 88 times by the Republic of Ireland. Cascarino proved a controversial figure during his time in the game for his off field gambling habit, and he was also arrested in 2008 for allegedly assaulting and threatening to kill his former wife.

CHAMBERS, John
Midfielder
Born: *Birmingham*
Playing career: *Aston Villa, Southend United, Bromsgrove Rovers (1968-1970)*

Chambers was a talented and skilful midfielder whom played in the Football League for Aston Villa and Southend United.H The local lad rose through the ranks at Villa Park and then moved on to Southend after only a solitary season in the Midlands. His senior professional career lasted only two years before he was forced to retire through injury. He also had a spell as manager of Kidderminster Harriers from 1979 to 1983, and became player-manager of Alvechurch in 1984.

CHAPMAN, Roy
Inside-forward
Born: *Birmingham* Died: 1983
Playing career: *Kynoch Works, Aston Villa, Lincoln City, Mansfield Town, Lincoln City, Port Vale, Chester-City, Stafford Rangers (1952-1975)*

Chapman never fully established himself at Villa Park under Eric Houghton, and left the club after 24 appearances and eight goals. An inside-forward equally as adept with both feet, what he lacked pace he made for in aggression and ball control. Chapman moved on to Lincoln and then Mansfield before he returned to Sincil Bank as the Imps player/manager/

In all he scored 200 goals in 415 games in the Football League. He was also given the management job at Rangers, and took charge there until 1975 when he was appointed at Stockport. His reign at Stockport was brief, and he became a coach before returning to Stafford for a second spell as manager in 1977. He proved very successful as Stafford boss, winning five trophies in six seasons including a treble of Northern Premier League, FA Trophy, and Staffordshire Senior Cup treble in 1972; He died four years later aged only 49 after suffering a heart attack whilst playing in a five-a-side tournament in Stoke.

CHAPEL, Frederick
Inside-forward
Born: *Bristol* Died: 1965
Playing career: *Aston Villa, Birmingham, Crewe Alexandra, Brentford, Bristol City, Blyth Spartans (1906-1920)*

He played as an inside forward in the Football League for Aston Villa, Birmingham and Bristol City and in non-league football for Crewe Alexandra, Brentford and Blyth Spartans where he finished his career. He played nine times for Villa, scoring three times in two seasons at the club under George Ramsay. Having retired in 1920, Chapple worked as a PE teacher, combining this work with a scouting position for Blyth Spartans. Chapple died in 1965 in Bristol, aged 80.

CHARLES, Gary
Defender
Born: *Newham*
Playing career: *Nottingham Forest, Leicester City, Derby County, Aston Villa, Benfica, West Ham United, Birmingham City (1987-2000)*

Charles has struggled with alcoholism since retiring from football and has twice been inside prison, firstly for drink driving and then for cutting his electronic tag off so he could go on holiday to Spain in 2005. He then received a suspended sentence and a community order for assaulting a woman in a taxi office, and then turning up to court drunk. He went back to prison in 2006 for committing a public order offence whilst on his suspended sentence. Due to his colourful personal, his flair and is skill, he was known as "the Brazilian". Charles holds a Diploma in Counselling and his experience and knowledge has given him a desire and drive to help fellow sportspeople when dealing with addictions, stress or anxiety and any other issues that arise in an athlete's life. See: https://www.gcsportscare.co.uk

CHARSLEY, Chris

Goalkeeper
Born: *Leicester* Died: 1945
Playing career: *Aston Villa (guest), Small Heath Alliance/Small Heath, WBA, Small Heath (1881–1894)*
Charsley will be remembered in the Midlands as a brilliant goalkeeper. He played for Small Heath Alliance, forerunner of Birmingham City F.C., and was capped for England in the game against Ireland at Perry Barr, in 1893. He turned out for Stafford Town and Stafford Rangers as an amateur, and guested for Villa. After retiring from the game he was recalled to play in the famous "test" match against Darwen, at Stoke, which took Birmingham into the First Division. In 1899, Charsley held the rank of inspector in the Hackney Carriage Department of the Birmingham police when he was appointed Chief Constable of Coventry. On retiring from the police force in 1919, he moved to Weston-super-Mare, Somerset, where he became deputy Mayor and served on the town council until his death at the age of 80. He died in 1945 in Weston - super - Mare.

CHATT, Bob

Wing-half/Inside-forward
Born: *Barnard Castle* Died: 1955
Playing career: *Cleator Moor, Middlesbrough Ironopolis, Aston Villa, Stockton, South Shields, Willington Athletic (1893–1898)*
A member of the Aston Villa team which won the Football League championship three times in the 1890, Chatt was credited with scoring the fastest goal in FA Cup Final history, scored after just 30 seconds in the 1895 FA Cup Final. Chatt later won the FA Amateur Cup with Stockton and is the only player to have winner's medals for both the FA Cup and the FA Amateur Cup.

He played 94 times for Villa between 1893 and 1898, scoring 26 goals. He was influential in a Villa side that was, at that point, considered the country's finest, winning the league championship three times in four seasons. On leaving Villa, Chatt played for South Shields and Willington Athletic before becoming the trainer of Doncaster Rovers (1904–1905). He held similar posts with Port Vale (1905–1906), Manchester City (1906–1916), South Shields (1919), Caerphilly (1921–1922) and Newport County (1922–1931). He died in 1955 aged 85.

CHATTERLEY, Lew

Midfielder
Born: *Birmingham*
Playing career: *Aston Villa, Doncaster Rovers, Northampton Town, Grimsby Town, Southampton, Torquay United (1962–1978)*
Chatterley retired in 1978, he played as an amateur for Barnstaple Town as well as running a guest house. He then moved to the United States, where he coached Chicago Sting. He made the move to Southampton in 1979 to become Assistant Manager before taking up a similar role at Sunderland. Then came a spell as Poole Town manager, and the Assistant's job at Reading where he briefly was handed the role of caretaker manager. He returned to Southampton in 1990 as a youth development officer but was later promoted to coach and then caretaker manager when Dave Merrington was sacked. He became a teacher and a football coach at Winchester College, he also briefly scouted for Newcastle United.

CHESTER, Reg

Forward
Born: *Long Eaton, Derbyshire* Died: 1977
Playing career: *Aston Villa, Manchester United , Huddersfield Town, Darlington (1935–1937)*
A prolific goalscoring winger, Reg Chester started his football career with Long Eaton Rangers in 1919 before joining Peterborough & Fletton United in 1920, moving again to play for Stamford Town in 1921. He joined First Division Aston Villa making his Football League and had 10 seasons at Villa Park without ever being more than a squad player, the most appearances he ever made in a season being 20 in 1929-30.

He was however a regular goalscorer when he played, attested to by 34 goals in 97 appearances over his decade with Villa. He joined Second Division Manchester United in the 1935 close season, his goal in 13 appearances helping them win the Second Division Championship in 1935-36. He scored seven goals in 25 appearances at Leeds Road for Huddersfield but after losing his place in October 1936 joined Darlington in the 1937 close season, scoring 11 goals in 33 appearances during 1937-38 before he joined non league Arnold the following summer. He also subsequently played for Woodborough United and Grantham. He worked in Liverpool on the docks during World War Two then later became a delivery driver. He died in 1977 aged 72.

CHILD, Paul
Forward
Born: *Birmingham*
Playing career: *Aston Villa, Atlanta Apollos, San Jose Earthquakes (indoor), Memphis Rogues, Atlanta Chiefs, Pittsburgh Spirit (indoor), Carolina Lightnin, Baltimore Blast (indoor), Los Angeles Lazers (indoor), Pittsburgh Beadling (1966-1988)*

Birmingham born Child signed with First Division side Aston Villa when he turned fourteen in 1966. He remained with the club for the next six seasons but never made a first-team appearance. In 1972 Child was loaned to the Atlanta Chiefs of the North American Soccer League. Went on to play for San Jose Earthquakes, Memphis, Pittsburgh Spirits, Carolina Lightning, Pittsburgh

Beading and indoor for LA Lazers and Baltimore Blast. He was capped twice at senior level for USA. Went on to manage Pittsburgh Stingers and Detroit Neon in the Continental Indoor Soccer League. He later coached of a youth team composed of young refugees, BW United, in suburban Pittsburgh and has been head coach at FC Pittsburgh since June 2018. Alongside that role, Child also holds a job outside of footballer where he works as a project manager at a millworks in the Pittsburgh area.

CLARK, Tom
Midfielder
Born: *Luton* Died: *1981*
Playing career: *Aston Villa, Walsall (1946)*

Also played cricket as part of the great Surrey side that won an unprecedented seven successive County Championship titles between 1952 and 1958. Clark was an opening batsman and a spin bowler. He began in Minor Counties cricket with Bedfordshire, that being the county of his birth, and played three matches for them in 2946 and then moved to Surrey. He had to retire from cricket in 1959 due to worsening arthritis. Before deciding to concentrate on cricket, he played football for Aston Villa, appearing in their reserve team but never making a senior appearance with the club. In May 1948 he moved to Walsall, for whom he scored three goals in nine first team games in the Third Division (South) as a midfielder. He died in 1981 aged 56.

CLARKE, Bill
Winger
Born: *Mauchline, Scotland* Died: 1940
Playing career: *Benburb, Crown Athletic, Third Lanark, Arthurlie, East Stirlingshire, Bristol Rovers, Aston Villa, Bradford City (1901-1908)*

Signed for Villa from Bristol Rovers after spells in the lower leagues of Scotland. Played 41 times at Villa Park between 1901 and 1905, scoring five goals. Winger Clarke became the first mixed raced player to score in the Football League in 1901 during his debut season at Villa. Signed for Bradford City for £200 after four years in the Midlands. After retirement, he worked as an adviser for the Scottish FA and then on the board of one of his former clubs East Stirlingshire. Clarke died in 1940 aged 62.

CLARKE, George

Outside-left
Born: *Bolsover*
Died: 1977
Playing career: *Mansfield Town, Aston Villa, Crystal Palace, QPR, Folkestone (1922-1934)*

Clarke began his playing career with then non league Mansfield Town having previously worked as a miner at Welbeck Colliery. Villa signed him for £500 but he only played once for the club, three years after joining them. In his first season with Crystal Palace, Clarke missed only one game and remained a fixture in the side for the next seven seasons. Ahead of the 1933-34 campaign, outside left Clarke moved to Queens Park Rangers but remained there for q single season, before moving into non-league football with Folkestone. He briefly served as player/manager of Folkestone but then became a sports consultant. He died aged 76 in 1977.

CLAYTON, Gordon

Centre-forward
Born: *Sunderland* Died: 1976
Playing career: *Shotton Colliery, Wolverhampton Wanderers, Aston Villa, Burnley (1932-1940)*

A coalminer, he played football for Shotton Colliery before being signed by Wolverhampton Wanderers, in October 1932. Unsurprising given Wolves quality and talent at the time, he struggled to hold down a regular place in the team. Clayton scored 39 goals in 54 goals for Wolves before joining Aston Villa in October 1937. He was described as a tall, strapping footballer, recruited to "bolster up Villa's attack during their Second Division championship-winning season." However, Clayton was not a success and only scored one goal in 11 games before being transferred to Burnley. Became a fitness instructor and later worked at a colliery in his native North East.

COLE, Carlton

Striker
Born: *Croydon*
Playing career: *Chelsea, Wolverhampton Wanderers (loan), Charlton Athletic (loan), Aston Villa (loan), Celtic, West Ham United (1996-2015)*

Cole earned a reputation as something of a mystery box striker, capable of providing delight and despair in equal measure. A much travelled forward, he turned out for eight different clubs including a brief season long loan at Villa in 2004-05. Surprisingly for a striker, he never mustered more than ten goals in a single Premier League season. Also played for Celtic and plied his trade in the USA and Indonesia for Persib Bandung. Capped seven times by England, Cole was declared bankrupt by a court in London in 2018. Cole now works for West Ham's academy and represents the club on the after dinner speaking circuit.

Carlton Cole

COLE, Joe

Attacking midfielder/Winger
Born: *Paddington, London*
Playing career: *West Ham United, Chelsea, Liverpool, Lille (loan), Aston Villa, Coventry City (loan), Coventry City (1994-2016)*

Made his name with West Ham and Chelsea but was sent off during his first league appearance for Liverpool in August 2010. He had a spell on loan in France with Lille in 2011. Played in the Premier League for Chelsea, Liverpool (twice), and had a loan spell at Villa (2014-16). He played 12 games and scored once in his time at Villa Park and was an unused substitute during the 2015 FA Cup final. Capped 56 times by England, he scored a stunning volley at World Cup 2006 against Sweden. Finished his career at Tampa Bay Rowdies and retired at the end of 2018. He has since taken up a coaching role at Chelsea, where he won three Premier League titles as a player. A clever, tricky and dazzlingly gifted goalscoring winger, Cole is known for his dribbling and direct running but yet many believe he never quite lived up to his early potential, mainly in part due to the string of injuries he suffered throughout his career.

COLLINS, James

Centre-back
Born: *Newport, Wales*
Playing career: *Cardiff City, West Ham United, Aston Villa, West Ham, Aston Villa, Ipswich Town (2000-2019)*

Welsh international Collins played 95 games for Villa (2009-2012), in between two spells at West Ham. He started out at Cardiff and broke through into their first team, making a senior debut in 2000. He most recently played for Ipswich Town and is currently a free agent having been released. Collins had been training at Aston Villa following his release from West Ham United and impressed manager Dean Smith, being offered a five-week contract in December. However, he injured his calf in his first training session after signing the short-term deal, potentially ruling him out for its duration, leading Collins to cancel the contract. A full recovery allowed him to resume playing and led to a contract with Ipswich Town in January 2019. Collins played 51 times for Wales, and played twice at Euro 2016. Collins was arrested but later released without charge after a driving incident with former Villa team-mate Barry Bannan when the pair crashed their car on the M1 in 2011.

COLLINS, Lee

Defender
Born: *Birmingham*
Playing career: *Aston Villa, Stoke City, Cambridge United (loan), Moor Green (loan), Moor Green, Solihull Moors, Hinckley United (1995-2010)*

Locally born centre back Collins began his career with Villa as a trainee. He rose through the ranks but never made it to the senior side. Tall and famed for his aerial ability, Collins moved to Stoke in 1998 but struggled to become a regular for the Potters. Played once in the FA Cup for Cambridge before he embarked on a career in the non league scene, most notably for Moor Green in the Midland Division. Captained Solihull in the National League for two years before he took up a role as player/coach at Hinckley United. Since retirement, he has taken a degree in Physiotherapy and returned to Solihull Moors as club physio in 2014. As of 2019, Collins works as a recruitment advisor in Birmingham.

COLLYMORE, Stan

Striker

Born: *Stone, Staffordshire*
Playing career: *Walsall, Wolverhampton Wanderers, Stafford Rangers, Crystal Palace, Southend United, Nottingham Forest, Liverpool, Aston Villa, Fulham (loan), Leicester City, Bradford City, Real Oviedo (1988-2001)*

Collymore played for his boyhood club Aston Villa for three seasons, playing over 50 times for 'The Villians' and scoring seven goals. A colourful and controversial winger/striker, he had moved to Villa Park under John Gregory for £7 million from Liverpool in 1997. Collymore was capped three times at full international level for England. He moved to Bradford City and then to Spain where he played for Real Ovideo before retirement. After hanging up his boots, he made a brief appearance alongside Sharon Stone in "Basic Instinct" 2. He has since done media work for TalkSport and was diagnosed with borderline personality disorder in 2017. The Staffordshire born forward has his own "Last Word with Stan Collymore" Podcast.

COMYN, Andy

Defender

Born: *Wakefield*
Playing career: *Manchester United, Alvechurch, Aston Villa, Derby County, Plymouth Argyle, West Bromwich Albion, (1989-1996)*

Although Comyn later reverted to a centre-back role, he played as a winger for Manchester United and Blackburn when he was still at school. He was released from Old Trafford without playing for the senior side. He was offered a trial, and then a contract, by Villa after writing to several clubs in the Midlands. He subsequently played for Derby, Plymouth and West Brom before leaving the professional game.

During his playing career, Comyn undertook a course in book-keeping and then, with life after football in mind, became an accountant. After retiring from playing, he worked for a number of leading accountancy companies, and in 2015 was appointed as vice-principal for financial strategy and control at Dudley College. He has continued in the financial trade to this day and now owns and runs his own accountancy business.

COOK, George

Inside-left

Born: *Evenwood* Died: 1980
Playing career: *Huddersfield Town, Aston Villa, Tottenham Hotspur, Brentford (1922-1932)*

Cook was a prolific hitman at Villa Park, as he netted 40 goals in 61 matches across two seasons at the club from central midfield. He moved on to Second Division Spurs, Third Division (South) club Brentford and then dropped into non league football with Colwyn Bay United where he retired after five years. He won the FA Amateur Cup with Bishop Auckland in 1914 and later went on to work for a restaurant in Sutton Coldfield. He died of cancer in Evenwood aged 85 on New Year's Eve 1980.

COOKE, Stephen

Midfielder
Born: *Walsall*
Playing career: *FA National School of Excellence, Manchester United, Walsall, Aston Villa, Bournemouth (loan), Wycombe Wanderers (loan), Bournemouth, Torquay United (loan), Halesowen Town, Weymouth, Halesowen Town, Bloxwich United, Pelsall Villa (2000-2010)*

Despite his size of 5ft 8, Cooke was considered to have a bright future in the game but despite a ten year career in the game, he was blighted by injuries. He signed for United as a trainee but never made the grade at Old Trafford and also played for England at youth level but again never got as far as a senior call up. His debut for the Villa came in a European tie against Celta Vigo in 2000, one of only four appearances he made in claret and blue under John Gregory. He went on to two spells at AFC Bournemouth before he signed for the Cherries permanently. He also played for Wycombe before Cooke dropped into non league football. Cooke's last club was Pelsall Villa. He now works as a player advisor and has also been a radio summariser for AFC Bournemouth.

COOPER, Neale

Midfielder
Born: *Darjeeling, India* **Died:** 2018
Playing career: *King Street, Aberdeen, Aston Villa, Rangers, Aberdeen, Reading, Dunfermline Athletic, Ross County (1978-1998)*

Born in India, Cooper began his career at Alex Ferguson's Aberdeen, where he won nine major honours in seven years at Pittodrie. Moving on to Villa, he played 20 times in two seasons before returning to his native Scotland with Rangers.

Also played for Aberdeen, Reading, Dunfermline and Ross County, he also won 13 caps for the Scotland Under 21 side. After retirement as a player, Cooper went on to manage Ross County, Gillingham and Peterhead and had two spells as boss of Hartlepool United (2003 - 2005 and 2011-12). Cooper collapsed and died at his home in Aberdeen in May 2018 aged 54.

CORNAN, Frank

Inside-left/Left-half
Born: *Sunderland*
Died: 1971
Playing career: *Sunderland Black Watch, Willington, Barnsley, Birmingham, Aston Villa, Spennymoor United, Barnsley, Nelson, Exeter City, Barnsley (1902-1915)*

Started his career with junior sides, Sunderland Black Watch and then Willington, but was snapped up by Second Division Barnsley in 1902. He was a big success at Oakwell during his three season stay as he netted 18 goals in 88 league appearances. He was transferred to First Division Birmingham City in 1905 and then moved to neighbouring Aston Villa for a fee of £350 in 1908, and stayed for two seasons, but never really established himself as a regular in the first team. After being released he returned to the North East and played for Spennymoor United for a short spell. Barnsley gave him another league opportunity when signing Cornan in 1909, but again he never made the first team and moved on to link up with Nelson for the 1909-10 season. He had a solitary season at Exeter in 1911 and then after retirement he worked as a tobacconist. Died in 1971.

COULTON, Frank

Defender
Born: *Walsall* Died: 1929
Playing career: *Walsall Swifts, Aston Villa (1888-1893)*

He played at amateur level for Walsall Swifts and Aston Unity before he signed on professional terms at Aston Villa in 1886 for a fee of £155. He turned out in 38 league matches and won the FA Cup in his first season and the league championship (1893/94) during his time at the club. Also played cricket for Aston and Warwickshire. After retiring, he became a pub licensee in Birmingham, including The Fluter's Arms in Deritend, The Red House on Broad Street, and also the White Horse on Constitution Hill (you can see more photos of old local pubs at birminghamhistory.co.uk).

COWAN, James

Half-back
Born: *Jamestown, Dunbartonshire*
Died: 1918
Playing career: *Renton, Vale of Leven, Aston Villa, Birmingham, Powderhall (1888-1914)*

When Cowan played for the club in the 1890s and early 1900s, they were the giants of the Football League and England's early pre-dominant side. While at Villa, he won five First Division titles and two FA Cup winners medals. In all he played 354 times for Aston Villa in 14 years at the club and is considered to be one of the finest players of the Victorian era. He was capped three times by Scotland at full international level between 1896 and 1898. After retiring from playing in 1902, he coached the Villa youth teams for a few years and then went on to manage QPR. He served as boss of the west London club for seven years, winning the Southern League title but denied promotion due to off the field issues. Cowan died in 1918 aged 50.

COWANS, Gordon

Midfielder
Born: *West Cornforth, County Durham*
Playing career: *Aston Villa,A S Bari,Blackburn Rovers,Derby County,Wolverhampton Wanderers,Sheffield United,Bradford City,Stockport County & Burnley.*

An energetic and combative box to box midfielder, Cowans is widely considered to be one of the greatest ever players to don the claret and blue. Popularly known as Sid, he left the club three times and returned on each occasion, latterly as a coach. He was Villa's inspiration during their glory years of the 1980s, winning the League, League Cup, European Cup and the Superb Cup during a glittering ten year career at Villa Park. He had three spells at Aston Villa and played a total of 453 league games for them scoring 49 goals.He won ten full caps for England between 1983-90. Since then he has been a coach and has been at Aston Villa again in various roles. He is now their Development Coach and represents the club at legends events. Cowans also served as a club ambassador.

COWE, Steve

Forward
Born: *Gloucester*
Playing career: *Aston Villa, Swindon Town, Newport County, Forest Green Rovers, (1993-2009)*

He rose through the ranks to become a full-time pro at Villa Park having risen through the ranks but he never made a senior appearance across three seasons in the Midlands. Steve McMahon then signed him for Swindon Town for 100,000 in 1995 and Cowe helped his new club win the old Division Two title. Cowe scored 12 goals in 117 first-team appearances for Swindon. He went on to play numerous non league clubs including Forest Green Rovers, Redditch, Cirencester and Cinderford. Since retiring he started up First Touch Academy and opened a new indoor football facility in Stroud.

"DID YOU KNOW?"

"The club was formed in 1874 by 4 members of the Villa Cross Wesleyan Chapel Cricket Team meeting under a gas-light ."

Gordon Cowans

COX, Gershom

Defender

Born: *Birmingham* Died: 1918
Playing career: *Excelsior, Walsall Town, Aston Villa, Willenhall Pickwick, Walsall Bruswick, Bloxwich Strollers (1888-1892)*

Cox signed for Villa in 1887, and - until 2013 - he was thought to have scored the first ever Football League goal. Cox won an FA Cup runners–up medal, appearing for Aston Villa in the 1892 final. He made 101 first–team appearances for Aston Villa (86 in the Football League) in all competitions. He retired from playing due to a broken leg. Cox was, for a while, a successful market trader, then he joined the Birmingham City Police Force then he left Birmingham for a brief stint as manager of Kent League club Gravesend United. Cox died in 1918.

COX, Neil

Defender

Born: *Scunthorpe*
Playing career: *Scunthorpe United, Aston Villa, Middlesbrough, Bolton Wanderers, Watford, Cardiff City, Crewe Alexandra (1990-2008)*

In 1991, Cox joined First Division side Aston Villa for a fee of £400,000, going on to make over 50 appearances for the side in all competitions, including playing in the club's victory over Manchester United in the 1994 Football League Cup Final. He went on to play for Middlesbrough, Bolton, Watford, Cardiff and Crewe before becoming player/manager at non league Leek Town.

He retired from playing to become Leek boss permanently, then became assistant to his former Watford team mate Neal Ardley at AFC Wimbledon. He was capped six times by England's Under 21 team. After retiring from professional football Cox became a property developer in Portugal.

CRABTREE, Jimmy

Full-back/Half-back

Born: *Burnley* Died: 1908
Playing career: *Burnley, Rossendale United, Burnley, Aston Villa, Plymouth Argyle (1889-1904)*

A full-back, Crabtree first represented Burnley-based Royal Swifts and, in an incident not widely recorded, he was stabbed in the chest after trying to break up a fight and underwent an immediate operation to save his life and career. In total, Crabtree played 14 times for England. Having signed for Villa, he struck up a formidable half back pairing with Howard Spencer and went on to share the captaincy of the club with him. He won League Championship medals with Villa in 1897, 1899 and 1900, he also lifted the FA Cup in as a part of the Aston Villa team that completed the Double in 1897. Crabtree joined Plymouth Argyle in January 1904 and made four appearances in the Southern League before injury forced him to retire. He then coached at several non-league clubs and later became a pub licensee in Birmingham. He died suddenly at the age of 36.

CRADDOCK, Miller
Winger
Born: *Ledbury, Herefordshire* Died: 1960
Playing career: *Newport C, Aston Villa (1946-1950)*
An explosive winger signed from Hereford United, he scored ten goals in 34 league games at Villa (1948 -1951) before having to retire aged only 25 due to a heart condition. He also had a brief spell at Chelsea, as well as guesting for Heenan and Froudin in Belgium during WW2. Craddock's short lived career was plagued by the heart condition that ultimately led to his death in 1960 at the age of 33.

CRAIG, Tommy
Midfielder
Born: *Glasgow, Scotland*
Playing career: *Aberdeen, Sheffield Wednesday, Newcastle United, Aston Villa, Swansea City, Carlisle United. Hibernian (1966-1985).*
A player who arrived at Villa with undoubted ability, but he never fulfilled his potential and his stay in claret and blue was short lived. Villa manager Ron Saunders cleared his squad in a bid to build the team that would go on to win the European Cup. He subsequently moved on to Swansea City, Carlisle United and Hibernian before becoming a coach. He earned one full cap for the Scotland national team. After retiring as a player, Craig was appointed as assistant at Hibernian. Became Billy McNeil's number two at Celtic and then stayed on at that club as a scout. Craig embarked on a managerial career where he took charge of Charleroi, St Mirren and the Scotland Under 21 side.

CRICHTON, Paul
Goalkeeper
Born: *Pontefract*
Playing career: *Nottingham Forest, Notts County, Darlington, Peterborough United, Swindon Town, Rotherham United, Torquay United, Doncaster Rovers, Grimsby Town, West Brom, Aston Villa, Burnley, Norwich City, York City, Accrington Stanley, Gillingham, Cambridge United, Brighton & Hove A*
In 2006 whilst with Gillingham, Crichton was given the role of player-goalkeeping coach which was a position he took up also with Cambridge United and Brighton before officially hanging up his boots in 2009. He was appointed as a full time goalkeeper coach at Norwich City in February 2009, but left the club exactly a year later.

In March 2010 he became custodian coach at Northampton Town. He also worked in the same role for QPR, Grimsby and Blackpool. As of 2019 he now lives in Florida and has continued to stay involved in the game as a coach for the PSA Academy.

CRISP, Richard
Midfielder
Born: *Birmingham*
Playing career: *Aston Villa, Scunthorpe United (loan), Telford United, Halesowen Town, Stourport Swifts (1987-1993)*
A defensive midfielder, not much is known about Crisp's career but he did start out at hometown club Villa on amateur terms. He played for the club at youth level and turned professional in 1990. He never made the first team and was loaned to Scunthorpe United in making 8 appearances in the Football League for them. After leaving Aston Villa in 1994, Crisp later played non-league football for several different sides including Telford United, Halesowen Town and Stourport Swifts. In later life, Crisp became a coach at Telford and then worked for the Professional Footballers Association (PFA) as an advisor and agent.

CROPS
The Alex Cropley Story
ALEX CROPLEY with TOM WRIGHT
With a foreword by ANDY GRAY and the last word by PAT STANTON

CROPLEY, Alex
Midfielder
Born: *Aldershot*
Playing career: *Hibernian, Arsenal, Aston Villa, Newcastle United (loan), Toronto Blizzard, Portsmouth (1968-1982)*

Holds the distinction of winning both the Scottish and English League Cup, with Hibernian and Villa respectively. Moved to Arsenal having started his career in his native Scotland, and then linked up with Villa in 1976. He won the League Cup as the club prevailed at the third attempt after two drawn finals with Everton. Having broken his leg, he was loaned to Newcastle and then returned to Villa. Later played in Canada and for Portsmouth. Forced to retire at 31 through injury, he went on to become a taxi driver in Edinburgh. During his playing career he earned two full caps for Scotland.

CROWE, Vic
Wing-half
Born: *Abercynon, Wales*
Playing career: *Aston Villa, Peterbro' (1954-1966).*

Served Aston Villa as player, coach and manager. Crowe played over 300 league games and skippered both his club and country (16 caps for Wales). Left Villa in 1974, and had a spell in the NASL with Atlanta Chiefs, before returning to England as an Aston Villa legend. As a manager, he took Villa to the 1971 League Cup final and got them promoted into the Second Division in 1972. As a player, he was captain of the claret and blue and led the team to Second Division title glory in 1960 before lifting the League Cup trophy the following year. Crowe also managed back across the pond in two stints as boss of Portland Timbers. Crowe died in 2009 after a long illness.

VIC CROWE

BEST FOR SPORT
EVENING DESPATCH

CROWTHER, Stan
Wing-half
Born: *Bilston* Died: 2014
Playing career: *Bilston Town, Aston Villa, Manchester United, Chelsea,Brighton & Hove Albion, Hednesford Town, Rugby Town (1955-1961)*

A tall and imposing wing-half, he joined Villa for £750 and quickly became a first team regular as he played in the 1957 FA Cup final. Villa beat Matt Busby's Man Utd 2-1 but a year later he played at Wembley again, this time in the red of United. He had hastily signed in an emergency in the wake of the Munich air crash. His time at Old Trafford was short-lived, however, and in December that year he joined Chelsea for £10,000; Arrived at the Bridge for £10,000 in 1958 and enjoyed two useful seasons at the club. Was never in Tommy Doc's long term plans and was sold to Brighton. Moved back to his native Black Country after quitting through disillusionment having dropped into non league football with Hednesford Town and Rugby Town. Crowther became a foreman at the Armitage Shanks factory in Wolverhampton until retirement. Crowther died in 2014.

CRUDGINGTON, Geoff
Goalkeeper
Born: *Wolverhampton*
Playing career: *Aston Villa, Bradford City, Crewe A, Swansea City, Plymouth Argyle (1970-1987).*

Crudgington made over 600 appearances in the Football League playing as a goalkeeper for six different clubs including Villa. Aston Villa, Bradford City, Toronto Metros, Crewe Alexandra, Swansea City and Plymouth Argyle. He went on to become Football in the Community officer and goalkeeping coach at Plymouth Argyle. Over the best part of the next decade, the 6ft 4 keeper brought experience, consistency and calm assurance to the various defences he played behind. He was a hero of the Plymouth side that reached the FA Cup semi-final in 1984 and incredibly solid between the sticks. Crudgington served as the club's Chief Scout but was forced to leave by mutual consent through financial difficulties. He then gained employment with former Plymouth Argyle sponsors, Beacon Electrical, but continued to be involved in the game, regularly coaching in the Plymouth area.

CRUZ, Ulises de la

Forward attacking midfielder Defender
Born: *Piquiucho, Carchi, Ecuador*
Playing career: *Deportivo Quito, Barcelona S.C., Aucas (loan), LDU Quito, Cruzeiro (loan), Barcelona S.C. (loan), Hibernian, Aston Villa, Reading, Birmingham City, LDU Quito (1991-2012)*

Now a governor of his country's National Assembly as a politician, de la Cruz played 89 times for Villa - scoring once - between 2002 and 2006. He was signed by Graham Taylor for Villa from Hibernian and quickly became cult hero at the club. He went on to play for Reading, Birmingham and then finished his career with LDU Quito in his homeland (his third spell with that club). He earned 101 caps for Ecuador and played at the 2006 World Cup in which his nation reached the knockout stages for the first time. De la Cruz is also a UNICEF ambassador.

CUELLAR, Carlos

Defender
Born: *Madrid, Spain*
Playing career: *Inter Argibay, Santa Ana, Pegaso, San Federico (loan), Numancia, Calahorra (loan), Osasuna, Rangers, Aston Villa, Sunderland, Norwich City, Almeria (2000-2015)*

Played for 12 clubs during an 18-year career, including a four season stint at Villa in which he featured over 100 times. He signed for the club for £7.8 million from Rangers (where he won both domestic cups and a UEFA Cup runners up medal). Reached the League Cup final at Villa Park under Martin O'Neill. He was mainly a right-back during his time in the Midlands, later going on to Sunderland, linking up with O'Neill again. Also played for Norwich, Almeria and then moved to Israel. Now aged 37, he continues to ply his trade with Israeli Premier League side Bnei Yehuda FC.

CUMBES, Jim

Goalkeeper
Born: *Manchester*
Playing career: *Runcorn, Tranmere Rovers, West Bromwich Albion, Aston Villa, Portland Timbers, Southport, Worcester City (1961-1982)*

Played cricket for four counties - Lancashire, Surrey, Worcestershire and Warwickshire - as a fast-medium bowler and lower order batsman. He also served as Chief Executive of Lancashire CCC. Cumbes enjoyed a varied professional football career as a goalkeeper with Tranmere Rovers, West Bromwich Albion, Aston Villa and Southport. All in all, he appeared in 376 Football League appearances in a 13-year career. He also played football in the North American Soccer League for the Portland Timbers, where he played against Pelé. During the 1970s, the eloquent Cumbes cemented his popularity as Aston Villa's goalkeeper by presenting a series of shows on BBC Local Radio in the West Midlands. Awarded an honorary Doctor of Business Administration by Manchester University in 2015 for his excellence on and off the pitch.

Jim Cumbes

Carlos Cuellar

Alan Curbishley

CUMMINGS, George
Full-back
Born: *Falkirk* Died: 1987
Playing career: *Aston Villa, Partick Thistle, Scotland (1930-1940)*

George Cummings had broken into the Scotland team by the time he joined Villa from Partick Thistle in November 1935 and his quality shone through throughout a 14-year association with the club. While he became a firm fans favourite for his spirit and no-nonsense style, Cummings was unable to prevent Villa's relegation in his debut season at the club. He earned a Second Division winners medal as well as a Wartime Cup tankard. A solid, resolute full-back, he was nicknamed "The Icicle" because of his ability to remain calm under pressure. He played 237 times for the claret and blue and was capped by Scotland. On retirement, Cummings returned to Villa to take up a role coaching their youth teams and later worked for the Dunlop Rubber Company and engineering firm Hardy Spicer Ltd.

CUNLIFFE, Arthur
Winger
Born: *Blackrod* Died: 1986
Playing career: *Blackburn Rovers, Aston Villa, Middlesbro, Burnley, Hull C, Rochdale (1929-1947)*

A cotton mill worker before he took up football professionally, Cunliffe was capped twice by England in 1932. Scored 47 goals in 129 league appearances for Blackburn Rovers, before he joined Villa, alongside Ronnie Dix in May 1933 for a 'substantial' fee, making 69 league appearances and scoring eleven goals. After retirement, he was appointed Rochdale manager and then worked at Bournemouth & Boscombe FC in a number of various roles - including coach, manager and physiotherapist.

CUNNINGHAM, John
Forward
Born: *Glasgow*
Playing career: *Rangers, Glasgow Thistle, Preston North End, Sheffield United, Aston Villa, Wigan County, Manchester United*

Cunningham was a well travelled forward who played for 12 clubs and was capped eight times for Scotland. Played at Villa for two seasons before he joined Manchester United.

Plied his trade at United for a single season then moved on again to Wigan where he became player/coach. Worked as a scout and player recruitment agent for Rangers in his native Glasgow. Later took employment at the docks on the River Clyde.

CURBISHLEY, Alan
Midfielder
Born: *Forest Gate, Essex*
Playing career: *West Ham United, Birmingham, Aston Villa, Charlton Athletic, Brighton, Charlton Athletic (1974-1993).*

Former England Schoolboy, youth, and Under 21 international who started at West Ham. Played 36 games for Villa in the 1983/84 season having moved from fierce local rivals Birmingham City. He was appointed joint manager at Charlton in July 1991 and was given full control four years later. His most recent post was at West Ham, who he joined in December 2006. Curbishley resigned in September 2008 and has been working as a TV pundit while being linked with numerous managerial vacancies. He masterminded Charlton's rise to Premier League status via the play-offs. Curbishley hasn't worked in football in any capacity since leaving the Hammers 13 years ago.

CURCIC, Sasa
Midfielder
Born: *Belgrade, SFR Yugoslavia*
Playing career: *OFK Belgrade, Partizan Belgrade, Bolton Wanderers, Aston Villa, Crystal Palace, New York & New Jersey MetroStars, Motherwell, Obilic Belgrade (1991-2001)*

Curcic signed for Villa in 1996 for £4million but the move was ultimately unsuccessful. He was regarded as a major flop in the Midlands, and he never saw eye to eye with manager Brian Little. He played only 29 times in two seasons at Villa, and described his move from Bolton as the "worst mistake I've made in my life." He was sold to Crystal Palace for £1million in 1998 and went to play overseas in America. Had a brief stint at Motherwell and returned to his native Serbia. Since retiring he has appeared on a number of reality TV shows including the Serbian equivalent of Big Brother. Currently a coach at the Crystal Palace Academy. He also turned out 14 times for the former Yugoslavia, scoring once.

CURTIS, George
Defender
Born: *Dover*
Playing career: *Coventry C, Aston Villa (1955-1971).*
As club captain, he skippered the Sky Blues of Coventry City from the Fourth Division to the First for the time in their history. He left in December 1969, having played a then club record 487 league games, scoring 11 goals. His next club was Aston Villa whom Curtis helped to win the Third Division title in the 1971–72 season. He went on to play a total of 51 games, scoring three times during his three year stint at Villa Park. After retirement as a player, Curtis became Commercial Manager at Coventry City in July 1974 and then Managing Director in September 1983. He managed the club between April 1986 and May 1987 and won the FA Cup as boss in 1987.

Cutler, Neil
Goalkeeper
Born: *Perton, Staffordshire*
Playing career: *West Bromwich Albion, Crewe Alexandra, Chester City, Aston Villa, Stockport C, Rotherham U, Bury, Scunthorpe U (1993-2011)*
During his time at Chester Cutler earned himself a move to Premier League side Aston Villa in October 1999, where he made one substitute appearance. He joined Stoke City in July 2001, playing a huge part in their promotion to the First Division in 2002. His final club was Rotherham United, where he had to retire from the game due to a persistent back injury. He joined Bury as a goalkeeping coach and is part of Just4keepers goalkeeping coaching company. Cutler currently works as goalkeeping coach at Villa Park.

Neil Cutler

DALEY, Tony
Winger
Born: *Birmingham*
Playing career: *Aston Villa,Wolverhampton Wanderers,Watford & Walsall.*
A diminutive winger, Daley played 233 league games for Villa between 1985-94. The Birmingham-born Daley gained seven full caps for England between 1991-92. He also played in the 1994 League Cup final triumph. After his playing career finished he gained a degree in Sports & Exercise Science and became Sheffield United's fitness and conditioning coach in 2003 moving on to Wolverhampton Wanderers in 2007. Daley now runs a fitness business called 7Daley. He states: "I had the honour of playing professional football for Aston Villa, Wolves & England, currently, I am a qualified fitness professional. Now, in my 50's, being a grandfather, my passion for working out and eating healthy is the same now as its always been". (See: https://7daley. co.uk/)

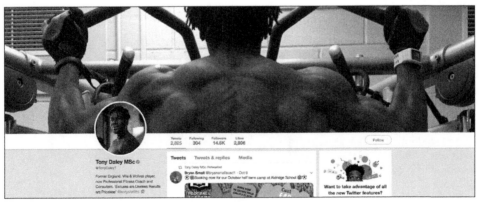

DALY, Pat
Defender
Born: *Dublin, Ireland* Died: 2003
Playing career: *Aston Villa, Shamrock R (1949-1952)*
Defender Daly was best known for his two
spells with League of Ireland side Shamrock
Rovers for whom he won the league in the
1951/52 season. It is often forgotten that he
played for Villa briefly in the 1949/50 season.
He only played three times for the club
and before he returned to Shamrock once
more. Daly won one cap for the Republic of
Ireland. Worked for the FAI and as a coach
at Shamrock Rovers after retirement, later
becoming player/manager of Rovers. He
died in 2003 aged 73.

DAVIS, Neil
Striker
Born: *Bloxwich*
Playing career: *Redditch United, Aston Villa, Walsall,
Hednesford Town, Newport County, Bromsgrove
Rovers, Coleshill Town (1990-2010)*
Davis played two Premier League games for
Villa in five seasons and had numerous loan
spells. Davis started his football career at
Reddich United before joining Villa in 1991
as an apprentice. He made his first-team
debut in the 1-0 win at Nottingham Forest
in 1996 and also appeared in Europe against
Bordeaux, and Atletico Madrid in the UEFA
Cup. Davis is still playing, for Midland
Football Alliance side Coleshill Town, at the
age of 45.

DAWSON, Frankie
Half-back
Born: *Birmingham* Died: 1938
Playing career: *Aston Unity, Aston Villa (1888-1889)*
Dawson made only three league
appearances for Aston Villa in the debut
season of the Football League, but played
in the 1886-87 FA Cup winning side. The
team overcame West Bromwich Albion
2-0 in the final at The Oval. A left-half, he
also represented non league Aston Unity
in the Birmingham Central League. After
retirement, he played cricket for Unity and
guested for Warwickshire before he became
a secretary for the Football League. Dawson
continued to live in the Midlands and died
in Birmingham in 1938 aged 79. Dawson was
believed to be a tenacious, tough-tackling
wing half - a full back in today's parlance.

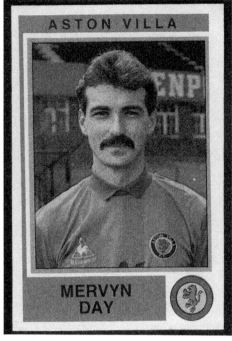

DAY, Mervyn
Goalkeeper
Born: *Chelmsford*
Playing career: *West Ham United, Leyton Orient,
Aston Villa, Leeds United, Luton Town, Sheffield
United, Carlisle United. (1973-1994).*
Former England Under 23 keeper. Day
played over 600 games for the Hammers,
Leeds and Villa, before joining Carlisle,
where after injury ended his career was
appointed first team manager in January
1996. He led them to promotion into
Division Two in 1997, but left shortly after
due to a falling out with the Chairman.
Day is known for his long association
with another former Villa player in Alan
Curbishley. He was first team coach under
Curbishley at Charlton for many years
before the pair both left the club at the end
of the 2005-06 season. In December 2006, he
was again named as Curbishley's number
two at West Ham manager but again left
the club at the same time as his boss in
September 2008. He won a Second Division
Championship with Leeds in 1990, where
he also worked as a scout. Day went on to
become Scouting and Talent Identification
Manager at Brighton and Hove Albion and
then was appointed head of recruitment at
West Bromwich Albion. Until recently he
was international scout at Bristol City.

DE BILDE, Gilles
Striker
Born: *Zellik, Belgium*
Playing career: *Eendracht Aalst, PSV, Sheffield Wednesday, Aston Villa (loan), Anderlecht, Lierse, Willebroek-Meerhof (1992-2007)*

A colourful and controversial striker, de Bilde was as notable for his off-field antics as he was for his glut of goals. After a prolific career in Belgium, de Bilde moved to England as he joined Sheffield Wednesday in 2000 and scored ten goals in his first full season at Hillsborough. He was unable to prevent Wednesday's relegation and moved on loan to Villa but things did not work out. He made only four appearances for the club before returning to Belgium. de Bilde was once arrested and given a suspended jail term for breaking an opponent's nose. He played 25 times for his country and played at Euro 2000. After retirement, de Bilde became a football analyst on Belgian television, he has also appeared on numerous celebrity challenge shows and had a modelling career.

"DID YOU KNOW?"

"Villa Park has played host to more FA Cup semi-finals than any other club ground."

DEACY, Eamonn
Left-back
Born: *Galway, Ireland* Died: 2012
Playing career: *West United, Sligo Rovers, Galway Rovers, Limerick, Galway Rovers, Aston Villa, Derby County (loan), Galway United (1975-1991)*

The full back left Galway Rovers for Aston Villa in February 1979, after writing 12 letters to the club requesting a trial. He went on to have an unforgettable five years at the club, during which time they won the League Championship, European Cup and European Super Cup. He was one of only 14 players used by Ron Saunders in the 1980–81 league-winning season, making enough appearances (11 in all, including six starts) to win a medal (he was Villa's number 12 on 19 occasions that season). He made one appearance for Villa in European competition against Juventus in the 1982–83 European Cup. He had a brief loan spell at Derby, and won 4 caps for the Republic of Ireland. He also played for the Republic of Ireland national football team amateur team that qualified for the 1978 UEFA Amateur Cup. He died following a heart attack in 2012. The Galway Football Association re-named Galway United's ground 'Eammon Deacy Park' in his honour.

DEAKIN, Alan
Wing-half
Born: *Balsall Heath*
Playing career: *Aston Villa, Walsall. (1959-1971).*

Deakin signed for Villa as a 15-year-old. He became a regular in the side during the 1960–61 season and collected a League Cup winners' tankard at the start of the following season. He recovered from an anke break and went on to skipper the side for the 1966–67 season. Deakin also played for the England under 23 team but never earned a senior cap .Deakin left Villa Park for Walsall in 1969, having made almost 300 appearances and scoring eleven goals. He went on to play 50 league games for Walsall before moving to Tamworth FC for a further 2 years of football then retiring in 1974. On retirement from the game he became a welder. He lived in Aldridge in the West Midlands and played a number of times for the Aston Villa "Old Stars." as well as representing the club at several charity galas. He died in January 2018 at the age of 76.

DEARN, Stephen

Inside-forward/Left-half
Born: *Halesowen*
Died: 1947
Playing career: *Halesowen Town, Aston Villa, Portsmouth, Brentford (1924-1929)*

He began his career as a trainee at Villa and rose through the ranks, but never played a senior match for their first team. Moved on to Division 3 (South) side Portsmouth in 1924 and they achieved promotion in his debut season with Pompey. He made over 100 appearances in total in his Football League career. He returned to Halesowen Town (where he started his career) and then later became a coach and a director at the club upon retirement in 1934. Worked in a greengrocer's during the war but died shortly afterwards in 1947 aged 46.

**JOHN
DEEHAN**
ASTON VILLA

DEEHAN, John

Striker
Born: *Solihull*
Playing career: *Aston Villa, West Bromwich Albion, Norwich City, Ipswich Town, Manchester City, Barnsley. (1975-1990)*

Capped seven times by England and became player/coach at Manchester City in July 1988 and switched to Barnsley in the same role in 1990. Returned to his old club Norwich to succeed Mike Walker in January 1994, however he left the following year after a string of poor results. Later managed Wigan and returned to Villa as caretaker boss in 2002. Deehan is currently the Director of football at Grimsby Town. Whilst at Norwich he won the League Cup and the Division 2 league title during unfancied Norwich's glory years.

DELANEY, Mark

Right-back
Born: *Haverfordwest, Wales*
Playing career: *Carmarthen Town, Cardiff City, Aston Villa (1995-2007)*

Began his career in his native Wales with Carmarthen Town and Cardiff City before he moved to Aston Villa in 1999. Made a Premier League debut that April under John Gregory. He made 193 first appearances for Aston Villa in all competitions, with two goals coming against Watford in August 1999 and Everton on Boxing Day 2005. He has also gained 36 international caps with the Wales national team. Retired due to persistent knee problems, as of 2019 he now works for Villa as a youth coach.

DEVEY, Harry
Defender
Born: *Birmingham* Died: 1924
Playing career: *Aston Villa (1888-1892)*
On of five brothers who all played professional football, Ted and Bob Devey for Small Heath and Jack, Harry and Will Devey for Aston Villa (see below). Another brother, Abel, was a cricketer with Staffordshire.Harry Devey played in Villa's first ever Football League match at Wolverhampton in August 1888. The club eventually finished runners up. He had begun his career at several amateur and non league clubs including Clarendon, Montrose Birmingham and Birmingham Excelsior before signing for Villa in 1887. After retirement he became a scout for Villa and then got involved in his family's embroidery business. He died in 1940 at the age of 80.

DEVEY, Jack
Striker
Born: *Newtown, Birmingham* Died: 1940
Playing career: *Wellington Road, Excelsior, Aston Unity, Aston Manor, West Bromwich Albion, Mitchells St George's, Aston Villa (1889-1902)*
Like his brothers, Devey was a multi-talented sportsman of considerable acclaim. Having signed for Aston Villa in March 1891; he would go on to become one of the club's greatest captains. He was Villa's leading scorer in the Championship winning side of 1893–94 season as he hit 20 goals.

Jack Devey

He was capped twice by England. For eight years, Devey captained Aston Villa during which time they won the League championship five times between 1894 and 1900 and the FA Cup twice. Including the famous 'Double' in the 1896–97 season. Devey also played cricket for Warwickshire as a top order batsman and medium pace bowler. He retired in April 1902 and was an Aston Villa director for the next 32 years.

DEVEY, Will
Centre-forward
Born: *Perry Barr, Birmingham* Died: 1935
Playing career: *Aston Unity, Small Heath, Wolverhampton Wanderers, Aston Villa, Walsall Town Swifts, Burton Wanderers, Notts County (1884-1899)*
The third of three Devey brothers to play for the Villains, he played as a striker in the Football Alliance and for many Midlands clubs in the Football League including Clarendon Montrose, Aston Unity, Small Heath, Walsall Swifts and Wellington Town. He was Small Heath Alliance's leading scorer for their first two seasons in the Football Alliance (1889–90 and 1890–91) before moving to Wolverhampton Wanderers where he became their leading scorer in the next Football League season. He played ten times for Villa and scored twice (1892 - 1894). Worked in his family's embroidery business in Birmingham with his other brothers having retired in 1900. He died in Birmingham in 1935 at the age of 70.

DICKSON, Ian
Forward
Born: *Maxwelltown* Died: 1976
Playing career: *Queen of the South, Aston Villa, Middlesbrough (1919-1921)*
A forward, Dickson represented Queen of the South in challenge games and minor cup competitions before he moved south to Villa in 1921 for £1,500. Still only 19, scored 28 goals in 42 games in his debut season in the Midlands to help Villa to fifth place in the First Division. Despite this prolific campaign, injuries began to bite and he was forced to retire only four years later, a disappointing end to a career that promised so much. He also played for Middlesbrough having signed from Villa for £3,000. He was the grandfather of another namesake who works as an Australian TV and radio personality. Died 1976.

DICKSON, William

Forward

Born: *Crail, Fife, Scotland* Died: 1910
Playing career: *Strathmore, Bolton Wanderers, Sunderland, Aston Villa, Stoke (1889-1896)*

Dickson played for Dundee club Strathmore before crossing the border to join English clubs Bolton Wanderers and then Sunderland. In 1889 he joined Football League side Aston Villa and was prolific for the second city side, scoring 34 goals in 64 matches. He joined fellow Midlands based club Stoke ahead of the 1892–93 season where he scored 11 goals as Stoke enjoyed their best season in the league up to that point. He scored 13 in the following campaign including five in six in the short lived United Counties League. Known for his versatility, Dickson regularly swapped positions between leading the line and dropping to full-back. He left the Victoria Ground in 1896 after scoring 48 goals in 128 matches for the "Potters". He is one of only two players to hold the distinction of scoring four goals in his only Scotland game - a 10-2 win over Ireland in 1888.

DINSDALE, Billy

Centre-forward

Born: *Darlington* Died: 1984
Playing career: *Darlington, Aston Villa, Lincoln City, Bradford PA, Lincoln City, Darlington (1921-1932)*

Lincoln City's top scorer in each of his four seasons at the club, Dinsdale played eight times for Villa during two years in the Midlands. He made the step up from Northern League Crook to First Division Villa, but was never able to establish himself in the senior side despite a prolific record for the reserves. Moved on to Lincoln, Bradford PA, Lincoln again and Darlington. He played only four further games and then retired from football at the age of 29. Dinsdale worked as a fitter for locomotive manufacturer Stephenson's in his native Darlington. In later life he was severely affected by arthritis. Dinsdale died in Darlington in 1984 at the age of 80.

"DID YOU KNOW?"

"Villa have scores more goals in the history of the FA Cup than any other league club ."

DIX, Ronnie

Striker

Born: *Bristol* Died: 1998
Playing career: *Bristol Rovers, Blackburn Rovers, Aston Villa, Derby County, Tottenham Hotspur, Reading (1928-1949)*

Began playing football with Bristol Schools before joining Bristol Rovers FC as an amateur. Dix left Rovers, a year later, after a hundred league appearances and 33 goals, when he joined Blackburn Rovers FC on 9 May 1932 for £3000. Another year, and he joined Aston Villa FC in May 1933 and 97 league appearances and thirty goals later, moved onto Derby County AFC in February 1937 and followed with 94 league appearances and 35 league goals. Transferred to Tottenham Hotspur FC in June 1939 and throughout WWII, he was playing for Blackpool FC. Left White Hart Lane for Reading FC on 6 November 1947 before retiring at the end of the 1948-49 season. He played once - and scored - for England against Norway. His record of being the youngest ever Football League goalscorer at 15 years and 180 days, is one that continues to stand to this day. He is believed to have returned to the Bristol area having hung up his boots.

DIXON, Arthur
Right-half
Born: *Matlock* Died: 1933
Playing career: *Aston Villa, Stoke (1888-1890)*
A defender, Dixon played for at amateur level before he signed for Villa ahead of the inaugural Football League season in 1888. His debut against Stoke was the first of only three games he made for the club. He was released at the end of the 1888–89 season and joined Stoke but he failed to make an appearance under Harry Lockett. Having retired he worked as a coach at former side Derby Midland (now known as Derby County) and also worked as a writer for the local press. Dixon died in 1933.

DIXON, Johnny
Striker
Born: *Newcastle upon Tyne* Died: 2009
Playing career: *Aston Villa (1946-1960)*
A one club man and Villa legend, he played over 400 games for the club in a 14-year career in the Midlands. He was part of the FA-Cup winning team in 1957 and captained the side as Villa beat Man United in the final. Dixon had moved south to Villa as an amateur from the non-league Spennymoor United in 1944 and was the club's top scorer with 28 goals from left-half in the 1951/52 season. In the 1958-59 season, Villa were relegated to the Second Division, but the following season Dixon helped them back into the First. He retired from playing in April 1961. For six years thereafter, he was a youth coach at Villa, and then worked as an ironmonger, a job from which he retired in 1985. He died in Sutton Coldfield in 2009 at the age of 85 after suffering with Alzheimer's disease.

DJEMBA-DJEMBA, Eric
Midfielder
Born: *Douala, Cameroon*
Playing career: *Nantes, Manchester United, Aston Villa, Burnley (loan), Qatar SC, OB, Hapoel Tel Aviv, Partizan, St Mirren, Chennaiyin, Persebaya Surabaya, Voltigeurs (2001-2016)*
Capped eleven times for Cameroon, Djemba - Djemba endured an inauspicious tenure in England. In 18 months at Old Trafford, the £3.5m signing found it difficult to maintain a period of sustained form, and he was unable to establish himself as a player capable of filling captain Roy Keane's shoes.

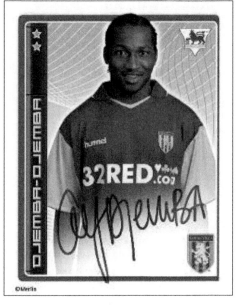

OWerfis

Djemba-Djemba was sold to Villa in the 2005 transfer window for a fee of £1.5 million but the move did little to restore his reputation. Started only twice in two seasons at Villa Park - eleven appearances in total - then loaned out to Burnley. Moved abroad and can now be found in the Swiss fifth division playing for FC Vallorbe.

DORIGO, Tony
Defender
Born: *Adelaide, South Australia*
Playing career: *Aston Villa, Chelsea, Leeds United, Torino, Derby County, Stoke City (1983-2001)*
As a teenager, Dorigo wrote to 14 top flight clubs in England. Aston Villa were the first club to respond and offered Dorigo a four-day trial. He was successful. He made his league debut for Aston Villa against Ipswich in 1984 as an 18-year-old and would go on to win the club's Player of the Year award during his time at Villa Park. Went on to play over 100 times for the club, scoring twice. Earned 15 caps for the full England team and played at Italia 90. The Australian-born defender chose to represent England over the country of his birth. Since retirement in 2001, Dorigo has worked as a football pundit for Bravo and Channel 5. Dorigo has also become a property developer and has earnt qualifications in order to obtain a UEFA Pro License. Twitter: https://twitter.com/tonydorigo

DORRELL, Arthur

Left-winger

Born: *Small Heath, Birmingham* Died: 1942
Playing career: *Carey Hall, R.A.S.C., Aston Villa, Port Vale (1919-1932)*

Birmingham born outside left Dorrell joined First Division Aston Villa in May 1919 and made his Football League debut at Derby County in September 1919 after the resumption of peacetime football. Dorrell rarely missed a match between 1920 and 1928 and was a regular goalscorer. He played 390 times for Villa including the FA Cup win in 1920. He won 4 caps for England between, and he also played twice for The Football League, before finishing his career with a season at Port Vale. He returned to Villa as a coach upon his retirement. Dorrell died in 1942 aged 46.

DORSETT, Dicky

Centre-forward

Born: *Brownhills* Died: 1999
Playing career: *Wolves, Aston Villa (1935-1953)*

Dorsett spent the entirety of his 17 year career in the Midlands with Wolves and then Villa, who he joined Aston Villa for £3,000 in September 1946. His career almost came to an end in 1950 when he was involved in a car crash, but he recovered and played on for three further seasons before retiring from the game in 1953. He stayed at Villa coaching the club's youth team before joining Liverpool in 1957 as assistant trainer, a job he held until 1962. He died in November 1999, aged 79.

Tony Dorigo

DOUGAN, Derek

Defender/Midfielder/Forward

Born: *Belfast, Northern Ireland* Died: 2007
Playing career: *Cregagh Boys, Distillery, Portsmouth, Blackburn Rovers, Aston Villa, Peterborough United, Leicester City, Wolverhampton Wanderers, Los Angeles Wolves (guest), Kansas City Spurs (guest), Shamrock Rovers XI (guest), Kettering Town (1951-1977)*

A strong and physical forward, Dougan retired from playing in 1975 after playing 532 League games scoring 219 goals together with 43 Northern Ireland caps. He also had a two-year stint as player/manager of Kettering between 1975 and 1977. Dougan was Chairman of the PFA and later returned to Molineux in August 1982 as Chairman and Chief Executive. He continued to live in the Wolverhampton area where he worked as a marketing and P.R. consultant. Died on 24th June 2007 at the age of 69. He won a League Cup winners tankard at Wembley in 1974 and a UEFA Cup runners up medal in 1972, whilst playing for Wolverhampton Wanderers. He stood as an Independent political for Belfast in 1997 and then became involved with the UK Independence Party.

DOWDS, Peter

Left-half
Born: *Johnstone, Scotland* Died: 1895
Playing career: *Aston Villa, Stoke, Celtic (1889-1895)*
Capped once by Scotland in 1892, the same year he moved to Villa from Celtic where he began his career. Made 20 appearances in the Midlands across four years at the club and scored three goals in the First Division. He then moved on to Stoke and then made a return to Celtic for the 1894–95 campaign however he fell ill with tuberculosis and died in September 1895 at the age of only 24.

DOWNING, Stewart

Winger/Attacking midfielder
Born: *Middlesbrough*
Playing career: *Middlesbrough, Sunderland (loan), Aston Villa, Liverpool, West Ham United, Middlesbrough (2001-2015)*
Downing started out at Middlesbrough, but following their relegation in 2009 he signed for Villa £12m under Martin O'Neill. He fell out of favour with O'Neill's successors Gerard Houllier and Alex McLeish, and then moved on to Liverpool, winning the League Cup - he was Man of the Match in the final - and a runners up medal in the FA Cup (he also played in Villa's 2010 defeat against United in the League Cup final at Wembley). Later played for West Ham and returned to Middlesbrough for another crack at the Premier League. As of 2019, he plays for Blackburn and has also represented England at every age group level - 35 caps for the senior side under four different managers.

DRAPER, Mark

Midfielder
Born: *Long Eaton*
Playing career: *Notts County, Leicester City, Aston Villa, Rayo Vallecano (loan), Southampton, Dunkirk (1988-2009)*
A talented midfielder, he became recognised by Notts County supporters as one of the greatest young players ever developed at the club. He spent most of his Premier League playing career at Aston Villa and Leicester City and retired from playing in 2003 after a spell at Southampton. He did however make a brief comeback in 2009 when he signed for non-league Dunkirk. Draper . It is fair to say that he enjoyed the best football of his career during his time at Villa where he was in the team that won the League Cup in 1996 and also earned two call ups to the England national side (although he was never capped). Upon retiring from playing Draper made the move into football coaching and joined his former side Notts County in a dual role as a coach and first team kit man in 2009. Leaving Meadow Lane in 2011, Draper then spent two years at Stoke City coaching within their academy set up. Having already obtained his UEFA 'A' and 'B' coaching badges, Draper joined non-league side Radford FC as a coach in 2012 before a brief spell in the same capacity at Arnold Town. He has since set up his own football academy with former team-mate David Norton where they coach 16-18 year olds.

Dion Dublin

DRINKWATER, Charlie

Outside-left
Born: *Willesden* Died: 1998
Playing career: *Aston Villa, Charlton Athletic, Watford, Ruislip Manor (1932-1953)*

Drinkwater signed for Villa as an amateur in August 1935. After two appearances, he joined another top flight club Charlton Athletic in July 1938, but made just three appearances before being released shortly before war broke out. An outside left, he had a spell coaching at Pinner FC, then joined Ruislip Manor as player/manager for the 1952/53 season. During the Second World War, Drinkwater served in the Royal Navy as a Physical Training Instructor. After the war, he worked at Mount Vernon Hospital as a remedial gymnast for three decades. He died aged 63 in 1998.

DROBNY, Vaclav

Centre-back
Born: *Czechoslovakia* Died: 2012
Playing career: *Strasbourg, Aston Villa (loan), Sparta Prague, Jablonec 97 (loan), FC Augsburg, Spartak Trnava, Bohemians Praha (1998-2011)*

The towering, commanding centre-back played twice for Czech Republic in 2004, after rising to prominence at French club Strasbourg. Drobny, 32, signed a season-long loan at Villa in August 2004 from Racing Strasbourg. At the time, he described the move as "the biggest opportunity of my football career." Unfortunately, he never quite fitted into manager David O'Leary's plans and failed to make a senior competitive appearance for the club, although he played 24 times for the reserves. He returned to his homeland with Sparta Prague, where he won the Czech League in 2007. Drobny died at the tragically young age of 32 when he skidded off piste in a bobsleigh and struck a tree in his native Czech Republic.

DUBLIN, Dion

Centre-forward /Centre-back
Born: *Leicester*
Playing career: *Norwich City, Cambridge United, Barnet, Manchester United, Coventry City, Aston Villa, Millwall, Leicester City, Celtic (1988-2008)*

Dublin started his career as a centre back with Norwich City, but made his name at Cambridge United as a centre-forward. He then went on to other clubs which include Manchester United, Coventry City, Millwall, Aston Villa, Leicester City and Celtic. Dublin is also an amateur percussionist, and invented a percussion instrument called "The Dube". In 2011, he accompanied Ocean Colour Scene in a gig at the University of East Anglia, Norwich. In 2015, he joined the presenting team on the BBC One daytime show Homes Under the Hammer. Dublin was capped four times for England. Dublin has also done some radio commentary work and has also appeared on Ford Super Sunday on Sky Sports.

DUCAT, Andy

Centre-forward/Right-half
Born: *Brixton, London*
Died: 1942
Playing career: *Southend United, Woolwich Arsenal, Aston Villa, Fulham (1903-1924)*

One of an elite group to have represented his country in both football and cricket. Became a Surrey regular and scored 52 centuries for the county, playing in one Test for England against Australia in the Ashes series of 1921. Ducat also had a successful football career. He started out playing for non-league Southend United before joining First Division Woolwich Arsenal in 1905. Eventually, he was sold for £1,000 to Aston Villa in 1912. He became a stalwart at Villa, captaining the club to their sixth FA Cup win in 1919–20. He moved to Fulham in 1921, and upon his retirement from playing in 1924, he succeeded Phil Kelso (his former boss at Arsenal) as Fulham manager. However, the Cottagers struggled in the Second Division with Ducat in charge. He was sacked in 1926. After his departure from Fulham, he continued to play amateur football for the Casuals. Also a sports reporter for the Daily Sketch and was cricket coach at Eton College. He won six caps for England and scored once. Died of a heart attack while playing at Lord's.

DUGDALE, Jimmy
Centre-half
Born: *Liverpool* Died: 2008
Playing career: *West Brownich Albion, Aston Villa, QPR. (1952-1962).*

Not many footballers can claim to have won FA Cup medals with two different West Midlands clubs, but Jimmy Dugdale held that distinction having lifted the famous trophy with WBA and Villa. For 25 years was a licensee, working in Perry Barr, Aston (at the Villa Lions Club), Hall Green, Moseley Rugby Club and the Hasbury Conservative club. He sadly had to have a leg amputated in 1990, forcing him to retire. He died in February 2008 aged 76 after a long illness. He won the Second Division (1960) and League Cup 1961 at Villa Park. Three caps for England B. Dugdale was a solid and dependable centre-back during his playing days and played over 200 games for the Villa. His uncle Ken Dugdale was also a professional player

DUGDALE, Ken
Striker
Born: *Liverpool*
Playing career: *Kirkby Town, Aston Villa, Wolverhampton Wanderers, Wigan Athletic, New Brighton, Burscough (1966-1972)*

Nephew of Jimmy (above), Dugdale spent his early career with Kirkby Town, Aston Villa and Wolverhampton Wanderers. He later played non-league football with Wigan Athletic, New Brighton and Burscough.

Andy Ducat

Dugdale later became a football coach, and was manager of the New Zealand national team from 1998 to 2002. He was in charge of New Zealand at the 1999 FIFA Confederations Cup, and has also managed the Football Kingz in the country. He has also managed Vollen UL in Norway.

DUNN, John
Goalkeeper
Born: *Barking*
Playing career: *Chelsea, Torquay United, Aston Villa, Charlton Athletic, Tooting & Mitcham United, Ford United (1962-1989)*

Signed from Essex Schools, he became the understudy to Peter Bonetti after the departure of Errol McNally. Accordingly, he found his chances limited despite being a competent and brave keeper. Dunn left for Torquay United on a free transfer in 1966 and later played for Aston Villa and Charlton. Now lives in Basildon, Essex and works as a PE teacher in Barking Abbey Sports College having worked a various other schools in the area since hanging up his boots.

"DID YOU KNOW?"

"Aston Villa is the only name ever used in the club's history ."

DUNNE, Richard
Centre-back
Born: *Tallaght, Dublin, Ireland*
Playing career: *Home Farm, Everton, Manchester City, Aston Villa, QPR (1994-2015)*
Dunne was one of Ireland's greatest defenders and will go down as one of the better defenders to have graced the top-flight. The Dublin native was a colossus for Manchester City and also had solid spells with Villa and QPR. He played his first top flight game in 1997 for Joe Royle's Everton and his last for QPR in 2015. He has also played internationally for the Republic of Ireland from earning 80 caps during 14 years served for the Republic. Dunne also held the Premier League record of being sent off and the Premier League record of scoring 10 own goals. Now works as a pundit on BT Sport.

DYER, Lloyd
Winger
Born: *Birmingham*
Playing career: *Aston Villa, West Bromwich Albion, Kidderminster Harriers (loan), Coventry City (loan), QPR (loan), Millwall, Milton Keynes Dons, Leicester City, Watford, Birmingham City (loan), Burnley (1999-2016)*
Dyer started his career with the Villa youth system in 1999, before joining West Brom in July 2001. He never played a first team game for the Villains. Had loan spells at Kidderminster, Coventry and QPR before moving on to Millwall. A tricky, much travelled winger, he currently plays for Burton Albion in League One. Best known for his time at Leicester as they earned successive promotions from the third tier to the Premier League between 2008 an 2014.

DYKE, Archie
Right-winger
Born: *Newcastle-under-Lyme* Died: 1955
Playing career: *Chesterton, Newcastle Congregational, Newcastle P.S.A., Stoke, Port Vale, Stoke, Aston Villa, Port Vale, Stafford Rangers, Coventry City, Blackpool (1909-1922)*
A diminutive and pacy winger, Dyke played for a number of clubs either side of the First World War. In 1913, Dyke was handed his Villa debut in a 3-2 win at The Wednesday on 14 February 1914, Brief spells at Coventry City and Blackpool followed before Dyke finally finished his career at Congleton Town in 1922. He served in the Army during the war. Dyke died in 1955.

ECCLES, Joe
Winger
Born: *Stoke-upon-Trent* Died: 1970
Playing career: *Walsall, Wolseley Motors, Aston Villa, West Ham United , Northampton Town, Coventry City (1922-1929)*
Eccles began his career as a trainee at Walsall but never made it to the senior team. He moved on to Birmingham League team Wolseley Motors then was signed by Aston Villa in 1924. He played ten games for the club and then moved down south to West Ham United and later Northampton. Finished his career at Coventry where he later became a coach and then a scout. His father Jack was also a professional footballer. Eccles died in Stoke in 1906.

EDWARDS, Rob
Centre-back
Born: *Madeley*
Playing career: *Aston Villa, Wolverhampton Wanderers, Blackpool, Barnsley, Fleetwood Town (loan), Shrewsbury Town (loan) (1999-2013)*
Edwards began his career with Villa, making his senior debut in the Premier League, he played eight games in total. He then moved to Wolves in 2004, where he spent four seasons at Championship level. He helped both Blackpool and Norwich to promotions to the Premier League and featured regularly for Barnsley in the Championship before retiring due to injury in 2013. Earned 15 caps for Wales and was interim manager of Wolves for two games in 2016. Also managed Telford in the 2017-18 season and is currently head coach of the Under 23 team at Wolves.

EHIOGU, Ugo
Defender
Born: *Homerton* Died: 2017
Playing career: *WBA, Aston Villa, Middlesbrough, Leeds United, Rangers, Sheffield United (1989-2009)*
Ron Atkinson brought him to Villa Park from West Brom for a £40,000 fee in August 1991. He became a regular and went on to win the League Cup in 1996 and earned a runners up medal after losing the FA Cup final to Chelsea in 2000. Won the League Cup for a second time having moved to Middlesbrough after nine years and over 300 games for Villa. He won four caps for England. Also played for Leeds, Rangers and Sheffield United. He had an unsuccessful trial at MK Dons in 2009, after which he retired and went into coaching. He was manager of Tottenham's Under 23 team when he collapsed and died at their training ground in 2017 at the age of 44.

ELLIOTT, Paul
Defender
Born: *Lewisham, London*
Playing career: *Charlton Athletic, Luton Town, Aston Villa, Pisa, Celti, Chelsea (1980-1994)*
Elliott was Chelsea's Player of the Year and had formed a solid partnership with Ken Monkou when, in 1992, aged 28, his career was ended as a result of a tackle from Liverpool's Dean Saunders. Whilst at Villa he played 57 times and scored seven goals across two seasons in claret and blue. He lost a subsequent court case, and faced court costs of around £500,000. Became a T.V. pundit, worked in Chelsea's sponsorship department, became an advisor to the Equality and Human Rights Commission, and was a member of the FA's bid for the 2018 World Cup. His work with youngsters and active campaigning against racism in the game was rewarded in 2003, when he was given the MBE. A defender of wonderful poise, he was good in the tackle, strong in the air and great heading ability.

"DID YOU KNOW?"

" In 1882, Arthur Alfred Brown and Howard Vaughton became the first Villa players to be capped by England"

Paul Elliott

ENCKELMAN, Peter
Goalkeeper
Born: *Turku, Finland*
Playing career: *Aston Villa, Blackburn Rovers, Cardiff City, St Johnstone, Hearts (1995-2014)*
His time at Villa will always remembered for the bizarre, infamous own goal in the derby against Birmingham in 2002, when the ball slipped under his foot from a throw in. He played 64 games for Villa between 1999 and 2004. Sold to Blackburn and went on to Cardiff - where he played in the FA Cup final of 2008. Had a spell in Scotland with St Johnstone and Hearts. Played 12 times for Finland and retired in 2015. Since he hung up his gloves, he has drifted out of the game and now works for DHL Express as a delivery driver. He also does TV work in his native Finland.

EPHGRAVE, George
Goalkeeper
Born: *Reading* Died: 2004
Playing career: *Guernsey Rangers, Northfleet, Aston Villa, Swindon Town, Southampton, Norwich City, Watford, Deal Town, March Town (1935-1955)*
Goalkeeper Ephgrave started off in the Southern League but Villa came calling for his services in 1936. During the war, he served his country and was captured and held as a prisoner of war whilst still contracted to Swindon. After his retirement, Ephgrave moved back to Guernsey, and he died in 2004 at the age of 86.

EVANS, Albert
Born: *Barnard Castle* Died: 1966
Playing career: *Aston Villa, WBA (1920-1924)*
He was a left back who made over 170 appearances in the Football League for Villa. After his retirement as a player he managed Coventry City and coached at Villa Park and Sarpsborg FK. Later in life he travelled the world and his jobs included sheep farming and gold prospecting in Canada.

He was a member of Villa's double-winning First Division and FA Cup team in the 1896/97 season, and won the league twice more during his time at the club.

EVANS, Allan
Defender
Born: *Dunfermline, Scotland*
Playing career: *Dunfermline Athletic, Aston Villa, Leicester City, Darlington (1973-1991)*
Initially signed as a striker to act as cover for fellow Scot Andy Gray, Allan Evans went on to become one of the best central defenders in Villa's history. Evans had played at centre-half early in his career and manager Ron Saunders saw the sense in playing him in that role alongside Ken McNaught. Only Charlie Aitken (660), Billy Walker (531), and Gordon Cowans (527) have bettered Allan's 475 appearances in claret and blue. He was also Brian Little's assistant manager when Villa won the League Cup in 1996. Evans won four caps for Scotland, all in 1982, and was a member of their 1982 World Cup squad. In 2007 Evans was appointed as a youth team coach at Plymouth Argyle F.C. Evans is the first team coach of Truro College's Football Development Programme.

Allan Evans

EVANS, Alun
Striker
Born: *Kidderminster*
Playing career: *Wolverhampton Wanderers, Los Angeles Wolves (guest), Liverpool, Aston Villa, Walsall, South Melbourne (1964-1983)*
Son of the former West Brom left-half of the same name, Alun Evans became Britain's first £100,000 teenage footballer when he was sold by Wolves to Liverpool in 1968. Also played for Aston Villa and Walsall before trying his luck in the America and then Australia, quitting soccer in 1980. Now lives near Melbourne in Australia where he has worked as a used car salesman, delivery driver at a fish market, and painter and decorator. Returned to the UK to live in Lancashire, where he has represented the county over-50's cricket team! He played for Liverpool in the 1971 FA Cup final.

EVANS, Billy
Centre-forward
Born: *Birmingham* Died: 1960
Playing career: *Aston Villa, Notts County, Gillingham, Grimsby Town (1946-1957)*
He had spent the Second World War making nuts and bolts and was 25 when he signed professional forms. He scored three goals in seven appearances at Villa. In the 1949-1950 season, Notts County clinched the Third Division (South) championship with Evans being an ever-present alongside England international Tommy Lawton. He retired as a player in 1957 having scored 28 times in 102 appearances at Blundell Park and became reserve team coach. He died of lung cancer in Grimsby in 1960, aged 38.

EVANS, Dave
Defender
Born: *West Bromwich*
Playing career: *Aston Villa, Halifax Town, Bradford City, Halifax Town, Brighouse Town (1978-1992)*
Locally born defender Evans began his career on the books at Villa. Despite playing for the youth team over three seasons, he only made two appearances for the senior team under Ron Saunders. He became best known for his time at Halifax - across two spells - and Bradford City where he won Division Three. Evans played over 500 games for his three clubs and after retirement he worked as a coach for non league Brighouse Town. Having left Brighouse he drifted out of the game and worked on the local council in Tamworth. He then moved onto the property ladder.

EVANS, David
Centre-Back
Born: *1935* Died: 2008
Playing career: *Aston Villa (1950-1954).*
A professional with Aston Villa who also played County Cricket for Gloucestershire and Warwickshire, he founded Office Cleaning Ltd in 1980 and became a Director of Luton Town in 1977. Took over as chairman seven years later and was behind the controversial idea to ban away fans from Kenilworth Road in 1987 to save on policing costs. He remained in charge until 1989, two years after being elected as Conservative Member of Parliament M.P. for Welwyn Hatfield. He retired in 2002 and died in Boston, USA, in October 2008.

EVANS, Robert
Left winger
Born: *Chester* Died: 1965
Playing career: *Saltney Ferry F.C, Chester, Wrexham, Aston Villa, Sheffield United (1904-1915)*
Evans was spotted by Villa, whom he signed in March 1906 for £300 and after sixteen league appearances, in which he scored four goals, Sheffield United FC signed him for £1100 +player, Peter Kyle a record at the time. After 204 league appearances, scoring 39 times, Evans retired during WWI. He later worked for the ShellMex Oil company in Ellesmere and turned out for their works team. He died in 1965 shortly after his 80th birthday.

EVANS, Walter
Full-back
Born: *Builth, Wales*
Died: 1897
Playing career: *Bootle, Aston Villa (1889-1897)*
As a promising young sportsman, he was multi-talented at a variety of sports including cricket, rugby and soccer. Having started his career with his local club, Builllth in Wales, he crossed the border to England in 1889 when he joined Bootle. In July 1890, Evans joined Aston Villa where he became a regular member of the team. He made a total of 23 appearances in 1891–92 and 28 in the following year. He was part of the Villa team that reached the FA Cup Final against local rivals West Brom. Evans won three caps for Wales. On returning to the Principality, Evans retired and became landlord of the Lamb Inn. He died in 1897 aged only 30.

EWING, Tommy
Left winger
Born: *Larkhall, Scotland*
Playing career: *Larkhall Thistle, Partick Thistle, Aston Villa, Partick Thistle, Greenock Morton, Hamilton Academical (1956-1971)*
Ewing's career was a case of what might have been, with injuries playing a major role as he never fulfilled his potential. He started in the juniors with Larkhall Thistle and joined Partick Thistle in 1955.

Keith Fahey

Playing mainly at outside left, having been converted from a left back, he played for Thistle in two League Cup Finals, losing both of them in 1956/57 and 1958/59. He moved to Aston Villa in February 1962 for £20,000 but was back at Firhill in the summer of 1964. He subsequently played for Morton and Hamilton Academical, a club he later went on to manage. Ewing also played twice for Scotland and turned out for the Scottish League XI.

EYRE, Edmund
Outside-left
Born: *Worksop* Died: 1943
Playing career: *Worksop West End, Worksop Town, Rotherham Town, Birmingham, Aston Villa, Middlesbrough, Birmingham (1907-1919)*
Eyre, a pacy winger who moved into the Football League with Birmingham in 1907 and was top scorer in his debut season for a struggling side who were relegated from the First Division. After scoring four goals in 15 games in the Second Division, he returned to the top flight with Aston Villa. He won a League Championship medal in claret and blue in the 1909/10 season. It was his final contribution at the club as he moved to Middlesbrough and then returned to Birmingham in April 1914. He retired from football in 1919, and died in Worksop in aged about 60.

FAHEY, Keith
Midfielder
Born: *Dublin, Ireland*
Playing career: *Aston Villa, Bluebell United, St Patrick's Athletic, Drogheda United, Birmingham City, Shamrock Rovers (1998-2015)*
A journeyman player, Dublin-born Fahey was more closely associated with the blue half of the second city. He earned Premier League promotion in 2006 and won the League Cup with Birmingham in 2011. Fahey represented Villa at youth level but never made it to the senior team. A hard-working winger, Fahey won 16 caps for the senior Republic of Ireland team. He finished his career in his homeland with St Patrick's Athletic, Shamrock Rovers and Bluebell United before he was forced to retire through injury in 2017. Fahey now works in the media and as a pundit for RTE in Ireland, also serving as a speaker at corporate events and hospitality dinners.

FARMAN, Alf

Outside-right /Inside right

Born: *Kings Norton, Birmingham* Died: 1896
Playing career: *Birmingham Excelsior, Aston Villa, Bolton Wanderers, Newton Heath (1888-1895)*

Farman proved a prolific and long serving forward for Newton Heath, the club that later became Manchester United. He hit 53 goals in 121 appearances for that club, and is noted for being the first player ever to score a penalty in England in 1891. Farman, Birmingham born, also played for Villa and Bolton as a professional. Not much is known about his career at Villa Park. When Farman retired in in 1897, he went on to become a factory work in Manchester. He died in 1922.

Blue collar: Gareth Farrelly

FARRELL, David

Midfielder

Born: *Birmingham*
Playing career: *Redditch United, Aston Villa, Scunthorpe United (loan), Wycombe Wanderers, Peterborough United, (1991-2009)*

The 46-year-old began his career at non-league Redditch United, before signing for his boyhood team Aston Villa.
Farrell didn't quite make the grade at Villa Park, but says he learned a valuable lesson from the experience, claiming that hard work allowed him to step up from non-league. It was these attributes that he took forward into the coaching career that followed his playing days. He signed for Villa in 1992 for a fee of £45,000 and made eight appearances in total across three years. The Brummie holds the full set of UEFA coaching licences and is currently Swindon's youth coach and head of Academy.

FARRELLY, Gareth

Midfielder

Born: *Dublin, Ireland*
Playing career: *Home Farm, Aston Villa, Rotherham United (loan), Everton, Bolton Wanderers, Wigan Athletic, Bohemians, Blackpool, Cork City, Warrington Town (1992-2010)*

Capped six times by the Republic of Ireland, Farrelly signed for Villa as a 16-year-old and went on to make eight appearances having risen through the ranks. He joined Everton for £700,000 in 1997. He had loan spells at Rotherham, Burnley and Bradford then played for a succession of lower league and non league sides. Player/boss of Bohemians before he was sacked and returned to England with Blackpool. Finished his career with Cork City and Warrington. Since retiring as a professional footballer, Gareth moved into a career in law. He undertook an LLB degree, before training as a solicitor in London. During his training he spent time on secondment in the legal team at Everton.

FASHANU, John
Striker
Born: *Kensington, London*
Playing career: *Norwich City, Crystal Palace, Lincoln City, Millwall, Wimbledon, Aston Villa (1979-1995)*

A Wimbledon legend and loved where ever he went, 'Fash' was a powerful and prolific centre-forward, most notably for the "Crazy Gang" at Plough Lane. He won the FA Cup in 1988 and scored over 100 goals in all competitions. He scored 134 league goals in a career lasting 17 years. He was also capped twice at senior level by England, but failed to score on either occasion. Following his football career he went on to co-host British television show Gladiators in the 1990s, and between 2003 and 2004 he managed his own Sunday league football side Fash FC on Bravo. He has also hosted Deal or No Deal.

FENCOTT, Ken
Forward
Born: *Walsall*
Playing career: *Aston Villa, Lincoln City (1959-1967)*

Fencott played as a striker for Walsall Boys before he joined Villa as an amateur in 1959, turning professional two years later. He never really hit the heights in claret and blue, playing only three games in the First Division and twice more in the League Cup before he was released in 1964. For the majority of his career, he plied his trade with Lincoln. He then joined West Midlands League side Tamworth, where he stayed for only one season before moving on again to Blakenall of the Midland Combination near his home town of Walsall. With his brief six year career over, Fencott turned his hand to snooker. He became a proficient amateur player at county level and ran a driving school business in Birmingham simultaneously. Now aged 75, he continues to reside in Walsall.

FENTON, Graham
Midfielder
Born: *Whitley Bay*
Playing career: *Aston Villa, West Bromwich Albion, Blackburn Rovers, Leicester City, Walsall, Stoke City, St Mirren, Blackpool, Darlington, Blyth Spartans, North Shields (1992-2010)*

He played as a striker, in the Premier League for Aston Villa, Blackburn Rovers and Leicester City, as well as in the Football League for West Bromwich Albion, Walsall, Stoke City, Blackpool and Darlington. He also spent a year in Scotland with St Mirren before later playing for Non-league Blyth Spartans.

John Fashanu

He was also capped once by England at under-21 level. Fenton joined Aston Villa as a trainee in June 1990, turning professional in February 1992. Made his debut for the club in the Premier League in February 1994 and played in the League Cup win over Man United the following month. Went on to Blackburn, Leicester City, Stoke, St Mirren, Blackpool, Darlington, and North Shields, who he went on to manage. Now joint manager of neighbours South Shields FC, he also earned one England Under 21 cap.

FERGUSON, Mike

Born: *Burnley*
Playing career: *Accrington Stanley, Blackburn Rovers, Aston Villa, QPR, Cambridge United, Rochdale, Halifax Town (1960-1976).*

Ferguson was a club record signing when he arrived from Blackburn Rovers in 1968, although his time at Villa Park was relatively short. He made a total of 42 appearances, scoring two goals, before moving to QPR 18 months later. Born in Burnley in March 1943, he was on Plymouth Argyle's books as a youngster and then played for Accrington Stanley, for whom he had the dubious distinction of scoring their final goal before they dropped out of the Football League in 1962. He then joined Blackburn before Villa manager Tommy Cummings made him the club's then-record signing. After retiring as a player, Ferguson tried his hand at management in England, with Rochdale, and overseas as boss of LA Akranes in Iceland and in Cyprus with APOEL and Evagoras Paphos, Ferguson died in August 2019 at the age of 76.

FERRARESI, Fabio

Midfielder
Born: *Fano, Italy*
Playing career: *Aston Villa, Chievo, Castel di Sangro, Avellino, Sora, Sangiovannese, Chiasso, Martina (loan), Pescara, Valle del Giovenco, Lecco (1997-2011)*

A journeyman player, he never spent more than three years at any of his 12 clubs. He was signed by Aston Villa in the late 1990s and never played a competitive game for the club, only playing in pre-season friendlies. He failed to make an impression on the Villa management and was sold to Chievo back in his homeland after a year at Villa Park. Played in Italy for the rest of his career, then became a player agent after retiring in 2012.

FINDLAY, Jake

Goalkeeper
Born: *Blairgowrie, Scotland*
Playing career: *Aston Villa, Luton Town, Barnsley (loan), Swindon Town, Peterborough United, Portsmouth, Coventry City (1969-1985)*

A big, imposing shot stopper, he signed for Villa just shy of his 15th birthday. Findlay went on to play 14 times for the claret and blue under Vic Crowe and later Ron Saunders. He was sold to David Pleat's Luton on the premise of first team football for the Hatters. Findlay represented Scotland at youth level but was never called up to the senior squad. Findlay moved on to Swindon Town in 1985, and after spells with Peterborough, Portsmouth and Coventry he retired from the game. He went on to take up a role as goalkeeping coach at Luton.

FISH, Ken

Forward

Born: *Cape Town, South Africa* Died: 2005
Playing career: *Railway Association, Aston Villa, Port Vale, Young Boys, Port Vale (1937-1939)*

He played for Port Vale and Swiss side Young Boys. He later served behind the scenes at Port Vale, Birmingham City, and Oxford United, winning the League Cup as trainer-coach of the latter in 1986 at the age of 72. Fish played for Railway Association (in South Africa) before moving to England to play for Aston Villa. He signed with Port Vale of the Third Division North for a sizeable fee in November 1937. He played just six games (five in the Football League and one FA Cup) and was sold to Swiss side Young Boys in October 1938. He returned to Vale as the assistant trainer in July 1939 and re-signed as a player the following month. Went on to fulfil the same role at Oxford after the war, during which he served as a warrant officer and remedial specialist. He also earned four caps for South Africa.

FISHER, Albert

Inside-forward

Born: *Birmingham* Died: 1937
Playing career: *Ashbury Richmond, Soho Caledonians, Aston Villa, Bristol City, Bristol City, Brighton & Hove Albion, Manchester City, Bradford Park Avenue, Coventry City (1902-1912)*

A striker, he scored 23 goals in 56 games during a Football League career spanning ten years and three clubs. He also played for Southern League clubs Brighton & Hove Albion, Bradford Park Avenue, Queens Park Rangers, Coventry City and Merthyr Town. He then dropped down into the non league game and led Merthyr Town to the Southern League Second Division title in 1911–12, and went on to manage Notts County. Fisher was born in Birmingham, and died in Nottingham at the age of 56 in 1937.

FISHER, Charles

Wing-half

Born: *Handsworth* Died: 1985
Playing career: *Kimberworth Old Boys, Aston Villa, Kidderminster Harriers, Brentford (1919-1922)*

Never made a senior appearance for Villa, despite spending two years in the Midlands. Moved on to Kidderminster Harriers then to Brentford. Was player/manager of Margate from 1925 - 1929. Upon retirement, he coached at Brentford and then went on to become a part time club director. Also worked in a shoe shop.

FISHER, James

Forward

Born: *Stirling* Died: Unknown
Playing career: *East Stirlingshire, St Bernard's, Aston Villa, King's Park, Manchester United (-)*

Played at amateur level for East Stirlingshire before he signed for Villa in 1886, playing in the FA Cup and friendly matches. He was part of Villa's team during their maiden Football League season. Joined United in 1900 where he earned the first of his three caps for Scotland. Retired in 1906, later worked in a cloth factory.

FLASH, Richard

Midfielder

Born: *Birmingham*
Playing career: *Aston Villa, Manchester United, Wolverhampton Wanderers, Watford, Lincoln City (loan), Plymouth Argyle (1992-1999)*

Flash was a highly rated player in the Birmingham area and had trials at both St Andrew's and Aston Villa – but he caught the eye of United's Midland scout and went to play for the Manchester Eagles. Mixing it with the Class of 92' at Old Trafford, he shared digs with a certain David Beckham, made the first team bench and was tipped for stardom. But his career was over before it even really began after he dislocated a kneecap. An all action midfielder, Falsh went on to play for Wolves, Watford, Lincoln and Plymouth before calling time on his career in 1999 – the same year the Class of 92 reached their peak winning the Treble. Flash went to university and did a Masters degree. He now works as the head of the academic department at UCFB - a higher education institution delivering degrees in sports and the football industries - based in Burnley and Wembley.

FLEMING, Jock
Centre-forward
Born: *Leith, Scotland* Died: 1934
Playing career: *Vale of Leven, Argyll and Sutherland Highlanders, Southampton St. Mary's, Aston Villa, Lincoln City, Larkhall Saints (1891-1893)*
John "Jock" Fleming was based India with the 93rd Argyll and Sutherland Highlanders before leaving the army in May 1892 to England and join First Division Aston Villa. He played four times for Villa before being signed by Lincoln City in 1892 and then return to his native Scotland the following year. Fleming died in 1934 aged 69.

FORD, Trevor
Striker
Born: *Swansea, Wales* Died: 2003
Playing career: *Swansea City, Aston Villa, Sunderland, Cardiff, Newport County. (1946-1960).*
A centre forward who played 38 matches for his national team, Wales, Ford ran a garage business but died in 2003. He was also a capable cricketer and was playing as a substitute fielder for Glamorgan in the match that Sir Gary Sobers set a new world record by scoring six sixes in one over.
He was the first Welsh international to score over 20 goals for his country. At the time of his transfer from Villa to Stoke, he set a new British record with a fee of £30,000 paid. He was very prolific during a fallow time for Villa collectively, and plundered 61 goals in 128 games.

Steve Foster

FORMAN, Matt
Midfielder
Born: Solihull
Playing career: *Aston Villa, Wolverhampton Wanderers, Burton Albion, Moor Green, Evesham United, Alvechurch FC, Bromsgrove Rovers*
Midfielder who played 30 games for Wolves in 1986/7 season. Injury and illness led to a degree course in photography. Started out at Villa as an apprentice but never made a senior appearance. Lived as an artist in Antwerp before training as a teacher in 1997. Has worked as an Art teacher in Manchester for the last 12 years.

FOSTER, Steve
Central defender
Born: *Portsmouth*
Playing career: *Southampton, Portsmouth, Brighton & Hove Albion, Aston Villa, Luton Town, Oxford United, Brighton & Hove Albion (1972-1996)*
Ian St John's decision to try 'Fozzie' in defence during a reserve game proved to be a key moment in the Portsmouth born player's career. Although he had scored goals regularly as a youngster, he immediately looked comfortable in the Centre-half position. Despite the club's poor form and subsequent relegation, Foster's performances stood out and ultimately earned a £130,000 move to Brighton who had just been promoted to the old First Division. Although he had to go through the agony of relegation at his new club he did win three England caps and captained his side in an FA Cup final replay against Manchester United. With a growing reputation, the fans' favourite was sold to Aston Villa and later played for Luton Town and Oxford United before ending his career back at the Goldstone Ground. He still lives in Brighton and runs a successful insurance business offering cover to professional footballers. At any one time they have about 4,000 of the top players on their books.

FOXALL, Frederick
Outside-left
Born: *Stourbridge* Died: 1926
Playing career: *Aston Villa, Blackheath Town, Southampton, Birmingham, Watford (1914-1924)*

Halesowen born winger Fred Foxall had signed for Aston Villa as an amateur in April 1915 but the Great War put paid to his Villa career. He signed for (then Southern League) Southampton in May 1919, making his Football League debut at Gillingham in August 1920. Indeed he was ever present that season, however at the end of the season he provoked controversy when he signed a contract with Aston Villa, although he was still registered with Southampton. He was ordered by The Football Association to re-join Southampton and he had played 28 games the following season (which saw him win a Third Division (South) Champions medal). Foxall, described as an "excellent" player, went on to ply his trade for Birmingham and Watford, where he was forced to retire after twice breaking a leg. He never fully recovered and died from complications two years later aged only 28.

FRASER, Cammie
Full-back
Born: *Blackford, Scotland*
Playing career: *Dunfermline Athletic, Aston Villa, Birmingham City, Falkirk (1958-1968)*

Played under legendary countryman Jock Stein at Dunfermline and won the Scottish Cup in 1961. He featured for the club throughout their run to the Cup Winners Cup quarter-finals, but a string of impressive performances inevitably attracted the attentions of a bigger club. He joined Villa for what at the time was a huge fee of £23,500. A runner up to fierce local rivals Birmingham City in the 1963 League Cup final. He started well at Villa but fell out of favour and moved across the city to the Blues, for £9,000 in May 1964. He returned to his native Scotland two years later with Falkirk and then hung up his boots. After football, Fraser worked for the Bank of Scotland and then joined his wife's hairdressing business. He also found employment in an oil company in Singapore and, returning home, had many short contract jobs. He has now settled in Australia with his wife.

FREEMAN, Bert
Centre-forward
Born: *Handsworth, West Midlands* Died: 1955
Playing career: *Aston Villa, Woolwich Arsenal, Everton, Burnley, Wigan Borough, Kettering Town, Kidderminster Harriers (1904-1924)*

Handsworth, Birmingham born double goals centurion Bert Freeman was a very successful centre forward and is a Burnley legend, not merely because he scored the winning goal in the 1914 FA Cup Final triumph over Liverpool, the only time the club have ever won the famous trophy. He began his football career playing junior football for Gower Street Old Boys in 1900 and Aston Manor in 1901 before joining his local First Division club Aston Villa in April 1904. He left Aston Villa without ever having appeared in claret and blue, signing for Woolwich Arsenal in November 1905. He earned five full caps for England, a number which doesn't seem right given the prolific nature of his career. He also guested for Birmingham during the conflict, during which he served in the Armed Force. His brother, Walter was also a footballer, playing for Aston Villa, Birmingham and Fulham.

FREEMAN, Walter
Inside-forward
Born: *Birmingham*
Playing career: *Aston Martin, Lowestoft Town, Aston Villa, Fulham, Birmingham, Walsall, Wellington Town, Walsall (1904-1915)*

A centre forward like his older brother Bert Walter Freeman started his football career with Aston Manor in 1903 and joined Lowestoft Town in 1904, before signing for hometown First Division club Aston Villa in May 1905. However he didn't make a first eleven appearance and joined Fulham in January 1906, helping them to their back to back Southern League Championship wins in 1905-06 and 1906-07, before being a member of their squad that joined the Football League in 1907. He played 2 seasons for Fulham in The Football League, scoring 12 goals in 23 appearances, before joining Birmingham in September 1909. At St Andrew's he scored 11 goals in 38 games before joining Walsall in 1911, subsequently having a spell at Wellington Town in 1914. After retiring from football, he drifted out of the game and worked in the cotton industry.

FRIEDEL, Brad

Goalkeeper

Born: *Lakewood, Ohio, United States*
Playing career: *USSF, Newcastle United (loan), Br√®ndby (loan), Galatasaray, Columbus Crew, Liverpool, Blackburn Rovers, Aston Villa, Tottenham Hotspur (1990-2015)*

Friedel set many records during his two decade career in the game. He is officially Aston Villa's oldest-ever player, a record he set in 2011, by playing in the club's Premier League fixture away at Manchester United at 39 years and 259 days old, surpassing the previous record held by Ernie Callaghan. In 2012, Friedel also became the oldest player to appear in a competitive match for Tottenham when he played in the club's Premier League fixture at former side Aston Villa, He holds another record as the most capped keeper in USA national team history with 82 appearances. Friedel played until he was 44 and once scored for Blackburn. He went on to coach the USA Under 19s team and manage New England Revolution. Friedel has also done punditry work and commentary for RTE in Ireland, Match of the Day and Radio Five Live.

Steve Froggatt

FROGGATT, Steve

Winger

Born: *Lincoln*
Playing career: *Aston Villa, Wolverhampton Wanderers, Coventry City (1989-2001)*

Froggatt began his career Aston Villa as a trainee, before turning professional and making his debut for the team in 1991.

He featured in the first ever Premier League season before going on to play for Wolves and Coventry. He has career wrecked by a horror tackle from Sunderland's Nicky Summerbee in 2000. It was an incident that ultimately led to his retirement at 27 years of age. He won a League Cup winner's medal at Villa in 1994 although he did not play in the final against United. He also won recognition from the England U21s, earning two caps during his career. Upon retiring, Froggart became the press officer at Coventry City and now works as a mortgage adviser and often appears on television and radio as a football summariser. Twitter: https://twitter.com/Froggy123Steve

Brad Friedel

GAGE, Kevin
Midfielder
Born: *Chiswick*
Playing career: *Wimbledon, Aston Villa, Sheffield United, Preston North End, Hull City (1980-1999)*
He started his career with Wimbledon and went on to make close to 500 league and cup appearances. In June 1987, Gage was bought by Aston Villa for £250,000 to be part of Graham Taylor's new regime to restore Villa to the top division after relegation the previous season. In his first season, Gage was a league and cup ever-present, as Villa gained promotion as Division 2 runners-up. In the following two seasons, Gage was used in a variety of positions, switching from full-back to midfield, and also a wing-back, as Aston Villa ran Liverpool very close to the league title, eventually finishing second in 1989-90 season. After Graham Taylor left for the England manager's job, and following Ron Atkinson's re-shaping of the team, Gage left for Sheffield Utd in Nov 1991. He retired from football through injury in 1999, going on to become a television pundit.

GALLACHER, Bernie
Defender
Born: *Johnstone, Scotland* Died: 2011
Playing career: *Aston Villa, Blackburn Rovers (loan), Doncaster Rovers(1985-1994)*
Bernie Gallacher was never a big star at Villa Park but he made a vital contribution to the club's history. The flame haired Scot was a member of the team who secured Villa's last promotion back to the old First Division under the management of Graham Taylor in 1987-88.The buccaneering left-back proved a virtual ever present as he played in 43 of Villa's 44 Second Division games that season. Only Kevin Gage and goalkeeper Nigel Spink featured in every game. Unfortunately, Gallacher's top-flight action was limited. Despite a total of 50 league and cup games in that promotion season, his total appearances in claret and blue amounted to 72. Born in Perthshire in March 1967, Gallacher joined Villa as a 16-year-old, graduating through the youth and reserve ranks before making his first team debut against Manchester United on the final day of the 1986-87 season. After spells at Blackburn, Doncaster and Brighton, he went on to become a player agent. Died in 2011 in Sutton Coldfield.

GARDNER, Tommy
Wing-half
Born: *Huyton* Died: 1970
Playing career: *Liverpool, Grimsby Town, Hull City, Aston Villa, Burnley, Wrexham (1929-1947)*
A wing-half, he signed for Villa for £4,500 from Hull in 1933. Something of a squad player in the Midlands, he passed through Villa on his journey from club-to-club and scored one goal in 77 appearances. He became Chester City's assistant trainer in the summer of 1954 and stayed in the post until May 1967, and was also a steward with the club. Later, Gardner set up a five a side league and became managing director of a sports clothing brand. He died in 1970.

GARRATY, Billy
Forward
Born: *Saltley, Birmingham* Died: 1931
Playing career: *Aston Villa, Leicester Fosse, West Bromwich Albion (1897-1911)* Garraty joined Aston Villa in August 1897 as an 18 year old after impressing in local football and sits ninth on the current list of all time Villa goalscorers with 111 (including 28 in 33 games in the 1899/1900 season), but for a man of such talent, he won only one cap for England. After retiring, he returned to Villa as a coach and then later became a pub owner and licensee in Birmingham. He is the great-great-grandfather of current claret and blue captain Jack Grealish.

GARVEY, Batty

Forward
Born: *Aston* Died: 1932
Playing career: *Aston Hall Swifts, Aston Shakespeare, Aston Villa (1888-1890)*
An inside who played in the first ever Villa Football League team. Only appeared in six more matches but scored four goals ibefore retiring through injury in 1895. Later became a PE teacher, combining that role with a position as manager of a leisure centre in Aston. He died in 1932 aged 46.

GEDDIS, David

Striker
Born: *Carlisle*
Playing career: *Ipswich Town, Luton Town, Aston Villa, Luton Town, Barnsley, Birmingham City, Brentford, Shrewsbury Town, Swindon Town, Darlington. (1976-1990)*
He was transferred to Aston Villa in 1979 for £300,000 and the following season won a league championship medal by being one of the 14 players Villa used that season. Won the FA Cup with Ipswich in 1978 and was on the bench in Rotterdam for Villa's victorious 1982 European Cup final. He went on to play for Brentford, Shrewsbury Town, Swindon Town and Darlington. Became first team coach at Newcastle, served as head of youth at Leeds United and also had a two game stint as caretaker manager at Elland Road in 2006. He was also a scout for England in the lead up to the 2006 World Cup.

GEORGE, Billy

Goalkeeper
Born: *Shrewsbury*
Died: 1933
Playing career: *Aston Villa (1897-1911)*
Billy George was signed by Aston Villa from the Army for £50 in 1897. While at Villa Park George kept goal in three of Aston Villa's League Championship winning sides, in 1899, 1900 and 1910 as well as keeping goal in their 1905 FA Cup winning team when Villa beat Newcastle United 2-0 at The Crystal Palace. His Villa career spanned 14 seasons, eventually leaving the club when he was sold to Birmingham City to become their player-trainer in July 1891. In total he made 399 appearances and is still regarded as one of the best goalkeepers to have played for the claret and blue in the club's history. Having won three caps for the England. football team, George also played 13 first class cricket matches as a right-handed batsman with Warwickshire between 1901 and 1906. In an era when it was not uncommon to play both sports, he was in the same Warwickshire team as Aston Villa team mate Jack Devey. He scored 342 runs in 18 innings at a respectable average of 21.37, with a high score of 71, one of three fifties he scored for the county on his occasional appearances. Worked on the cricket club's board after retiring and also at Birmingham as a coach.

1905 FA Cup Final

GERRISH, Billy
Inside-forward
Born: *Bristol* Died: 1916
Playing career: *Bristol Rovers, Aston Villa, Preston North End, Chesterfield Town (1905-1913)*
Known as 'Willy' Gerrish, he played for Villa and Preston North End in the Football League, winning the First Division with the former in 1909-10. An inside-forward forward of considerable strength, he also played for Freemantle as an amateur, Bristol Rovers and Chesterfield. In 1915, six months into the First World War, Gerrish enlisted in the 17th (Service) Battalion of the Duke of Cambridge's Own (Middlesex Regiment). He was severely wounded in both legs by a shell blast and subsequently died later that day. He scored 17 goals in 55 appearances for Villa between 1909 and 1912.

GETTINS, Alfred
Forward
Born: *Manchester* Died: 1949
Playing career: *Bolton Wanderers, Blackpool, Luton Town, QPR, Aston Villa, Brighton & Hove Albion , Fulham, Portsmouth, Partick Thistle, Dumbarton, Stenhousemuir (1904-1923)*
A much travelled journeyman striker, he played for Villa in the 1908-09 season as part of a 19 year professional career. He only made one first division appearance at the club. Represented England at age group level but is best known for his time at Dumbarton where he made over 50 appearances and later became a scout Also worked in the construction industry but died in 1949 aged 63.

Najwan Ghrayib

GHENT, Matthew
Goalkeeper
Born: *Burton upon Trent*
Playing career: *Aston Villa, Lincoln City, Forest Green Rovers, Barnsley (1996-2009)*
Embroiled in an ugly legal wrangling after assaulting his then girlfriend, Ghent was a controversial goalkeeper who started out as the youngest ever stopper to appear on a Premier League teamsheet. He had only just turned 17 when he was named on the bench in 1997 against Southampton. That would be as good as it got for Ghent as he never made a senior appearance for the club. Ghent admitted he lost his love for the game and ended up selling shampoo. He was convicted of harassment after the incident with his girlfriend, and given a ten-week suspended sentence in 2013.

GHRAYIB, Najwan
Defender
Born: *Nazareth, Israel*
Playing career: *Maccabi Haifa, Hapoel Petah Tikva, Hapoel Haifa, Aston Villa, Hapoel Haifa, Maccabi Ahi Nazareth, Hapoel Petah Tikva (1990-2006)*
Aston Villa paid out £1 million for his transfer from Hapoel Haifa in 1999, but Ghrayib saw very little first-team action, playing only five times in two years at the club in his solitary foray outside of his native Israel. He was sold back to hometown side Hapoel Haifa. Earned 18 caps for Israel, and then, having retired as a player, moved into the dugout. Now manager of Maccabi Ahi Nazareth for his second spell as boss, he has also had a spell in charge of another Israeli side Hapoel Bnei Lod in 2010.

GIBBON, Malcolm
Half-back
Born: *North Shields*
Playing career: *Port Vale, Aston Villa, Eastwood, Congleton Town, Milton United (1967-1975)*
Gibbon started with Port Vale and made four appearances in the Fourth Division for the Valiants under Stanley Matthews as boss. Having been released, he was signed by Villa but never made an appearance for the club, going down as one of their more obscure names. He also turned out for Eastwood, Congleton Town and Milton United, spending two seasons with Congleton for whom he played over 50 times.

GIBSON, Colin

Left-back /Midfielder
Born: *Bridport*
Playing career: *Aston Villa, Manchester United, Port Vale, Leicester City, Blackpool, Walsall. (1978-1994)*

Gibson started his career at Aston Villa in 1978 and made around 200 appearances for the club in seven years, as well as winning the First Division title, the European Cup and the European Super Cup. He moved on to Manchester United in 1985, and during his five years at United he played 79 league games. He signed with Leicester City in 1990, after a short loan at Port Vale. After a four-year spell with the "Foxes" in which he helped the club to win promotion to the Premier League via the play-offs in 1994, he transferred to Blackpool, before finishing his career by winning promotion out of the Third Division with Walsall in 1995. Won one cap for England Under 21s and the B team. Worked as an agent for BBC Radio Leicester then moved to BBC Radio Derby as senior sports reporter after retirement.

GIBSON, Colin

Outside/inside right
Born: *Normanby* Died: 1992
Playing career: *Cardiff City, Newcastle United, Aston Villa, Lincoln City, Stourbridge (1948-1957)*

Gibson was born in Middlesbrough in 1923 and payed for Cardiff before joining Newcastle where he made 23 appearances and five goals. Later played for Villa, Lincoln City and Stourbridge. He played for Villa for seven years during which time he earned recognition for both England 'B' and the Football League XI.

Joined Villa for £17,500 in 1949, and went on to play over 100 times for the club. He finished up his playing career with Lincoln and in the non league game with Stourbridge. He died in 1992 aged 68. After retirement he worked as a delivery driver and also as a labourer.

GIBSON, Dave

Inside-left
Born: *Edinburgh, Scotland*
Playing career: *Livingston United, Hibernian, Leicester City, Aston Villa, Exeter City (1956-1974)*

Opened a pet food and garden shop in Exmouth before moving back to Leicestershire where he was a postman for twelve years and was also co-owner of a residential rest home in Whetstone before retiring to Dorset. Considered to be one of the finest and most skilful players in Leicester's history, he was the playmaker and creative force of the great Leicester side of the 1960s under Matt Gillies, including the "Ice Kings" side that fell just short of winning the double in 1962–63. He scored in both legs of Leicester's 1964 League Cup final victory and also played in a further 3 cup finals for the club. Gibson earned seven caps and scored three goals for Scotland.

GIBSON, Jimmy

Half-back
Born: *Scottish*
Died: 1978
Playing career: *Kirkintilloch Rob Roy, Ashfield, Partick Thistle, Aston Villa, Rangers (1917-1936)*

Regarded as an excellent, tall defender at right-half with a superb reading of the game, he played almost 200 games for Patrick before he crossed the border to Villa for £7,500. He went on to play over 200 times for the club and was capped eight times by Scotland at international level. Gibson came from a prestigious sporting family, with his father Nelly and brothers Neil and Willie were also professional players. He stayed at Aston Villa for nine full seasons, playing his last game in April 1936 and retiring after their relegation that season. In total he scored 10 goals in 227 appearances for The Villains and was twice a runner up with them in the League Championship, in 1931 and 1933. He died in 1978 aged 77.

GIDMAN, John
Right-back
Born: *Liverpool*
Playing career: *Liverpool, Aston Villa, Everton, Manchester United, Manchester City, Stoke City, Darlington (1970-1989)*

Gidman played for the Liverpool youth team without every making it to the senior side, before he joined Villa in 1971. He won the League Cup with Villa in 77' but left two years later. He played once for the full England team. Joined United in 1981 in the same deal that took Mickey Thomas and £50,000 to Everton to become Ron Atkinson's first signing for the club. He soon became a favourite of the Stretford End but a number of injuries dented the impact that he made at the club. He was a FA Cup winner in 1985. He played almost 100 league matches before joining Man City in 1986 after becoming surplus to requirements. Former Kings Lynn manager, has been living in Marbella on the Costa del Sol since the mid-1990s.

GILLIBRAND, Ernest
Centre-forward/Outside-forward
Born: *Prestwich* Died: 1976
Playing career: *Northwich Victoria, Glossop, Aston Villa, Nelson, Rossendale United, Manchester North End, Stalybridge Celtic, Buxton, Denton United, Hyde United, Denton United, Buxton, Droylsden, Ashton National, Stalybridge Celtic (1920-1937)*

A winger turned striker, Gillibrand had something of a nomadic career, turning out for 12 clubs across 17 years. He began in non league as an amateur with Northwich

Victoria and Glossop, before he signed for Villa. Gillibrand never made the first team and moved on to Nelson, Rossendale then Preston. Whilst playing for Hyde United, he reportedly scored 87 goals in one season. Later in his life, he was player/manager of Ashton and also took over as boss of Staybridge Celtic's youth team.

GILSON, Alf
Right-back
Born: *Lichfield* Died: 1912
Playing career: *Whittington Royal, Burton Swifts, Aston Villa, Brentford, Bristol City, Clapton Orient, Brentford (1899-1905)*

Played two games for Villa in the 1900-01 season. A right-back, he spent the majority of his playing days at Ashton Gate with Bristol City. Gilson also represented Brentford and Clapton Orient. After suffering from a chest condition which forced his retirement from football in September 1910, Gilson spent time recovering in Bournemouth. He then fell unconscious and died from pneumonia and pleurisy one month later. He was only 30.

GINOLA, David
Winger/Forward
Born: *Gassin, France*
Playing career: *Toulon, Racing Club Paris, Brest, Paris Saint-Germain, Newcastle United, Tottenham Hotspur, Aston Villa, Everton (1985-2002)*

A former forward, he played football for ten seasons in his native France before making the move from Paris Saint-Germain to Newcastle United in the English Premier League in July 1995. He continued playing in the Premier League for Tottenham Hotspur, Aston Villa and Everton before retiring in 2002. Since his retirement from the game he has become involved in several new pursuits, including acting. Ginola is a regular contributor to BBC, BT and CNN. He hosts 'Match of ze Day' ('MozD'), a program which broadcasts live Premier League matches on Canal+. He has also done modelling work. On 16 January 2015, Ginola announced his intention to run for the FIFA presidency. However, 14 days later, on 30 January 2015, Ginola withdrew his bid for the FIFA presidency, after failing to receive the required backing of at least five national football associations. Played 17 times for France.

David Ginola

GIVEN, Shay
Goalkeeper
Born: *Lifford, County Donegal, Ireland*
Playing career: *Celtic, Blackburn Rovers, Swindon Town (loan), Sunderland (loan), Newcastle United, Manchester City, Aston Villa, Middlesbrough (loan), Stoke City (1991-2015)*

The most capped keeper in Republic of Ireland history having played 134 times for his country, he joined Aston Villa for a fee believed to be around £3.5 million, signing a five-year contract in 2011. Played in the 2015 FA Cup final for the club, and also had a two game spell as interim first team assistant boss to Paul Lambert at the end of the previous season. Played in the 2002 World Cup and Euro 2012, and also won the FA Cup with Manchester City. Currently works as goalkeeping coach at Derby County.

GLOVER, Dean
Born: *Birmingham*
Playing career: *Aston Villa, Sheffield United, Middlesbrough, Port Vale.(1981-1999)*

A cultured, stylish, ball playing defender, Glover started out at Villa where he spent the next seven years. He was restricted to only 39 appearances in that time, though, scoring once, and never became a constant presence in the first team. He then helped Middlesbrough to promotion before spending nine years with Port Vale, for whom Glover played 363 league games, becoming one of the Valiants' all time greats. After retirement, he stayed at Vale Park as a trainer and then as a scout. He later became the club's manager. Glover is also a graduate of the LMA's Certificate in Applied Management at Warwick University.

GODFREY, Brian
Striker
Born: *Flint, Wales* Died: 2010
Playing career: *Everton, Scunthorpe, Preston NE, Aston Villa, Bristol Rovers, Newport C. (1959-1975)*

Godfrey started his professional football career at Everton and in an 18-years career played for six league clubs and was capped for Wales at U23 and full international level, earning three caps and scoring twice. He joined Villa from Preston North End in 1967 and played over 160 games including captaining Aston Villa in the 1971 League Cup Final. He went on to manager Bath City, Exeter City, Weymouth and had two spells as Gloucester City boss. The former forward also turned for the Villa legends and the Aston Villa Old Boys teams. Godfrey died in 2010 after a battle with leukaemia.

GOFFIN, Billy
Striker
Born: *The Riddings, Amington* Died: 1987
Playing career: *Amington Village, Aston Villa, Walsall, Tamworth (1936-1958)*

Known as "Cowboy", Goffin signed for Villa as an amateur and went on to play over 200 times for the club, scoring an impressive 89 times. Later managed Tamworth and combined his role with a job as a collector for the East Midlands Electricity Board and worked for the council. Coffin died in 1987.

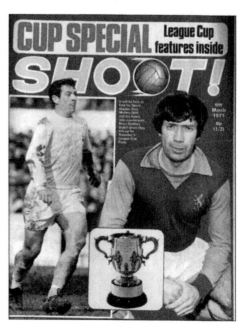

GOODALL, Archie

Half-back/Forward

Born: *Belfast, Ireland* Died: 1929
Playing career: *Preston North End, Aston Villa, Derby County, Wolves (1887-1905)*

Goodall had an effective but brief spell as inside-right at Villa, scoring 7 goals in 14 appearances, and this was followed by over a decade at Derby County. At Derby his stamina and sheer physical presence made him one of the most effective backs in the English game. He won ten caps for Ireland, scoring twice for his country. Goodall left Derby County in 1903, where he had been club captain, after 425 games and 52 goals. He joined Plymouth Argyle of the Southern League and then became player-manager of Glossop. At the age of 41 years 153 days he is the oldest player ever to feature for Wolves, where he finished his career. After retiring as a player, Goodall travelled Europe and the United States as part of a strongman act before settling in London, where he lived out his remaining years.

GRAHAM, George

Midfielder/Forward

Born: *Bargeddie, North Lanarkshire, Scotland*
Playing career: *Aston Villa, Chelsea, Arsenal, Man United, Portsmouth, Crystal Palace. (1962-1977)*

Known as 'Stroller', began his career as a youngster at Villa Park, signing on his 17th birthday and going on to play 8 games in the early 1960's. He went on to enjoy phenomenal success both as a player and manager at Arsenal. He later joined Portsmouth from Manchester United in the twilight of his career as part of a straight swap that took Ron Davies to Old Trafford. His playing days drew to a close after a summer in America with California Surf. He coached various clubs before taking charge of Millwall. Later moved back to Arsenal where he enjoyed a very successful reign before accepting an 'unsolicited gift' from Norwegian agent Rune Hauge and was sacked. Has since managed Leeds and Spurs but is now a media pundit.

George Graham

GRAHAM, John
Forward
Born: *Leyland*
Playing career: *Blackburn Rovers, Aston Villa, Wrexham, Rochdale, Bradford City (1945-1954)*
Graham played for Leyland Works, Blackburn Rovers, Aston Villa, Wrexham, Rochdale and Bradford City as a strong and hard-working centre forward, equally as adept on either wing. For Bradford City he made 18 appearances in the Football League, scoring once. Having guested for Villa in wartime (10 apps, three goals), when football resumed after World War Two he went on to play for the club until 1949, making twelve appearances and scoring three goals. He retired in 1954 and went on to work as a labourer in Preston.

GRAHAM, Tommy
Midfielder
Born: *Glasgow, Scotland*
Playing career: *Aston Villa, Barnsley, Halifax Town, Doncaster Rovers, Motherwell, Scunthorpe United, Scarborough, Halifax Town, (1978-1992)*
Graham began his football career with Arthurlie before moving to England where, after a brief spell with Aston Villa, he signed for Barnsley in late 1978 for a £25,000 fee. Having failed to make a senior appearance in claret and blue, he moved on to Halifax, Doncaster, Motherwell, Scunthorpe, Scarborough, and finally Frickley Athletic.

Andy Gray

He became best known for his unstinting service for Scarborough and 'Scunny', playing a combined 300 games for the two clubs and getting promoted with the former. His brothers were also all professional players on both sides of the Anglo-Scottish border. He continues to live in Barnsley and works as a Surgical Chiropodist in the town.

GRAY, Andy
Striker
Born: *Glasgow, Scotland*
Playing career: *Clydebank Strollers, Dundee United, Aston Villa, Wolverhampton Wanderers , Everton, Aston Villa, Notts County (loan), West Bromwich Albion, Rangers, Cheltenham Town (-)*
A League Cup winner at Midlands powerhouses Villa and then Wolves, he was a key cog at Goodison Park in Everton's glory years. 20 caps for Scotland, seven goals. Relegated into the Second Division on his return to Villa in 1986-87. After retiring as a player, Gray entered coaching as an assistant to Ron Atkinson at Aston Villa before focusing full-time on his television work. He was the lead football pundit for Sky Sports until his dismissal in January 2011, following multiple allegations of sexism. Gray, along with former Sky Sports anchor Richard Keys, then signed for talkSPORT in February 2011. They now both work for beIN Sports in Doha, Qatar.

GRAY, Andy
Midfielder/Striker
Born: *Lambeth*
Playing career: *Corinthian Casuals, Dulwich Hamlet, Crystal Palace, Aston Villa, QPR, Crystal Palace, Tottenham Hotspur, Swindon Town (loan), CA Marbella, Falkirk, Bury, Millwall (1980-1998)*
Gray - no relation to the 'other' Andy Gray (above), is best known for his association across two stints with Crystal Palace, from whom he played in the 1990 FA Cup final against United. He began his career as a forward but then moved into the midfield where he made his name. During his two seasons at Villa, he helped Graham Taylor's claret and blues to promotion. He played once for the full England team in 1991 and later managed Sierra Leone. Gray has since continued to represent Palace at charity functions, legends events and as an after dinner speaker.

GRAY, Stuart
Midfielder
Born: *Withernsea*
Playing career: *Nottingham Forest, Bolton W, Barnsley, Aston Villa, Southampton. (1980-1994)*
Gray moved to Villa Park in 1987 and quickly became a fans favourite for his all-action displays at the heart of the midfield. Villa won promotion in his second season and then finished as runners up in the First Division in 1990. He made over 100 appearances for the club and also served Barnsley FC with distinction. After retiring as a player, Gray remained strongly involved in the game as a coach and manager. He took charge of former club Southampton, briefly managed Villa as caretaker boss in 2002 and then managed Wolves, Northampton, Burnley, Portsmouth (caretaker), Sheffield Wednesday and Fulham (interim).

GRAYDON, Ray
Winger
Born: *Bristol*
Playing career: *Bristol Rovers, Aston Villa, Coventry City, Oxford United. (1965-1980).*
Moved to Villa in 1971 for £50,000 from Bristol Rovers. Scored the winning goal as the club beat Norwich in the 1975 League Cup final. Played almost 200 games in a six year career at Villa Park. After retiring as a player, he worked as a coach at Southampton, became manager of Walsall and later returned to Bristol Rovers as boss. Also managed in China and was first team coach at Leicester in 2006. He lives in Bristol and later worked in the motoring trade.

GRAYSON, Simon
Defender
Born: *Ripon*
Playing career: *Leeds United, Leicester City, Aston Villa, Blackburn Rovers, Sheffield Wednesday, Stockport County, Notts County, Bradford City, Blackpool (1988-2005)*
A defender in his playing days, Grayson has had an extensive, well travelled career as both player and manager.
Grayson moved to Aston Villa in 1997 and made 49 Premier League appearances at Villa Park before he moved on to Blackburn in 1999. He lost his place in the team the following season and spent most of the next two years on loan, with spells at Sheffield Wednesday, Stockport County, Notts County and Bradford City. Grayson signed for Blackpool on a free transfer in 2002. He made more than 100 appearances for the Seasiders and captained the side. In 2004 he started the final as Blackpool won the 2003–04 Football League Trophy. After retiring as a player, he remained at Bloomfield Road as reserve team coach. Following the departure of Colin Hendry, he was named as first team interim manager. He remained with the club as boss for the next three years, then went on to manage Leeds, Huddersfield, Preston, Sunderland and Bradford. In 2019, he returned to Blackpool as manager for a second time.

GREEN, Haydn

Born: *1887*
Died: 1957
Playing career: *Nottingham Forest, Manchester United, Aston Villa, Newport County, Reading (-)*

A versatile player with excellent distribution, he was perhaps best known for his time at Old Trafford. In a long playing career, he also went on to play for Nottingham Forest, Villa, Newport County and Reading. Once Green had hung up his boots, he went on to manage Ebbw Vale, Bangor, Hull City - where the club won Division Three under his tutelage - Swansea and Watford. He died in 1957 at the age of 70 in his home town of Hereford.

GREEN, Tommy

Forward
Born: *Worcester*
Died: 1923
Playing career: *Aston Villa (1888-1889)*

Became known for scoring Aston Villa's first ever goal in the Football League. He played for Dreadnought F.C., Mitchell St George's, Aston Unity F.C., Great Lever, West Bromwich Albion, Kidderminster Harriers and Worcester Rovers as well as guesting for several teams, including Wolverhampton Wanderers, the club he had scored Villa's first league goal against. He played in Albion's 1886 and 1887 FA Cup finals, losing both (the latter against Villa). Green played one season in the Football League (1888-1889), the inaugural season. After retirement, he worked for the Football League as a board member and secretary. He scored 14 goals in 22 league games for Villa and was described as a hard-working player. Died aged 60 in 1923.

GREENHALGH, Brian

Striker
Born: *Chesterfield, Derbyshire*
Playing career: *Preston North End, Aston Villa, Leicester City, Huddersfield Town, Cambridge United, Bournemouth, Torquay United, Watford, (1965-1975).*

Greenhalgh was a graceful, flaxen-haired striker whom plundered 20 goals in 47 games for Villa. He formed a potent partnership with Brian Godfrey at Villa Park - the duo were nicknamed the BG's - a role they later reprised together at Deepdale. He hit the peak of his career at Cambridge, where he scored 47 in 116 league apps.

Greenhalgh helped Cambridge, who had only been elected to the Football League in 1970, win promotion from Division Four in 1973, before going to Bournemouth and then Watford. He then played for a string of non-league teams, including Dartford, Carshalton, Maidenhead and Staines, while working as a sales rep for a food firm. Greenhalgh later became a business partner in a St-Albans based firm selling optics and bar equipment. Worked for Everton and former club Watford as a scout.

GREENHALGH, Sam

Centre-half
Born: *Eagley, Lancashire*   Died: 1955
Playing career: *Eagley, Turton, Aston Villa, Bolton Wanderers, Chorley (1902-1913)*

Played at amateur level for Birtenshaz Wesleyans, Eagley United and Turton before he signed for Bolton. Moved on to Villa and played 50 times in 18 months at the club. A centre half, he earned an FA Cup runners up medal for Bolton in 1904. He rejoined Wanderers in 1907 and went on to Chorley where he later had a brief spell as player/ manager. Retired from football and drifted out of the game to run a greengrocer's in Manchester. Represented England at youth level. No relation to Brian Greenhalgh (above).

GREGORY, Harry

Midfielder
Born: *Hackney, London* Died: 2016
Playing career: *Orient, Charlton Athletic, Aston Villa, Hereford United, Chelmsford City (1962-1976)*

He joined Villa in 1970, making 29 appearances for the club and scoring two goals - in consecutive Third Division matches against Doncaster Rovers and Swansea City - before joining Hereford United two years later. He went on to Chelmsford and later became a coach at that club. He continued to reside in Essex until his death in 2016 at the age of 72 after a battle with cancer.

"DID YOU KNOW?"

"Although Wesley Moraes cost £22m in June 2019, a total of £24m was paid for Darren Bent in 2011."

GREGORY, John

Midfielder
Born: *Scunthorpe*
Playing career: *Northampton Town, Aston Villa, Brighton & Hove Albion, QPR, Derby County, Plymouth Argyle, Bolton Wanderers (1972-1990)*

After a successful playing career, the former England midfielder went on to take charge at numerous clubs in the Uk and even in Israel. One of the few men to have both played for and managed Villa. Gregory was widely considered a success at Aston Villa. Despite playing two divisions higher than he had ever reached previously, he wasn't out of place in the First Division and scored 10 goals in 65 games over the next two seasons. During his two years in claret and blue, Gregory became the only player to play in every outfield position, wearing every number from 2 to 11 over his two seasons with the club, which remains a record.

GRIFFITHS, Thomas

Centre-half
Born: *Moss Valley, Wrexham, Wales* Died: 1981
Playing career: *Wrexham, Everton, Bolton W, Middlesbrough, Aston Villa, Wrexham (1922-1939)*

A tall, rangy, centre half Griffiths earned 21 caps for Wales and signed for Aston Villa in November 1935. However his spell at Villa brought his third relegation of his career as they went down at the end of the season. Finished up at Wrexham. Died in 1981.

GROVES, Willie

Striker
Born: *Glasgow, Scotland* Died: 1908
Playing career: *Hibernian, Celtic, West Bromwich Albion, Aston Villa, Hibernian, Celtic (1885-1896)*

Willie Groves. The world's first £100 player when he joined Aston Villa from West Bromwich Albion in 1893. Groves was the most charismatic - and controversial - footballer of his day and, more than a century on, his family still features in the West Midland sporting scene. His great, great nephew is Warwickshire batsman Jim Troughton. Villa were forced to pay the £100 to West Brom and were fined by the Football Association amidst allegations that Groves and Jack Reynolds had been illegally poached by the club. He ended up working as a labourer for Edinburgh Corporation and died aged only 38.

GUDJONSSON, Joey

Midfielder
Born: *Akranes, Iceland*
Playing career: *Betis, Aston Villa (loan), Wolves (loan), Leicester City, AZ, Burnley, Huddersfield Town, iA, Fram Reykjavik, Fylkir (1994-2015)*

The Icelandic midfielder's previous clubs include Real Betis, Aston Villa, Wolves, Leicester City, AZ Alkmaar and Burnley. He was on loan at Villa in the 2003/04 season, playing eleven times. He has played in five top-flight leagues across Europe. He earned 34 caps for the Iceland national team between 2001 and 2007 and is the current manager of IA in his homeland. Gudjonsson also managed another Icelandic side, HK, in the 2016/17 season.

GUZAN, Brad

Goalkeeper
Born: *Evergreen Park, Illinois, United States*
Playing career: *South Carolina Gamecocks, Chicago Fire Premier, Chivas USA, Aston Villa, Hull City (loan) (2003-2011)*

A runner up in both domestic cups during his time at Villa, although he did not play in the 2015 cup run with his understudy Shay Given deputising. Guzan played over 150 games in claret and blue. Also played for Hull City and Middlesbrough in England, and continues to ply his trade in his native USA for MLS side Atlanta United. Capped for his country at Under 23 level, he has played 60 times for the full US national side including in two World Cup finals. He won the MLS Cup with United in 2018.

HACKETT, Bernard
Forward
Born: *Ramsbottom*
Playing career: *Birmingham City, Aston Villa, Aston Villa, Chester. (1953-1960)*
He played for Worcestershire at county level in both football and cricket. Having chosen the beautiful game ahead of leather on willow, he played for Birmingham City as a junior before being snaffled up by arch rivals Villa. He turned professional in 1953 but left two years later without making a league appearance. Hackett later combined an amateur football career with a job in the building trade.

HADJI, Mustapha
Midfielder
Born: *Morocco*
Playing career: *Nancy, Sporting CP, Deportivo, Coventry City, Aston Villa, Espanyol, Emirates Club, FC Saarbrucken, Fola Esch (1991-2010)*
Hadji was a goalscoring attacking midfielder with great pace and trickery. Having started out in France, Portugal and Spain, he signed for Coventry and became something of an enigmatic genius. After Coventry were relegated in 2001, he joined Villa, having scored against them three times in the previous season. However he never nailed down a regular starting spot and was released on a free transfer to Espanyol in Spain where he remained until June 2004. He was capped 63 times by Morocco and played in two World Cup finals.

Mustapha Hadji

He is currently number two to Vahid Halilhodzic as assistant manager for the Moroccan national team.

HADLEY, George
Half-back
Born: *Darlaston, Staffordshire* **Died:** 1954
Playing career: *Southampton, Aston Villa, Coventry City (1913-1922)*
West Bromwich born wing half Hadley joined Villa in March 1919. He managed only four first team appearances for Villa before moving on to Second Division Coventry City. His career ended through injury and Hadley later worked as a press-tool setter with a lock manufacturer. He diesd in 1954

HADLEY, Harry
Wing-half
Born: *Barrow-in-Furness* **Died:** 1942
Playing career: *Colley Gate United, Halesowen, West Bromwich Albion, Aston Villa, Nottingham Forest, Southampton, Croydon Common, Halesowen, Merthyr Town (1895-1919)*
A button-maker by trade, Hadley had a short spell at Aston Villa but later became manager at Chesterfield and Gillingham before going back to take over at Merthyr Town for a third time. Scouted for Chelsea and Bangor City before he passed away in West Bromwich in 1942, at the age of 67.

Hale, Alfie
Inside-forward
Born: *Waterford, Republic of Ireland*
Playing career: *Waterford, Aston Villa, Doncaster Rovers, Newport County, Waterford (1956-1983)*
A legend in the League of Ireland, Hale came from a sporting family (his father and three of his uncles had all played for Waterford). He earned 14 caps for the Republic of Ireland and scored an extraordinary rate for Waterford, hitting 21 in 33 games between 1958 and 1960.

Hale was signed by Aston Villa for £4,500 in June that year, although he went on to only make seven first team appearances in claret and blue, scoring once. Despite this, his debut for the Republic came whilst at the club. He went on to Doncaster and Newport before returning across the Irish Sea. After his playing days ended, he remained in his native homeland and became a manager for five clubs including his hometown club Waterford over three different spells.

HALL, Proctor
Inside-forward
Born: *Blackburn*
Playing career: *Oswaldtwistle Rovers, Manchester United, Brighton & Hove Albion, Aston Villa, Bradford City, Luton Town, Chesterfield, Hyde, Preston North End, Newport County, Mardy (1903-1910)*

He played for various clubs, including Brighton & Hove Albion, Bradford City, Chesterfield and Manchester United. Hall never played a senior match for the claret and blue and was sold to Bradford in 1906. Hall was a diminutive inside forward whom was known for his tenacious tackling and fleet of foot. Finished his career in non league football in Wales, and became Caernarfon FC's first ever scout. Having retired from the game, he worked in the metal production industry.

HALSE, Harold
Forward
Born: *Stratford, London* **Died:** 1949
Playing career: *Clapton Orient, Southend United, Manchester United, Aston Villa, Chelsea, Charlton Athletic (1905-1923)*

Started repaying his £350 transfer fee when he opened his goal scoring account in the first game of his United career. A top opportunist marksman of his day, he won League Championship and FA Cup winner's medals, he became the first player to appear in three Cup Finals with different clubs. He also netted six times in the 1911 Charity Shield win over Swindon Town. Halse was capped once by England in 1909. He was sold to Aston Villa for £1,200 and won the FA Cup with the club in 1913. Scouted for Charlton for a couple of years before opening a tobacconist's shop in Walton on Naze. Died in Colchester County Hospital in March 1943, aged 63.

HAMILTON, Ian
Midfielder
Born: *Streatham, London*
Playing career: *Chelsea, Southend United, Aston Villa, Sheffield United, Minnesota Kicks (NASL), Minnesota Kicks (NASL indoor), San Jose Earthquakes (1966-1982)*

Hamilton still in the record books as the youngest player ever to play a league game for Chelsea. He made a goal scoring debut against Spurs in May 1967 aged only 16 years and 138 days. However, he was only at the club for another eight months before being sold to Southend for £5,000. Whilst in the claret and blue of Villa he carved out a long career as a midfielder, helping the club win the Third Division title in 1972, and playing in two League Cup finals – they lost in 1971 and won in 1975. Enjoyed success with Aston Villa and lived in the States for a number of years, where he coached at the Tommy Washington High School in Ohio. Upon his return to this country; he worked for the Nike organisation as a coach, and then as a play scheme organiser coaching a girls team in Sheffield.

"DID YOU KNOW?"

"George Ramsey was manager/ secretary for almost 40 years!"

HAMILTON, Willie
Forward
Born: *Chapelhall, Scotland* Died: 1976
Playing career: *Sheffield United, Middlesbrough, Hearts, Hibernian, Aston Villa, (1954-1972)*
At the peak of his powers - under the watchful eye of Jock Stein whilst at Hibernian - he was an extraordinary talent capable of penetrative passes and single-handedly changing the outcome of a game. Celtic were apparently keen on signing Hamilton, but a move never materialised and without the influence of Stein he was deemed surplus to requirements at Hibernian and sold to Aston Villa for £24,000 in August 1965. His time at Aston Villa came to an abrupt halt after he was involved in a horrific car crash and he headed back to Edinburgh to sign for Hearts again in the summer of 1967. He earned a solitary cap for Scotland in 1965. He emigrated to Canada where he worked as a bricklayer. Hamilton died of a heart attack in 1976.

F. & J. SMITH'S CIGARETTES

ASTON VILLA.
H. HAMPTON,
O.H.M.S.

HAMPSON, Jack
Half-back
Born: *Oswestry, Wales* Died: 1960
Playing career: *Oswestry Town, Northampton Town, Leeds City, Aston Villa, Port Vale (1921-1924)*
Hampson played for Oswestry Town, Northampton Town, Leeds City and Aston Villa, before joining Port Vale for a £1,000 fee in June 1921. He played 14 times in claret and blue and over 100 times for Vale. Known for his strength and positioning, he also played for Wales at youth level but never got a senior call up. He sustained a number of knee injuries and was forced to retire in 1926. Later became a pub landlord in his home town of Oswestry. Died in 1960.

HAMPTON, Harry
Forward
Born: *Wellington* Died: 1963
Playing career: *Wellington Town, Aston Villa, Birmingham, Newport County (1902-1925)*
The second highest goalscorer in Villa history, Hampton hit 242 goals in 376 games across a 16 year career. Between 1913 and 1914 Hampton was capped by England four times, scoring twice. He won the FA Cup with Villa in 1904/05 and 1912/13, as well as a league First Division medal in 1910. Hampton served on the Somme during the First World War and suffered from the effects of mustard gas poisoning. Following his retirement from playing, Hampton was a coach at Preston and another former club, Birmingham. He later ran a catering business in Rhyl, where he died in 1963 at the age of 77.

HANDLEY, Brian
Centre-forward
Born: *Wakefield* Died: 1982
Playing career: *Goole Town, Aston Villa, Torquay United, Bridgwater Town, Rochdale (1957-1966)*
Handley combined his career as a footballer with a career as a cricketer. He played for Yorkshire Second and First XI's in the County Championship while also proving to be a prolific scorer for Villa. His career at Villa Park was frustratingly brief, and he's best known for his four-year stint at Torquay United where he hit 32 goals in 80 games under Eric Webber. After retiring following a brief spell at Rochdale, Handley coached at Torquay but died at the young age of 45 in 1982.

HARDY, Sam
Goalkeeper
Born: *Chesterfield* Died: 1966
Playing career: *Chesterfield, Liverpool, Aston Villa, Nottingham Forest (1898-1925)*

Widely regarded as one of the greatest keepers of his generation, Hardy joined Villa from Liverpool in 1912 for a fee of £1500. He won two FA Cups at the club and played for 14 years as England's first choice goalkeeper. Upon retirement, Hardy became a publican, keeping pubs and billiard halls in the Chesterfield area and remained so until his death aged 84 in October 1966.

HARE, Charlie
Forward
Born: *Yardley, Birmingham* Died: 1947
Playing career: *Aston Villa, Woolwich Arsenal , Small Heath, Watford, Plymouth Argyle, Warwick County, Birmingham United (1891-1904)*

A tricky inside forward , Hare signed for Villa in March 1891 but was mainly a fringe player before he was transferred to Woolwich Arsenal in February 1895 He later became the player-coach of Green Waves in September 1904 before his eventual retirement. Hare later took up a job in a steelworks.

HAREWOOD, Marlon
Striker
Born: *Hampstead, London*
Playing career: *Nottingham Forest, Haka (loan), Ipswich Town (loan), West Ham United , Aston Villa, Wolverhampton Wanderers (loan), Newcastle United (loan), Blackpool, Barnsley (loan) , Guangzhou R&F, Nottingham Forest, Barnsley, Bristol City, Hartlepool United, Nuneaton Town (1996-2015)*

A former striker, Harewood led the line for 15 clubs during a 20-year, 571-game professional career. Martin O'Neill signed Harewood for £4m in 2007 where he was mainly utilised as a "super sub" player. FA Cup runner up with West Ham in 2006. Known as a penalty box predator, he was mostly associated with the 'other' claret and blue capital club but hit five goals in 29 games for Villa. Played in Europe under O'Neill but eventually fell out of favour and then embarked on a vast journeyman career. He also played for Wolves, Newcastle, Blackpool, Barnsley (twice), Bristol City, Hartlepool and in China. After retiring in 2016, Harewood set up and ran his own bespoke car supplier business AC13 Premier in Nottingham. More: https://twitter.com/Mazer_9

Marlon Harewood

105

HARKUS, George
Half-back
Born: *Newcastle upon Tyne* **Died:** 1950
Playing career: *Aston Villa, Southampton, Olympique Lyonnais, Southampton (1921-1934)*
Newcastle born centre half Harkus turned professional in 1922 but his opportunities at Villa Park were limited and he signed for Southampton for £250. He finished his career becoming player-coach at Southport in September 1932 although he never played for their first team. Harkus was later awarded an MBE and remained in the RAF after the war. He served on the committee at Southampton but died in 1950 aged 52.

HARPER, George
Inside-forward
Born: *Aston, Birmingham* **Died:** 1914
Playing career: *Aston Villa, Hereford Thistle, Wolverhampton Wanderers, Grimsby Town, Sunderland (1897-1903)*
An inside forward, Harper's time in claret and blue promised much but offered little. He never made a first team appearance for the club and instead became more widely known for his time at their west Midlands rivals Wolves. He scored 19 goals in 61 appearances at Molineux. Harper also turned out for Grimsby Town and Sunderland where he finished his league career. Harper later coached at Wolves but was only 37 when he died in 1914.

HARPER, Roly
Outside-right
Born: *Lichfield* **Died:** 1949
Playing career: *Walsall Wood, Small Heath/ Birmingham, Burton United, Aston Villa, Notts County, Mansfield Invicta (1904-1910)*
Harper started out at amateur local club Walsall Wood before he was scouted by Small Heath, now known as Birmingham City. He signed for First Division Blues in 1904 and went on to play 22 times for the club, scoring once. Moved to Burton United then on to Villa for the 1907/08 season. Harper played only two games for Villa's first team before being sold together with Jimmy Cantrell to Notts County in March 1908. After making only ten league appearances in two seasons he dropped into non-league football with Mansfield Invicta. Harper died in Birmingham in 1949 aged 68.

HARRIGAN, Duncan
Centre-forward
Born: *Paisley, Scotland* **Died:** 2005
Playing career: *St Mirren, Crewe Alexandra, Aston Villa, Chester-City, Colwyn Bay (1945-1949)*
He never made a senior appearance for Villa and moved on to Chester for £350 in 1948. He retired in 1949 to become a bank clerk.

HARRIS, George
Goalkeeper
Born: *Headless Cross* **Died:** 1910
Playing career: *Aston Villa, Wolves , Grimsby Town, Portsmouth, Kidderminster Harriers (1893-1908)*
A goalkeeper who played one league match during Villa's title winning season before moving on to Wolves and Grimsby. He finished his career with Kidderminster Harriers, then became the owner of a sports wear shop before his death in 1910.

HARRISON, Jimmy
Defender
Born: *Leicester* **Died:** 2004
Playing career: *Leicester City, Aston Villa, Coventry City, Corby Town (1946-1953)*
Played as a left back for Villa, Coventry City and Leicester City. He scored once in eight appearances in claret and blue in the 1949/50 season. He never pinned down a regular starting role at Villa Park, something which saw him move on to Coventry before his career more locally with Corby Town and Hinckley Athletic. Upon retirement, he remained involved with the game as secretary of the local Leicestershire leagues.

HARRISON, John
Fullback
Born: *Leicester*
Playing career: *Aston Villa, Colchester (1948-1956)*
John Harrison played 249 games for the U's as a right-back during his six-year spell at the club in the 1950s and notched one goal. After being born in Leicester, he was on the books of Midlands giants Nottingham Forest and Aston Villa without ever making an appearance for the first team, and joined the U's in September 1950. A knee injury curtailed Harrison's career in 1956 and he took up a job at engineering firm Woods of Colchester for the rest of his working life. He played over 200 games for Colchester, including in the first ever Essex derby between the U's and Ipswich.

HARRISON, Thomas
Forward
Born: *Birmingham* **Died:** 1942
Playing career: *Coombs Wood, Aston Villa, Halesowen, Handsworth Richmond (1888-1889)*
A pacy, dangerous winger, Harrison made his one and only league appearance for Aston Villa in 1888/89, the inaugural professional Football League season in England. He became a factory worker in Solihull and died in his home town of Birmingham in 1942 aged 75.

HARROP, Jimmy
Defender
Born: *Sheffield, Yorkshire* **Died:** 1958
Playing career: *Sheffield Wednesday, Denaby United, Rotherham Town, Liverpool, Aston Villa, Sheffield United, Burton All Saints (1900-1924)*
Won the FA Cup with Villa in 1912, 1-0 over Sunderland in the final. His father was a grinder and he followed in his footsteps in that trade until earning enough from his football. He played over 100 times for Liverpool before signing for Villa. He finished his career at Sheffield United then became assistant coach for local amateur side Burton All Saints. Known as "Heads up" Harrop, he made 171 appearances for Villa scoring four goals. Died in 1958.

HARVEY, Alf
Born: Aston **Died:** 1943
Playing career: *Aston Villa (1881-1884)*
Earned one cap for England as a full back in 1881. He was playing for Wednesbury Strollers at the time, and also played representative football for Staffordshire. He played for Holte Villa and Birmingham Excelsior before he joined Villa in 1882 until 1884. He returned to Villa in 1885 to play two matches as a goalkeeper and went on to work in an engineering and arms factory in Birmingham. He died in 1943 aged 87. Harvey was described in the Football Annual of 1881 as a "clever, intuitive and hard working full back."

HARVEY, Howard
Centre-forward
Born: *Aston* **Died:** 1904
Playing career: *Walsall Town Swifts, Small Heath, Aston Villa, Burslem Port Vale, Manchester City, West Bromwich United, Burton United, Watford, Darlaston, Glentoran (1894-1903)*

He started out at Walsall Town Swifts and then moved across town to Small Heath, now known as Birmingham City. He never made a senior appearance at the club and swapped colours to join neighbours and fierce local rivals Aston Villa for £75 in 1894. In a solid if unspectacular career in claret and blue, he scored three goals in eleven games before moving on to Port Vale. Harvey died in 1904 at the age of 26 after suffering turbeculosis.

HATELEY, Tony
Striker
Born: *Derby* **Died:** 2014
Playing career: *Notts County, Aston Villa, Chelsea, Liverpool, Coventry City, Birmingham City, Notts County, Oldham Athletic. (1958-1973).*
Became the first £100,000 signing in club history when Tommy Docherty signed him for Chelsea from Aston Villa to partner Tommy Baldwin after Peter Osgood broke his leg. One of the best headers of the ball in the game, he never really justified his fee despite scoring the winner against Leeds to book the Blues first ever appearance in a Wembley Cup Final. He was sold at the end of the season to Liverpool with Chelsea getting their money back. Upon retiring from the game, set up his own business until 1978. Later became Lottery Manager at Everton and then a drinks rep before moving to the Preston area. Hateley ran a stall at Southport's indoor market selling Christmas decorations. Father of England striker Mark, he died in 2014 after a long illness.

HAZELDEN, Wally
Forward
Born: *Ashton-in-Makerfield* **Died:** 1941
Playing career: *Aston Villa, Aston Villa, Wigan Athletic (1956-1961)*
Hazelden still stands in the record books to this day as the youngest goalscorer in Villa history, when he netted against West Brom on his debut aged 16. He holds the unique feat of scoring in his first and last games for the club even though the club lost on both occasions. Hazelden played for England at youth level and then moved on to Wigan. His time at the Latics was the last known trace of Hazelden's professional career but it's thought he then went on to work in the financial trade. He continued to live in the north West.

HAZELL, Reuben
Defender
Born: *Birmingham*
Playing career: *Aston Villa,Tranmere Rovers,Torquay United,Kidderminster Harriers,Chesterfield,Oldham Athletic,Shrewsbury Town (1998-2012)*

A much travelled defender and utility player, Hazell started his career at Villa in 1998. He never played for the first team and moved on to Tranmere where he featured in the 2000 League Cup final. Hazell managed the Panjab football team at the 2018 ConIFA World Football Cup. Since retiring, Hazell has set up his own football team TBTK in Birmingham and is the founder and director of the "Lazy Lunch" corporate catering business. Also a player adviser and mentor for SideKick Management Consultancy. More: https://twitter.com/reubenhazell?lang=en

HEARD, Pat
defender/midfielder
Born: *Kingston upon Hull*
Playing career: *Everton, Aston Villa, Sheffield Wednesday, Newcastle United, Middlesbrough, Hull City, Rotherham, Cardiff City, Hull City. (1978-1992)*

The 59-year-old spent four years at Villa Park during which time he made 24 appearances and scored two goals. He will be forever enshrined in club folklore as a member of the squad which won the European Cup in May 1982. Heard was a non-playing substitute on the night Villa beat Bayern Munich 1-0 through Peter Withe's historic strike. Heard left Villa for £60,000 in 1983 for Sheffield Wednesday having played 24 league games for Villa and scored two goals.

After football, Heard embarked on a variety of careers including as a publican in both Hull and Chesterfield, a summariser for Free Radio Birmingham, a stage hypnotist. Most recently, as an Approved Driving Instructor, Heard taught Villa youngsters Barry Bannan, Benji Siegrist, and Andreas Weimann to drive. More: https://twitter.com/patheardavfc?lang=en

HEATH, Adrian
Midfielder
Born: *Newcastle-under-Lyme*
Playing career: *Stoke City, Everton, Aston Villa, Manchester City, Burnley, Stoke City (1979-1995).*

Worked for Peter Reid at Sunderland, Leeds and Coventry where he had two spells as caretaker boss, managed Burnley and Sheff Utd, took charge of Austin Aztex FC in the USSF D2 Pro League. Now head coach of Minnesota United FC having previously been in charge of Orlando City. In May 2011, he jointly set up a first year new franchise aiming at MSL participation. He won two league Championship medals with Everton. Heath's brief career at Villa spanned nine games in the 1989/90 season under Graham Taylor.

Pat Heard

HENDERSON, Wayne
Goalkeeper
Born: *Dublin, Republic of Ireland*
Playing career: *Aston Villa,Brighton & Hove Albion, PrestonNorth End, Grimsby Town (loan) (2000-2011)*
His first professional club was Aston Villa where he spent six years without ever playing for the first team. He played at every level for the Republic of Ireland including six caps for the full senior side. Henderson had to retire in 2009 through a spinal injury sustained in training with Grimsby Town. He currently works as an FA Intermediary with player management company YMU.

0121 777 7792   info@thebugsgroup.com

HENDRIE, Lee
Midfielder
Born: *Birmingham*
Playing career: *Aston Villa,Aston Villa,Stoke City (loan),Sheffield United,Derby County, Bradford City, Bandung. (1993-2014)*
A one cap wonder for England, Hendrie was known for his dead ball expertise and ability to score 'worldies' from distance. He was sent off on his Villa debut but went on to turn out over 300 times in the claret and blue and was a fans favourite for his enigmatic but occasionally inspirational performances. Hendrie later became a journeyman in the lower divisions and non league game and also played overseas in Indonesia with FC Bandung. Declared bankrupt in 2012, he has twice tried to take his own life. Now recovered and having got back on the straight and narrow, the former midfielder is also a director of FootyBugs which provides football-based activities for children aged two to seven.

HENSHALL, Horace
Outside-left
Born: *Hednesford*   **Died:** 1951
Playing career: *Bridgetown Amateurs,Crewe Alexandra,Aston Villa,Notts County,Sheffield Wednesday,Chesterfield (1910-1934)*
Hednesford born winger Henshall scored eleven goals in 50 appearances for Villa before moving to Notts County in the summer of 1912 for a then club record fee.

He remained in Nottingham, serving as landlord of the Navigation Inn near the club's Meadow Lane ground. He died in 1951 aged 62.

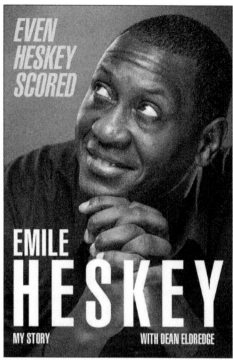

HESKEY, Emile
Striker
Born: *Leicester*
Playing career: *Leicester City, Liverpool, Birmingham City, Wigan Athletic, Aston Villa, Newcastle Jets, Bolton Wanderers (1987-2014)*
A powerful targetman with pace and strength, Heskey divided opinion amongst fans and pundits alike. Never a truly prolific scorer, he was known for his hold up play and work rate. He scored 15 goals in 111 appearances in claret and blue during three years in the Midlands. He earned his reputation with Leicester and Liverpool and also represented Birmingham, Wigan, Newcastle Jets and Bolton. Heskey played for England at every age group level and in three major tournaments at senior level - 2002 and 2010 FIFA World Cup finals and at Euro 2004. He won 62 caps and scored seven goals. Since retiring, Heskey has done some punditry work for Five Live and BBC Radio Midlands.

HICKSON, Dave
Striker
Born: *Salford* Died: 2013
Playing career: *Everton, Aston Villa, Huddersfield Town, Everton, Liverpool, Bury. (1951-1963).*
His physical approach as centre forward, coupled with his determination soon made him a crowd favourite. Hickson's 25 goals in the 1953-54 season helped Everton gain promotion to the old First Division. After just one season back in the top flight with Everton, Hickson was sold to Aston Villa for £17,500. He never settled at Villa Park and played just 12 games in a brief stay. Went to Ireland as player/manager of Ballymena, then took a job as a bricklayer and later worked in a pub. He worked for Everton as a tour guide at the age of 80 but died in 2013 after a short illness.

HINCHLEY, Albert
Goalkeeper
Born: *Warwick*
Died: 1922
Playing career: *Aston Villa (1891-1892)*
Warwick born Hinchley began his career in the Birmingham&Midland League at amateur level for Warwick County before he signed for Villa in 1890. He made eleven appearances for the claret and blue in the 1891/92 season as a squad player, and kept eight clean sheets in the process between the sticks. Signed for Cape Hill Smethwick having left Villa in 1892. After retirement he became a hotelier.

HIRD, Sam
Centre-back
Born: *Doncaster*
Playing career: *Aston Villa, Leeds United, Doncaster Rovers, Grimsby Town, Chesterfield (1997-2012)*
Currently playing for National League side Barrow. Hird signed terms with Aston Villa at a young age after catching the eyes of scouts but he never made the grade and was released. He moved on to sign for Leeds United. Once again, Hird had to taste rejection as he never featured for The Whites. Initially a striker, he reverted to a defender at Elland Road. Hird also played for Leeds' Yorkshire rivals Donny and went on to captain Chesterfield, playing over 200 times for the club. Whilst still actively plying his trade for Barrow, he has begun working towards his UEFA coaching badges.

HISBENT, Joe
Right-back
Born: *Plymouth* Died: 1953
Playing career: *Aston Villa, Portsmouth, Brentford, Darlington, Middlesbrough (1905-1914)*
Hisbent played twice in Villa's pre-war side of 1905/06 as an attack minded right-back. He also played for Pompey, Brentford and Darlington and Middlesbrough before doing his bit for to the war effort. He died in his home city of Plymouth in 1953 aged 71.

HISLOP, Percy
Forward
Born: *Glasgow, Scotland* Died: 1929
Playing career: *Aston Villa (1891-1892)*
Hislop was lured down south by Aston Villa in 1891 before quickly returning home. He remained in his native Scotland and became a factory worker in Clyde.

HITCHENS, Gerry
Centre-forward
Born: *Rawnsley, Staffordshire* Died: 1983
Playing career: *Highley Miners Welfare,Kidderminster Harriers,Cardiff City,Aston Villa,Internazionale,Torino,Atalanta,Chicago Mustangs (loan),Cagliari, (1952-1971)*
Despite the fact that Villa had won the FA Cup the previous season, boss Eric Houghton knew that he needed a fast, goalscoring centre-forward. In December 1957, Houghton got his man when Cardiff accepted a £22,500 bid from the Midlands club. Hitchens formed deadly strike partnership with fellow striker Peter McParland, Hitchens' time with Villa is still remembered fondly by those lucky enough to have seen him play. Four seasons would return a yield of 96 goals, the highlight being a five-goal haul in an 11-1 victory over Charlton in 1959. Unsurprisingly, the lethal Hitchens soon attracted the attention of the upper echelons of English football, and he also went on to earn full England honours, earning seven caps and scoring give goals. Hitchens played in the 1962 World Cup in Chile. Considered one of the club's greatest ever strikers, he also made a successful fist of playing in Italy. He managed an ironworks in Wales upon retirement and then took over his brother in law's timber firm in Prestatyn. Hitchens died in 1983 aged 48 when playing in a charity match in 1983.

HOBAN, Mick
Midfielder
Born: *Tipton*
Playing career: *Aston Villa, Aston Villa, Atlanta Chiefs, Atlanta Apollos, Denver Dynamos, Portland Timbers (1969-1978)*

He never played a senior competitive game in claret and blue having signed as a youth player in 1969, although he did twice make the first team bench. He was loaned out to the Atlanta Chiefs two years later and began his career in the US. He went on to play for Atlanta Apollos, Denver Dynamos and the Portland Timbers, and was also capped once for the US national team in 1973. During his years playing in the NASL, Hoban also served in various front-office capacities in preparation for his career after football. He served as Business Manager with the Atlanta Apollos (NASL – 1973), Director of Community relations with the Denver Dynamos (1974) and the Portland Timbers (1976–1978). He went on to become assistant manager to Dennis O'Meara with the University of Portland team. He still lives in the States.

HOCKEY, Trevor
Midfielder
Born: *Keighley, West Riding of Yorkshire* Died: 1987
Playing career: *Bradford City, Nottingham Forest, Newcastle United, Birmingham City, Sheffield United, Norwich City, Aston Villa*

Hockey turned professional with Bradford City in May 1960 and went on to play for 12 clubs in a professional career spanning 16 years. In total, he made over 600 appearances and played nine times for Wales. In March 1976, Hockey became player-manager at Athlone Town before taking his footballing talents across the pond and a spell with San Diego Jaws in the North American Soccer League. Hockey returned to England the following year and took on the manager's role at non-league Stalybridge Celtic before another spell in the States as head coach with both San Jose Earthquakes and Las Vegas Quicksilvers. He returned home in 1981 to reform - and run - his home town club Keighley FC, yet by the end of the decade they would again be defunct. Hockey died of a heart attack during a five a side tournament in his home town, aged 43.

HITZLSPERGER, Thomas
Central midfielder
Born: *Munich, West Germany*
Playing career: *VfB Forstinning, Bayern Munich, Aston Villa, Chesterfield (loan), VfB Stuttgart, Lazio, West Ham United, VfL Wolfsburg, Everton (1988-2013)*

As a player he spent the early part of his career playing for Aston Villa in England (accompanied by a short loan spell at Chesterfield), before returning to Germany to play for Stuttgart, where he won the Bundesliga in 2007. In 2010, he signed for Italian side Lazio, before moving back to England to join West Ham United later that year. He then had brief spells with Wolfsburg and Everton. Hitzlsperger also represented the German national team, earning 52 caps and being selected for the 2006 World Cup and Euro 2008. Following a series of injuries, he retired from football in September 2013. After his retirement, he came out as gay, the highest-profile male footballer to do so. In February 2019 he became head of football operations at Vfl Wolfsburg.

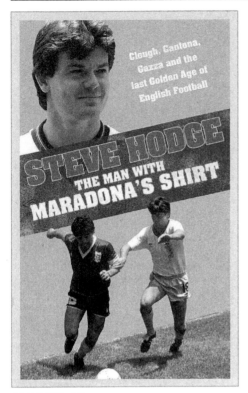

HODGE, Steve
Midfielder
Born: *Nottingham*
Playing career: *Nottingham Forest, Aston Villa, Tottenham Hotspur, Leeds United, Derby County, QPR, Watford, Leyton Orient (1980-1998)*
He moved across the Midlands from East to West to sign for Villa from Forest in 1985. He won the League Cup twice under Brian Clough at the City Ground. He won 24 caps for England, playing in two World Cups (1986 and Italia 90). He inadvertently set up Diego Maradona's infamous Hand of God goal in the latter tournament.Ironically given his Forest connections, had a brief stint as caretaker manager at Notts County in 2013. Also worked at County as development squad coach.

HODGETTS, Dennis
Forward
Born: *Birmingham* Died: 1945
Playing career: *Aston Villa, Small Heath (1888-1896)*
Hodgetts signed for Aston Villa in February 1886 and the following season he played a major part in Aston Villa's first FA Cup final triumph. In 1895 he collected another FA Cup winners medal with the club Hodgetts

- described as remarkably clever and good with both feet' - was also a key member of the club's Football League title-winning sides of 1894 and 1896. He was also part of the club's first ever Football League tie. In total Hodgetts played 181 times for and scored 62 goals before transferring to local rivals Small Heath. He went on to become a publican, and in 1930 was elected Aston Villa's vice-president, a position he held until his death in 1945.

HODGSON, Gordon
Forward
Born: *Johannesburg, South Africa* Died: 1951
Playing career: *Pretoria, Transvaal, Liverpool, Aston Villa, Leeds United (1919-1939)*
Only Ian Rush and Roger Hunt have ever scored more for Liverpool than Hodgson. Despite his prolific reputation, he was allowed to leave Anfield for Villa for £4,000 in 1936. His stay in the Midlands last only one season, though, scoring eleven goals in 28 appearances before moving on to Leeds. He played twice at full international level for his native South Africa, and also represented the senior England side on three occasions. He later had five years as Port Vale manager (1946 - 51), and playedcricket for Lancashire, winning the County Championship in 1928 and 1930. Died in 1951.

HOGAN, Cornelius
Centre-forward
Born: *Malta* Died: 1909
Playing career: *Aston Villa,Millwall Athletic,New Brighton Tower,Watford,Burnley,Fulham,Swindon Town,Nelson,Rossendale United (1897-1906)*
A Maltese striker, he played for New Brighton Tower, Burnley and Swindon in the Football League. Started his career at Villa but never made a senior appearance for the club. The son of an army sergeant, he himself enlisted in the Royal munster Fusiliers as a boy solider before Villa came calling and brought him out of the services. He worked in a munitions factory but was only 30 when he died.

"DID YOU KNOW?"

"Villa have spent 100 seasons in the top-flight and only Everton have spent more."

HOLE, Barrie

Midfielder
Born: *Swansea* Died: 2019
Playing career: *Cardiff City, Blackburn Rovers, Aston Villa, Swansea City. (1959-1971)*

Swansea-born Barrie hailed from a footballing family - his father had been a professional player for Swansea Town before World War II and his brothers Colin and Alan also played for their hometown club. He had a stint at Villa in the late sixties, before returning to his home town in 1970. He joined Swansea for £20,000, playing for the club for a couple of years before retiring in 1972. Hole represented Wales on 30 occasions in the 60s and 70s. After hanging up his boots he ran his family's newsagent business. Hole died in March 2019 aged 76.

HOLMAN, Brett

Attacking midfielder
Born: *Bankstown, Australia*
Playing career: *Northern Spirit,Parramatta Power,Feyenoord,Excelsior (loan),N.E.C.,AZ,Aston Villa,Al Nasr,Emirates Club (2001-2015)*

Holman has been on quite the journey throughout a career that has seen him play in Holland, England and Dubai before eventually returning back home to play for Brisbane Roar. He also has over 60 caps for his national side, during which he featured for the Socceroos at the 2010 FIFA World Cup finals. Holman made 27 appearances in claret and blue during a single, turbulent 2012/13 season at the club under controversial choice of manager Alex McLeish. A solid and dependable midfield grafter, Holman moved abroad to UAE-based club Al Nasr. He last played for Brisbane Roar in his native Australia.

HOLT, Grant

Striker
Born: *Carlisle*
Playing career: *Carlisle United, Workington, Halifax Town, Sengkang Marine, Barrow, Sheffield Wednesday, Rochdale, Nottingham Forest, Shrewsbury Town, Norwich City, Wigan Athletic, Aston Villa (loan), Rochdale (1999-2016)*

Holt scored one goal in ten appearances whilst on loan at Villa from Wigan, as part of a lengthy and nomadic career as journeyman striker. Holt, who played for 13 clubs in his career, spent 2018/9 as a player-coach at National League side Barrow.

The Carlisle-born striker is best remembered for goalscoring runs at Norwich, Forest and Rochdale across a career that spanned 18 years.The 37-year-old works as academy coach at Norwich - as well as trying out being a professional WAW wrestler

HOMER, Tom

Forward
Born: *Winson Green* Died: 1967
Playing career: *Birmingham, West Midlands, Soho Caledonians, Erdington, Aston Villa, Stourbridge, Kidderminster Harriers, Manchester United (-)*

Although originally from Winson Green, Tom Homer wrote himself into Manchester United club history by becoming the first United player to score at Old Trafford in a defeat to Liverpool in February 1910. A centre forward, small in size but significant in stature, he only spent three years at the club. Homer found chances limited with Enoch West preferred, despite an highly impressive games to goals ratio. He also played for Erdington at amateur level, Villa, Stourbridge and Kidderminster. A knee injury forced his early retirement. He became a licensee back in Birmingham.

113

HOPKINS, Robert
Winger
Born: *Birmingham*
Playing career: *Aston Villa, Birmingham City, Manchester City, West Bromwich Albion, Birmingham City, Shrewsbury Town (1979-1991)*
He started his playing career at Villa and was a member of the team which won the FA Youth Cup in 1980. He played in more than 300 Football League matches for Villa, Birmingham City (in two spells), Manchester City, West Bromwich Albion, Shrewsbury Town and Colchester United. He also played in Hong Kong for Instant-Dict and for non-League clubs Solihull Borough and Bromsgrove Rovers. A Birmingham City legend, Hopkins now lives in Solihull and works as a delivery driver. He has also written a column for a local newspaper.

HORNE, Stan
Midfielder
Born: *Clanfield*
Playing career: *Swindon Town, Aston Villa, Manchester City, Fulham, Chester-City, Denver Dynamos, Rochdale (1960-1975)*
Horne was the first black player in the history of his first three teams - Aston Villa, Manchester City and Fulham. He also played for Chester, Denver Dynamos and Rochdale, making a total of 201 appearances in the League. He was forced to retire from football due to high blood pressure.

HORTON, Ezra
Right-half
Born: *West Bromwich* Died: 1939
Playing career: *George Salter's Works ,West Bromwich Albion (amateur), Port Vale (guest), Aston Villa (guest), West Bromwich Albion (1882-1891)*
He played as a guest trialist for Port Vale and Aston Villa in the days before the inception of the Football League. Born in West Bromwich, Horton - an agile and uncompromising right half - initially played football for George Salter's Works in 1880 and joined his hometown team the following year. He retired from playing football in June 1891, and in 1895 he became a referee and also a hockey international.

"DID YOU KNOW?"

"The 12–2 victory over Accrington in 1892 is still the club's record win."

HOUGHTON, Eric
Winger
Born: *Billingborough*
Died: 1996
Playing career: *Aston Villa, Notts County. (1926-1948).*
A dead ball specialist, Houghton signed for Aston Villa as a seventeen-year-old and played in the Villa side for over 20 years scoring 170 goals in 392 games. He played a major part in the club's Second Division championship triumph of 1938 and also won seven caps for England. After taking charge Notts County whom he also played for, he went on to become Aston Villa manager, guiding Villa to a record seventh FA Cup triumph in 1957. He later returned to Villa as a director, the only person ever to serve the claret and blue as player, boss and board member. Former flying winger Houghton also played seven first-class matches as a right-handed batsman and a right-arm bowler for Warwickshire County Cricket Club (1946–1947) and also minor counties cricket for Lincolnshire County Cricket Club. He also played club cricket for Sleaford, Aston Unity and Olton Cricket Clubs.

HOUGHTON, Ray
Midfielder
Born: *Glasgow, Scotland*
Playing career: *West Ham United, Fulham, Oxford United, Liverpool, Aston Villa, Crystal Palace, Reading. (1981-1999)*
After 202 appearances and 38 goals in his five successful years at Liverpool, Houghton joined Aston Villa for £900,000 in 1992. Villa manager Ron Atkinson fought off attempts by Chelsea manager Ian Porterfield to bring Houghton to West London. He won the League Cup with the club in 1994 with victory over United in the final. Houghton is now a media pundit and is a consultant for the popular computer game Championship Manager. He played in three major tournaments during an international career in which he earned 73 caps for the Republic. Houghton has now taken up a post as an ambassador for the Football Association of Ireland (FAI). Funny video can be seen at: https://www.belfastlive.co.uk/sport/football/football-news/hilarious-video-shows-ray-houghton-16190420

HUGHES, Aaron
Defender
Born: *Cookstown, Northern Ireland*
Playing career: *Newcastle United , Aston Villa, Fulham, QPR, Brighton, Melbourne City (1996-2015)*
Sold to Villa from Newcastle for £1m in 2005 and went on to play 64 appearances in two seasons for the club. He has also features 112 times for Northern Ireland. Went on to play for Fulham, QPR, Brighton, Melbourne City, Kerala and Hearts. He retired from football in the summer of 2019 aged 39. He is renowned for diligent and disciplined defending, having played 455 Premier League games without ever getting sent off. Hughes earned 110 caps for his country, the second most in the history of Northern Ireland, making his tournament debut at the age of 36 at Euro 2016. He is now a pundit for BT Sport and in India.

HUGHES, Tommy
Goalkeeper
Born: *Dalmuir, Scotland*
Playing career: *Chelsea, Clydebank, Aston Villa, Brighton & Hove Albion (loan), Hereford United, Trowbridge Town (1966-1982)*

A Scottish under-23 international who arrived at Villa Park from Clydebank. As understudy to Peter Bonetti, he found first team opportunities few and far between and was forced to leave Stamford Bridge to seek regular football. Suffered a broken leg and John Phillips was signed from Aston Villa and when he recovered he was sold to Villa for £12,500 to replace his replacement. Had a short spell as Hereford boss but settled in the town where he owns a carpet cleaning business.

HUNT, David
Midfielder
Born: 1959
Playing career: *Derby County, Notts County, Aston Villa, Mansfield Town (1977-1989)*
He began playing at the age of five before he was scouted and signed by Derby on apprentice terms, eventually joining as a professional. Making five first team appearances for the Rams, he moved to Notts County £45,000 and played over 300 games for them. He spent nine years with the club before he moved on to Villa to join up with ex England boss Graham Taylor. Hunt gained his UEFA A coaching badges and now runs the David Hunt Soccer Schools Academy, coaching kids in Ashby. See: https://www.davidhuntsoccerschool.co.uk

"DID YOU KNOW?"

"Villa's first ever opponents were a team called St Marys, which was made up of rugby players!"

HUNT, Steve
Winger
Born: *Birmingham*
Playing career: *Aston Villa, Coventry City, West Bromwich Albion, Aston Villa (1974-1987)*
Despite not making the grade as an Aston Villa player in the mid-1970s, Hunt - a winger - became a star player in a Pele-inspired Cosmos team that won the North American Soccer League in 1977 and 1978. In that first season Hunt, a left-winger rejected by Villa boss Ron Saunders, played in 28 of the 32 games scoring 12 goals. He developed from a fast, tricky winger with a penchant for long distance shooting to one of the country's most accomplished midfield play-makers with a cultured left foot capable of unlocking the tightest of defences. He eventually rejoined Aston Villa and suffered the ignominy of relegation before he was forced to retire in November 1987 with a recurring knee injury. Hunt went on to manage non league Willenhall Town, VS Rugby and Wessex League club Cowes Sports on the Isle of Wight.

HUNTER, Andy
Striker
Born: *Joppa, Ayrshire, Scotland* Died: 1888
Playing career: *Aston Villa, Ayr Thistle, Third Lanark, Vale of Leven (-)*
The younger brother of Aston Villa captain Archie Hunter, Joppa, Ayrshire born forward Andy Hunter played for Ayr Thistle, Third Lanark and Vale of Leven.

He eventually came to England to link up with his brother at Aston Villa, where he played for several years before they joined The Football League. He died of a heart attack in June 1888 aged only 24. He scored Villa's first ever FA Cup goal against Stafford Road Works in 1879.

HUNTER, Archie
Forward
Born: *Aston, Birmingham*
Died: 1894
Playing career: *Ayr Thistle, Aston Villa (1878-1890)*
Brother of Andy (above) Archie Hunter was the first Villa captain to lift the FA Cup, in 1887, scoring in ever round. He became one of the first household names in the English game, synonymous with the club's status as Victorian era powerhouses. Hunter played at Third Lanark, Ayr Thistle as an amateur and whom he signed for the claret and blue in August 1878, just four years after their formation. His Villa career began a decade before the commencement of the first Football League season, so his early games were FA Cup games and friendlies. His tally of 33 goals in the former remain a club record, and in competitive marches he played 73 matches and scored 42 goals. One source described the auburn-haired Hunter as one of the greatest players of the time. Like his brother Andy, he died of a heart attack at the young age 35. Hunter collapsed and died during a game.

1887 FA Cup Final

HUNTER, George
Half-back
Born: *Nowshera, British India*
Died: 1934
Playing career: *Maidstone United, Croydon
Common, Aston Villa, Oldham Athletic, Chelsea,
Manchester United, Croydon Common, Southampton ,
Brentford, Birmingham, Portsmouth (1907-1919)*

A fiery wing half nicknamed 'Cocky' who
had suffered from discipline problems
before his time at Pompey, and it is reported
that his manager nor his team mates could
control him. Wrote a light hearted football
book before going onto serve as a sergeant-
major in the army in the Royal Sussex
Regiment during World War One seeing
action in France and Gallipoli. The Indian
born enigma served three months hard
labour in August 1930 for deserting his wife
and children and died in February 1934 aged
46. He worked as a sports writer and as a
fitness instructor having hung up his botos.

HUSBANDS, Michael
Winger/Forward
Born: *Birmingham*
Playing career: *Aston Villa,Hereford United
(loan,Southend United,Bristol Rovers,Walsall,Port
Vale,Macclesfield Town,AFC Telford United
(loan),Oxford United,Redditch United (2002-2012)*

The midfielder dropped out of the
professional game in 2008 before signing for
local non-league side Redditch United in
2012. Husbands accepted a call-up to the St
Lucia national team in 2012 and joined the
Royal Marines. He has spent time coaching
the West Brom fans' team, Boing FC. A box
to box player, he was part of Villa's famed
FA Youth Cup-winning team in 2002. Now
aged 35, Husbands has yet to officially retire
from the game but has not played for a club
since being let go by non league Redditch
United in 2012.

HUTTON, Alan
Right-back
Born: *Glasgow, Scotland*
Playing career: *angers, Tottenham Hotspur,
Sunderland (loan), Aston Villa, Nottingham Forest
(loan), Mallorca (loan), Bolton Wanderers (loan)
(2000-2014)*

Hutton left Villa Park in summer 2019 after
an eight-year stint with the Claret and Blues,
during which time he made more than 200
appearances for the club. The 34-year-old
ended his tenure in B6 on the ultimate high
by helping the club secure promotion to
the Premier League through the Sky Bet
Championship play-offs in May. Capped
50 times by Scotland, Hutton has played
for seven different clubs on both sides of
the Anglo-Scottish border and in Spain for
Mallorca. Won the league with Rangers in
2005. Hutton has reportedly contemplated
retirement and remains without a club.

Alan Hutton

HYNES, Peter
Forward
Born: *Dublin, Ireland*
Playing career: *Aston Villa, Dublin City, Dundalk, Derry City, Limerick, Drogheda United, (2001-2014)*
He began his career as a trainee at Villa and was a member of the famed claret and blue-clad team to lift the 2002 FA Youth Cup. Despite this promise, the Dublin-born forward never made it into the first team and Hynes went on to ply the majority of his trade in the League of Ireland. He won the cup with Drogheda United in 2012 and went on to do some coaching work with that club. Played for 15 clubs in a 12-year career as a journeyman forward. Hynes is a free agent but has not yet officially hung up his boots.

IVERSON, Bob
Wing-half
Born: *Folkestone* Died: 1953
Playing career: *Lincoln City, Wolverhampton Wanderers, Aston Villa (1933-1948)*
Iverson played 135 games and scored nine times for Villa between 1937 and 1948. Upon retirement he stayed with the club as first team coach, scout and then head of youth. Iverson also played with Villa during World War 2 as a guest. (178 - 61 goals). A wing half, he also guested for Birmingham City, Bournemouth, Kidderminster, Leicester, Northampton Town, Notts County, Nottingham Forest and Sutton Town during the conflict as competitive football was suspended. He died in 1953 aged 42.

JACKSON, Dennis
Full-back
Born: *Birmingham* Died: 2014
Playing career: *West Bromwich Albion, Hednesford Town, Aston Villa, Millwall, Rugby Town (1954-1961)*
In 1952 he joined the British Army for his compulsory two-years National Service. Following his demob, Dennis played in a trial at Aston Villa in June 1954, then signed for Hednesford in July 1954 for a three-month spell before finally signing professional forms for First Division Villa in October 1954. He went on to play 80 times for Millwall. He later managed Villa Old Stars. Jackson retired in May 1966, with a career total of 91 first-class games under his belt, and became a bookmaker before working in a bakery in the 1970s. Died aged 82 in 2014.

JACKSON, Tommy
Goalkeeper
Born: *Kingston upon Hull* Died: 1975
Playing career: *Aston Villa*
Tommy Jackson began his football career playing during the First World War and played Army football while serving with The Northumberland Fusiliers. He joined First Division Aston Villa from Durham University in 1920, making his Football League debut at Sunderland in February 1921. Having lost his place as first choice in 1927, he made only occasional appearances and joined Kidderminster Harriers. Jackson went on to become a mechanic.

JAMES, David
Goalkeeper
Born: *Welwyn Garden City*
Playing career: *Watford, Liverpool, Aston Villa, West Ham United, Manchester City, Portsmouth, Bristol City, Bournemouth, Kerala Blasters (1986-2014)*
James is on the list of all-time Premier League appearances, having played in 572 top-level matches, and held the Premier League record for most clean sheets with 169 until Petr Čech surpassed this record. He was capped 53 times by England between 1997 and 2010, and was first choice goalkeeper during the team's Euro 2004 and 2010 World Cup campaigns. He was appointed a Member of the Order of the British Empire (MBE) in the 2012 Birthday Honours for services to football and charity. Having started his career with Watford, James went on to feature in the Premier League for Liverpool, Aston Villa, West Ham United, Manchester City and Portsmouth. Managed Kerala Blasters in India and also a BT Sport pundit. Most recently, could be seen as a contestant on BBC1's 'Strictly Come Dancing'.

JASZCZUN, Tommy
Defender
Born: *Kettering*
Playing career: *Aston Villa, Blackpool, Northampton Town, Rochdale, Cambridge United (1998-2013)*
Jaszczun began his career with Villa and rose through the ranks in the Midlands. He featured only once for the club's senior side and is one of the more obscure players to have turned out for the claret and blue. Jacszczun played his one and only game as a sub in a League Cup tie with Chelsea. Having retired, he joined United Counties League side Wellingborough Whitworth as player/assistant manager. Managed Wellingborough in 2015-2016 season and later became a players' agent.

JENAS, Jermaine
Midfielder
Born: *Nottingham*
Playing career: *Nottingham Forest, Newcastle United, Tottenham Hotspur, Aston Villa (loan), Nottingham Forest (loan), QPR (1999-2014)*
Jenas was a promising talent who never fulfilled his potential through a combination of injuries, fitness and losing Bobby Robson as his manager at Newcastle. He joined Villa on a season long loan in the 2011/12 season, but only played five times for the club. He also featured for the Toon, Spurs, hometown Nottingham Forest and QPR before retiring with injury in 2014. Having hung up his boots, Jenas moved into media work as a pundit, a role which he has continued ever since, most recently for the BBC on Match of the Day, as well as BT Sport. Jenas played 21 games for England.

JENKINS, Lee
Midfielder
Born: *West Bromwich*
Playing career: *Aston Villa, Port Vale, RoPS, Birmingham City, FinnPa (1977-1986)*
One of 28 men to represent both sides of the Second City rivalry, albeit showing only a fleeting glimpse of his ability. A West Bromwich born box to box midfielder, Jenkins played three games for Villa in the 1979/80 season, and one game for the Blues five years later, where he broke his ankle on debut. Jenkins also played for England at youth level, he also turned out for Port Vale and FinnPa in Finland. Since retiring, he has worked in the travel industry.

playertrader

Get Seen
Get Scouted
Get Signed

Do you want to play football at a professional club, but can't get the chance to be seen by them?

JOACHIM, Julian
Striker
Born: *Peterborough*
Playing career: *Leicester City, Aston Villa, Coventry City, Leeds United, Darlington (1992-2014)*
During his professional career he initially played from 1992 until 2011, but he came out of retirement in 2013. Joachim notably played in the Premier League for Leicester City and Villa, having also played for Coventry City, Leeds United, Walsall, Boston United and Darlington before moving into the Non-League game. Over the course of his career in professional football, he has scored over 100 league goals and accumulated over 450 league appearances. Whilst at Aston Villa he played in the 2000 FA Cup Final. After retirement, Joachim signed for Notts Senior League side Aslockton & Orston. A year later, he joined Gibraltar National League side Europa Point as a player and advisor, as part of the club's collaboration with Player Trader (https://playertrader.com/).

JOHNSEN, Ronny

Centre-back Defensive midfielder
Born: *Sandefjord, Norway*
Playing career: *Lyn Oslo, Lillestrom, Besiktas, Manchester United, Aston Villa, Newcastle United, Valerenga (1992-2008)*

A Norwegian international who was capable of playing in defence or midfield, Johnsen was snapped up by United from Turkish side Besiktas for £1.5 million in 1996, and helped the club to four Premier League titles, an FA Cup and a Champions League winner's medal as a mainstay of the Treble winning side. After forming a solid partnership with Jaap Stam, he remained with United until the end of the 2001-2002 season when his contract expired, and was given a free transfer following fellow Norwegian Oyvind Leonhardsen to Villa Park. He has played for Norway in the International Masters Tournaments and now deals in Real Estate in Tonsberg, Norway.

JOHNSON, George

Forward
Born: *West Bromwich* Died: 1934
Playing career: *West Bromwich Baptists, West Bromwich Albion, Walsall, Aston Villa, Plymouth Argyle, Crystal Palace (1895-1904)*

He played local football for Wrockwardine Wood before joining West Brom in May 1895. Johnson scored 23 goals in 55 games for his new club and in April 1898 he was sold to Aston Villa for £300. He joined a team that included forwards of the quality of George Wheldon, John Devey, and Stephen Smith. Despite the competition Johnson played in 24 league games that season. He rewarded the club with scoring nine goals and Villa won the First Division title that season. During his time at Aston Villa Johnson scored 47 goals in 110 appearances. Johnson died in Walsall in May 1934.

JOHNSON, Tommy

Striker
Born: *Gateshead*
Playing career: *Notts County, Derby County, Aston Villa, Celtic, Everton, Sheffield Wednesday, Kilmarnock, Gillingham, Sheffield United, Scunthorpe United, Tamworth, Rocester (1989-2007)*

A treble winner with Celtic, Johnson had a distinguished 19-year playing career that also included two promotions with Notts County, a League Cup triumph with Villa and seven caps for England at under-21 level. He moved into coaching with Notts County in 2007, prior to joining Leicester City as Chief Scout and then the Northern Ireland under-17 and under-21 setups as assistant manager. Johnson is currently head of recruitment at Blackpool. The 48-year-old has also held senior scouting positions at Championship and Premier League level with Cardiff City, Blackburn Rovers, Watford and Nottingham Forest.

JONES, Alf

Full-back
Born: *Walsall* Died: 1935
Playing career: *Walsall Swifts, Scotland, Howard Vaughton, Wales, Great Lever, Bolton, Aston Villa, Burnley (1880-1888)*

Having played for Walsall Swifts, he joined Aston Villa for the 1885/86 season via a brief spell at Burnley. He holds a unique place in Walsall footballing history; being the only man to play for the Swifts, Town and Town Swifts teams. Full-back Jones also played three times for England.

JONES, Keith

Goalkeeper
Born: *Nantyglo, Wales* Died: 2007
Playing career: *Stourport Swifts, West Bromwich Albion, Kidderminster Harriers, Aston Villa, Port Vale, Crewe Alexandra (1946-1960)*

A goalkeeper, he made 295 league appearances in a 13-year career in the Football League, and won one cap for Wales in 1949. He spent May 1946 to July 1957 at Aston Villa, and made 199 appearances in all competitions, though was usually the club's second choice goalkeeper. He was sold on to Port Vale for £3,500, and helped the "Valiants" to win the Fourth Division title in 1958–59. He moved on to Crewe Alexandra in April 1959, before leaving the club the following year.

JONES, Les

Full-back

Born: *Mountain Ash, Wales* Died: 2016
Playing career: *Luton T, Aston Villa (1950-1959)*

Played five games for Villa in the 1957-58 season before he moved to non league Worcester City the following year. Also played for Luton and Wales age group sides. He served in the forces as a First Battalion Fusilier and represented the Army football team. Played in the Birmingham League as an amateur before returning to his native Wales where he served as president of the south Wales Football Association. Jones died aged 86 in Birmingham in 2016.

JONES, Mark

Full-back

Born: *Warley*
Playing career: *Aston Villa, Brighton & Hove Albion, Birmingham City, Shrewsbury Town, Hereford United, Worcester City (1979-1991)*

He played as a full back in the Football League for a number of clubs during the 1980s. He featured in the 1982 European Super Cup in which Villa defeated Barcelona 3–1 on aggregate. Signed professional for the claret and blue in 1979 and won the FA Youth Cup the following year. Despite five years at Villa Park, Jones - described as a tough-tackling full-back - only made 24 appearances for the club.

Hassan Kachloul

KACHLOUL, Hassan

Midfielder

Born: *Agadir, Morocco*
Playing career: *Metz, Southampton, Aston Villa, Wolves (loan) , Livingston (1988-2005)*

Moroccan playmaker Hassan Kachloul joined Southampton in 1998 having played for Nimes, Metz and St Etienne in France's Ligue 1, and became a crowd favourite before spells with Aston Villa, Wolves, and Livingstone, where he still enjoys cult status. After retiring in 2005, Kachloul swapped boots and balls for bricks and mortar by entering the housing trade. Kachloul was capped 12 times by Morocco. He played 22 games in claret and blue under three different Villa managers, mainly John Gregory, the man who signed him. Kachloul was frozen out by Gregor's successors Graham Taylor and David O'Leary which resulted in his 2004 departure from Villa.

KAPENGWE, Emment

Midfielder

Born: *Broken Hill, Northern Rhodesia* Died: 1988
Playing career: *Atlanta Chiefs, Aston Villa, Kitwe United, Atlanta Apollos, City of Lusaka (1957-1976)*

Kapengwe became the first Zambian to play for an English club when he moved to Villa. He only made three appearances for the claret and blue, however. A 42-cap Zambia international, he went on to manage City of Lusaka FC (whom he also played for) in his native homeland. Died in 1988 aged 45 having suffered a stroke.

KEANE, Robbie

Striker
Born: *Dublin, Ireland*
Playing career: *Crumlin United, Wolverhampton Wanderers, Coventry City, Inter Milan, Leeds United (loan), Leeds United, Tottenham Hotspur, Liverpool, Tottenham Hotspur, Celtic (loan), West Ham United (loan), LA Galaxy, Aston Villa (loan) (1995-2012)*

All time top scorer for the Republic of Ireland (68 goals in 146 games), Keane is currently assistant manager with both his country and Middlesbrough. Best known for two prolific spells at Spurs in the Premier League and across the pond with LA Galaxy in the MLS, his Villa career was only a brief one. He played for the club on loan in 2012, but despite only playing six games he scored three goals demonstrating his prolific ability. He retired in 2018 after a spell as player/manager of ATK in India. A talented, quick and agile player, Keane was versatile and capable anywhere across the front.

KEARNEY, Mike

Forward
Born: *Glasgow* Died: 1953
Playing career: *Aston Villa Shrewsbury Chester Reading Chester Reading.*

Signed for Villa on a youth scholarship but never made a senior appearance for the club.

He moved on to play in the Football League for Shrewsbury - where he was prolific - Chester and Reading. Ended his career at Basingstoke Town who he also briefly managed. Kearney was not an out and out scorer but was an intelligent and skilful footballer, and so he was often effectively used in a number of roles from striker to the occasional game in the heart of the defence. After he retired, he continued to work for as a scout and as player promotion manager.

KEARNS, John

Full-back
Born: *Nuneaton* Died: 1949
Playing career: *Coventry City, Birmingham, Aston Villa, Bristol City (1903-1915)*

Kearns began his career in the local amateur Birmingham leagues before the pacy full-back was signed by Coventry. After 61 games and three years across the city in Blue, Kearns joined Aston Villa and sporadically contributed to their title success of 1909/10 and the runner up season that followed. He joined Bristol City where he played another 100 games. After retiring he took a job in a factory and later worked in the construction industry.

KEELAN, Kevin

Goalkeeper
Born: *Calcutta, India*
Playing career: *Aston Villa, Stockport County, Kidderminster Harriers, Wrexham, Norwich City, New England Tea Men, Jacksonville Tea Men (indoor), Tampa Bay Rowdies (1956-1981)*

He spent the majority of his career with Norwich City, though he also played for Aston Villa briefly. He also served as assistant boss and goalkeeping coach for theTampa Bay Rowdies, as well as a short spell as interim manager of the University of Tampa. After retirement, he has worked for a company that manufactures contact lenses and distributed them all over the world. A commanding keeper, he made five appearances for Villa in the 1960/61 season.

"DID YOU KNOW?"

"Villa moved from Aston Park to Perry Bar in 1876 to play on a pitch rented from a local butcher."

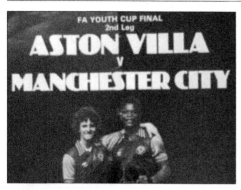

KENDALL, Mark

Goalkeeper

Born: *Nuneaton*

Playing career: *Aston Villa, Northampton Town, Birmingham City, Tamworth, Mile Oak Rovers, Hitchin Town, Worcester City, Atherstone Town, Bedworth United, Willenhall Town, Polesworth North Warwick (1976-1985)*

He joined Aston Villa in 1976. A goalkeeper, Kendall played in Aston Villa's youth teams which lost in the final of the 1978 FA Youth Cup but were winners two years later. While with Villa, Kendall was capped for England at youth level. He played 18 games for the reserves, but never appeared for the club's senior team. He joined Fourth Division club Northampton Town on a free transfer in 1982. He went on to play for number of non-league sides and coached in the Tamworth Junior League upon hanging up his boots.

KENNING, Mike

Right Winger

Born: *Birmingham*

Playing career: *Aston Villa, Shrewsbury Town, Charlton Athletic, Norwich City, Wolves, Charlton Athletic, QPR, Watford (1959-1973)*

Played three games for his boyhood club Villa in the 1960/61 season, but was most notable for his time at Charlton for whom he turned out over 100 times. Kenning had signed for the Addicks in November, 1962 for £10,500 and, in four seasons, struck 43 goals in 154 Division Two games. Kenning's career spanned over 400 appearances in total and the goalscoring winger had a goal ratio of better than one in five. He also played for Norwich, Wolves, QPR and Watford. He later Moved to South Africa where he found a job working as a Sales Rep for a safety equipment company.

KEOWN, Martin

Defender/Defensive midfielder

Born: *Oxford, Oxfordshire*

Playing career: *Arsenal, Brighton, Aston Villa, Everton, Leicester City, Reading (1984-2005)*

Keown was brought to Villa Park in 1986 in the hope of improving the team's recent poor form. Despite experiencing relegation in his first season, he did become a mainstay in the side and helped regain a place in the top flight the following year. His good form resulted in Everton parting with £750,000 to take him to Goodison Park in August 1989. In total, he had made 122 appearances and scored 3 goals during his stay. He went on to make his England debut in 1992 against France and went on to win 43 caps for the national side over the next 10 years. Keown represented England at four major international football finals including the 1998 and 2002 World Cups. He came out of retirement in 2012 and briefly played for Combined Counties League Premier Division side Wembley in their FA Cup fixtures. Since retirement Keown briefly worked as a coach for non-league side Newbury, before returning to Arsenal as a part time coach and scout. He now works as a television football pundit for the BBC.

Martin Keown

KERNS, Frederick

Forward
Born: *London* Died: 1908
Playing career: *Aston Villa, Birmingham, Bristol Rovers (1906-1909)*

A forward, it appears that Kerns only played one game in his senior professional career. That came with Villa's city rivals Birmingham, in the 1908/1909 season during the Blues second division campaign. He failed to impress at St Andrew's and move on to Bristol Rovers where he again never played. Kerns had joined Birmingham from Aston Villa as a makeweight deal which took Edmund Eyre to Villa and Fred Chapple the other way. Kerns did not turn for Villa and died in 1912 at the young age of 29.

KERR, Paul

Midfielder
Born: *Portsmouth*
Playing career: *Aston Villa, Middlesbrough, Millwall, Port Vale, Leicester City, Wycombe W. (1983-1994)*

Kerr began his career at Villa in 1982, before moving on to Middlesbrough in January 1987. He helped the club to win promotion into the First Division and played in the Full Members Cup final in 1990, before he moved on to Millwall in March 1991. He was sold on to Port Vale in July 1992 for a fee of £140,000, and helped the "Valiants" to win the Football League Trophy in 1993 and then to win promotion out of the Second Division in 1993–94. Loaned out to Leicester City in March 1994, he then ended his career at Wycombe Wanderers. Became a financial consultant to the PFA until 2002 when he founded Paul Kerr Associates where he is principal in Stockton-on-Tees (see: https://paulkerrwm.com).

KIMBERLEY, Walter

Left-back/Right-half
Born: *Aston* Died: 1917
Playing career: *Aston Manor, Aston Villa, Coventry City, Walsall (1906-1914)*

Kimberley worked as an engraver and a packer before he joined Villa. While playing for Coventry City, Kimberley worked at the Coventry Ordnance Works and was an army reservist. Served as a Lance Corporal in the Goldstream Guards during the first World War when he was captured by the Germans and spent two months in a prisoner of war camp. He played seven times for Villa across two seasons as a left back/right half in the First Division before the outbreak of the war. Walter died in 1917 at the age of 32 in Aston having developed tuberculosis.

KING, Phil

Defender
Born: *Bristol*
Playing career: *Exeter City, Torquay United, Swindon Town, Sheffield Wednesday, Notts County, Aston Villa, West Bromwich Albion, Swindon Town, Blackpool, Brighton & Hove Albion (1985-2004)*

Won the League Cup with Sheffield Wednesday in 1991 but best remembered for his time with Swindon, he played four Premier League games for Villa between 1994 and 1997 having been signed by Ron Atkinson for £250,000. Scored a winning penalty against Inter Milan in the UEFA Cup for Villa for which he is still remembered as a cult hero. Played once for England B. Since retirement King has turned out playing for the Aston Villa Masters team as well as still having close connections with Swindon Town. He also co-commentates on Swindon games for BBC Radio Wiltshire. Now runs the Dolphin public house in Rodborne, Swindon.

KINGABY, Herbert

Outside right
Born: London **Died:** 1934
Playing career: *Clapton Orient, Aston Villa, Fulham, Peterborough City (1906-1911)*

Kingaby worked in a wool production factory in London throughout his football career and so he was was only available to play at weekends or on bank holidays. He was the subject of a famous and groundbreaking legal case when, supported by the Players Union, he challenged the 'retain and transfer" system. Villa signed the full back for the maximum wage of £4 a week but things did not work out and he made only four appearances for the club in the 1905/06 season, but things did not work out. Unwilling to pay £300, his wages were blocked and he eventually moved back to Fulham in the Southern League. After retirement, Kingaby worked as a prominent member of Leyton Borough council and was a director/secretary of a tiling firm. Kingaby is believed to have committed suicide.

KINGDON, Billy

Half-back
Born: Worcester **Died:** 1977
Playing career: *Kepex (Worcester), Kidderminster Harriers, Aston Villa, Southampton (1924-1946)*

Right half Kingdon played junior football in the Birmingham and District League for Kidderminster Harriers before he joined Villa, initially on amateur forms, turning professional in 1926. In his time at Villa Park, Villa were moderately successful, finishing runners-up in the League Championship twice, in 1930-31 and 1932-33, and a third place in 1928-29. Kingdon was part of their teams that reached the FA Cup semi final in both 1929 and 1934 as Villa lost to eventual winners Manchester City. After relegation, Kingdon left Villa in the summer of 1936 to join Southampton having played 240 games. At Southampton he displayed "a nice line in distribution and looked to be an asset". He briefly became club captain at Saints. Later, he joined Yeovil & Petters United as player-manager after a single goal in 49 appearances for The Saints. He remained with Yeovil for the duration of the Second World War, but left to accept the position as manager at Weymouth. He returned to his trade as a carpenter and ran the Fountain Hotel in the town.

KINSELLA, Mark

Midfielder
Born: *Dublin, Ireland*
Playing career: *Home Farm, Colchester United, Charlton Athletic, Aston Villa, West Bromwich Albion, Walsall, Lewes (1988-2008)*

Kinsella began his career at Colchester United, before spells at Charlton Athletic, Aston Villa, West Bromwich Albion, Walsall and Lewes. He played 48 times for the Republic of Ireland, scoring three goals and playing in the 2002 FIFA World Cup in Japan and South Korea. Kinsella has also enjoyed an extensive coaching career with Walsall (caretaker manager), Charlton Reserves (head coach), Daventy Town manager, Colchester United's assistant, and since 2016 has been in charge of Drogheda United in his native Ireland. Both of Kinsella's children are heavily involved in sport with daughter Alice an international gymnast and son Liam also a footballer.

KINSEY, George

Left-half
Born: *Burton upon Trent* **Died:** 1936
Playing career: *Burton Crusaders, Burton Swifts, Birmingham St George's, Wolverhampton Wanderers, Aston Villa, Derby County, Notts County, Bristol Eastville Rovers/Bristol Rovers, Burton Swifts, Burton Early Closing (1891-1900)*

Kinsey started his football career with junior clubs Barton FC Burton Crusaders, Burton Swifts and Birmingham St George's. He won the FA Cup with Wolves in 1893 and was capped four times by full senior England squad. He signed for Aston Villa in July 1894 but played only 3 times in Villa's 1894-95 season before moving to Derby County in July 1895. He returned to his home town to end his career, firstly re-joining by now Second Division Burton Swifts in 1900, scoring once in 8 appearances, and later moving on to non league Gresley Rovers in 1902 and Burton Early Closing in 1903 before his retirement. Kinsey later worked as a labourer and in a factory.

"DID YOU KNOW?"

"Tom 'Pongo' Waring, still holds the record for most goals scored in a season - he bagged 50 in 1930–31."

KIRALY, Gabor
Goalkeeper
Born: *Szombathely, Hungary*
Playing career: *Haladas, Hertha BSC, Crystal Palace, West Ham United (loan), Aston Villa (loan), Burnley, Munich, Fulham, Haladas (1993-2015)*

Known for his eccentric style and unusual attire of tracksuit bottoms, Kiraly spent most of his 25-year career in Germany. He played at Villa Park on a month-long emergency loan in the 2006/07 season following injuries to regular keepers Thomas Sorensen and Stuart Taylor. He has also amassed a record number of caps for Hungary, having played 108 times for his country and he featured at Euro 2016 aged 40. Kiraly has claimed that the tracksuit bottoms bring him luck. He retired at the end of the 2018/19 season after four seasons with Haledes in his homeland.

KIRBY, Alan
Winger
Born: *Waterford, Ireland*
Playing career: *Johnville F.C., Aston Villa, Waterford United, Longford Town, St Patrick's Athletic, Sporting Fingal, Sligo Rovers, Longford Town (1994-2012)*

Regarded as a tricky winger with blistering pace, Kirby joined Villa at 16 and spent four years at the club without ever making a first team appearance. He returned to his native Waterford and spent the remainder of his career in the League of Ireland. He would go on to win a bronze medal with the Republic of Ireland U20 team at the 1997 World Cup, win back-to-back FAI Cups with Longford Town, and play for various other League of Ireland clubs. Kirby now works on the FAI board.

KNIGHT, William
Goalkeeper
Born: *Toogates, Tamworth*
Playing career: *Walsall, Aston Villa, Stourbridge, Southampton (1907-1913)*

He began his career with Walsall before being scouted and signed by Aston Villa in 1907. Described as a "vigilant and agile keeper". After retirement he worked on Southampton docks. He served in the Navy during WWI and died in Romsey aged 50.

KNIGHT, Zat
Centre-back
Born: *Solihull*
Playing career: *Rushall Olympic, Fulham, Peterborough United (loan), Aston Villa, Bolton Wanderers, Colorado Rapids, Reading (1999-2015)*

Knight had extended spells at Aston Villa, Bolton Wanderers and Fulham in the Premier League and the Championship. He finished his career at Reading in the Championship. Knight represented England at under-21 and senior international levels. He earned two caps for the full England team in 2005. He signed for his boyhood club Villa in 2007 for £3.5 million. Unbeknownst to many, Knight was arrested and bailed after a police raid at his home on the day of his transfer to Villa. His agent dealt with the incident and no mention was ever made of it. Knight currently works as a player liaison officer at former club Fulham.

KUBICKI, Dariusz
Right-back
Born: *Kozuchow, Poland*
Playing career: *Aston Villa, Wolves, Tranmere Rovers (loan), Carlisle United, Darlington (1981-1999)*

Kubicki played little part in the Villa teams which came second in the 1993 Premier League and won the 1994 Football League Cup, but played a more active role in Sunderland's promotion to the Premier League in 1996. Kubicki played 46 times for the Polish national team, scoring once, and featured at the 1986 FIFA World Cup.
In October 2007, Kubicki was arrested by the police due to a bribery scandal involving the sale of one of the Warsaw sport centres. Due to this scandal, Kubicki was suspended as manager of Lechia Gdańsk. He is currently the head coach of Olimpia Grudziadz in his native Poland.

Zat Knight

KYLE, Peter
Centre-forward
Born: *Rutherglen, Glasgow, Scotland* Died: 1961
Playing career: *Clyde, Liverpool, Leicester City, West Ham United, Tottenham Hotspur, Woolwich Arsenal, Aston Villa, Sheffield United, Watford (1899-1909)*

Certainly one of the most travelled players in British football history in a career beset by disciplinary problems and disputes with both clubs and team mates. Having begun his career in his native Scotland, he played five games in claret and blue between 1907 and 1909 before he joined Sheffield United for £1,100. Kyle later became a coach at his last club Watford. He died in Calder, Lanarkshire, in 1961 aged 81.

LAMPTEY, Nii
Midfielder
Born: *Tema, Ghana*
Playing career: *Anderlecht, PSV Eindhoven, Aston Villa, Coventry City, Venezia, Union Santa Fe, Ankaragucu, Uniao Leiria, Greuther Furth, Shandog Luneng, Al-Nassr, Jomo Cosmos (1990-2008)*

The Ghanaian international had ten games on loan at Villa Park and told Birmingham Live that "the move to Aston Villa was the worst decision of my career that I still regret today." Well travelled, he also turned out for clubs in Portugal, Argentina, Germany, South Africa and China. Capped 38 times by his country, Lamptey became the assistant manager of Sekondi Wise Fighters in 2009. Is now the proprietor of a football academy in the country's capital Accra.

LARSEN, Henrik
Midfielder
Born: *Lyngby, Denmark*
Playing career: *Hellerup, Lyngby, Pisa, Lyngby (loan), Aston Villa (loan), Waldhof Mannheim (loan), Lyngby, Copenhagen (1983-1999)*

Larsen was part of the Denmark team's shock Euro 1992 triumph and was joint top scorer in the tournament. He eventually moved to Villa on a loan deal in January 1993. His stay at Aston Villa was short, as he had trouble forcing his way into the team under manager Ron Atkinson and never played a minute. He has since managed a number of Danish clubs and also the Faroe Islands. He was most recently boss of Lyngby Boldklub whom he also played for.

LAURSEN, Martin
Defender
Born: *Farvang, Denmark*
Playing career: *Horn/Farvang IF, Silkeborg, Hellas Verona, Parma, Milan, Aston Villa (1995-2009)*

Made 84 appearances in five years at Aston Villa and also played for AC Milan. He was most recently manager of BK Sollerod - Vedbaek in his homeland. Laursen was signed by the claret and blue for £3million, he went on to captain the team and became a fans' favourite for his no nonsense defending and leadership ability. He has also worked as a pundit for Sky Sports.

LEAKE, Alex
Half-back
Born: *Birmingham* Died: 1938
Playing career: *Hoskins & Sewell, King's Heath Albion, Saltley Gas Works, Singer's, Hoskins & Sewell, Old Hill Wanderers, Small Heath, Aston Villa, Burnley, Wednesbury Old Athletic (1892-1911)*

He won five caps for his country and made 407 appearances in the Football League playing as a half back for Small Heath, Aston Villa and Burnley. After retiring from playing he took up coaching, both with professional clubs and at school level. Leake won the FA Cup with Villa in 1905 and was described as a hard-working player who was safe and solid rather than showy. Leake died in his native Birmingham at the age of 66.

LEE, Alan
Forward
Born: *Galway, Ireland*
Playing career: *Aston Villa, Torquay United (loan), Port Vale (loan), Burnley, Rotherham United, Cardiff City, Ipswich Town, Crystal Palace, Norwich City (loan), Huddersfield Town, Ipswich Town (1995-2014)*

A well-travelled striker, Lee now works as an academy coach at Ipswich, for whom he played over 100 times during his lengthy 19 season career. He spent his final year as a player/coach at the club. Lee earned ten caps for the Republic of Ireland and began his career as a trainee with the Villa in 1995.

He never made a first team debut at Villa Park and moved on to Torquay United. A winger-turned-striker, he enjoyed the best spell of his career whilst with Rotherham and scored 42 goals in three seasons with the Millers. Lee made his Ireland debut in 2003. The Aston Villa website describes Lee a very strong and quick striker with no little skill.

LEE, Gordon
Right-back
Born: *Cannock*
Playing career: *Aston Villa, Shrewsbury Town. (1958-1966).*

Lee played in the Villa team of the late 50s and early 60s under manager Eric Houghton. He won the inaugural League Cup with the club and was also part of the Villains team to lift the FA Cup in 1956/57 although he did not play in the final against Manchester United. Lee made 142 appearances for Villa as a right back before he moved on to Shrewsbury in July 1966. After retirement as a player Lee became a successful manager in his own right, taking charge of Port Vale, Blackburn, Newcastle United, Everton, Preston, Reykjavik in Iceland and caretaker boss at Leicester in 1991. He later settled down to retirement in Lytham St Anne's.

LEE, Jimmy
Goalkeeper
Born: *Brierley Hill* Died: 1955
Playing career: *Cradley Heath, Wulfrunians, Aston Villa, Stoke, Macclesfield (1919-1922)*

Lee joined Villa in 1919. He played 18 times in two seasons and left for Stoke in 1921. A talented, dependable custodian, Lee then moved on to Macclesfield, his last club before retirement. He became an accountant and financial advisor having retired in 1925.

LEIGH, Harry
Outside-right
Born: *Lymm* Died: 1919
Playing career: *Aston Villa, Barnsley, Stoke, Winsford United (1908-1912)*

Cheshire born Leigh earned a trial at Villa ahead of the 1907/1908 season and was subsequently signed by the club. He left for Barnsley without ever making an appearance for the claret and blue. He later coached at Winsford United before taking up a job in a factory during WW1.

LEONARD, Keith

Striker
Born: *Birmingham*
Playing career: *Aston Villa (1972-1974)*
Won the League Cup and Second Division title with Villa as a player and then moved on loan to Port Vale. He joined Vic Crowe's side in 1972 having played at non-league level for Darlaston and Highgate. A knee injury forced his retirement four ears later after Villa had turned down a £5,00 bid from Port Vale to make his loan permanent. Took up coaching at Villa under Ron Saunders and then moved to fierce rivals Birmingham where he had one game as caretaker boss in 1986. He went on to coach at West Bromwich Albion before leaving football to work at the Solihull Land Rover plant.

LEONHARDSEN, Oyvind

Midfielder
Born: *Kristiansund, Norway*
Playing career: *Molde, Rosenborg, Wimbledon, Liverpool, Tottenham Hotspur, Aston Villa, Lyn Oslo, Stromgodset (1989-2007)*
He retired after the 2007 season, ending a career with nine years in English football at clubs Wimbledon, Liverpool, Tottenham Hotspur, and Aston Villa, and in Norway he played for Molde, Rosenborg, Lyn, and Strømsgodset. Leonhardsen now works as a youth team coach for Norweigan side Lyn Oslo. He played 86 times for his country, scoring 19 goals, and represented Norway in the 1994 and 1998 World Cups.

LESCOTT, Aaron

Defender
Born: *Birmingham*
Playing career: *Aston Villa, Lincoln City (loan), Sheffield Wednesday, Stockport County, Bristol Rovers, Cheltenham Town (loan), Walsall, Halesowen Town (1995-2013)*
Older brother of namesake Joleon (below), he started his career with Aston Villa but only made one FA Cup appearance for the club. Unable to establish himself at Villa, he had a loan spell with Lincoln City in 2000, before signing for Sheffield Wednesday in October of the same year for a fee of £100,000. Went on to Stockport County, Bristol Rovers (twice), Cheltenham, Walsall and Halesowen Town, his last club.

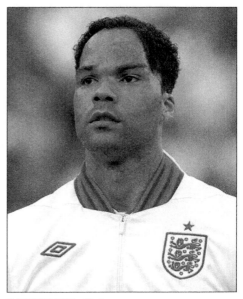

LESCOTT, Joleon

Defender
Born: *Birmingham*
Playing career: *Wolverhampton Wanderers, Everton, Manchester City, West Brom, Aston Villa (1999-2015)*
He currently works as a loanee player liaison agent for Manchester City, for whom he also played for five seasons. Won two league titles and both domestic cups. He played 26 times for England and was relegated from the Premier League with both Wolves and the Villa. Infamously known for his "phone in the pocket" tweet of an expensive car in the hours after Villa's relegation in 2016. Lescott had also done some coaching work with the England Under 21 team.

LIDDLE, Craig

Defender
Born: *Chester-le-Street*
Playing career: *Aston Villa, Blyth Spartans, Middlesbrough, Darlington (1990-2005)*
Liddle is most closely associated with the North East, having played over 400 games for Middlesbrough and another 271 for Darlington, and later went on to coach and manage at both clubs. Liddle started out at Villa in 1990 but did not make the grade and was released after only one season because he was deemed too small. Since retiring as a player, Liddle has stayed heavily involved in the game and is Professional Development Lead coach at the Riverside. He has also worked for Sunderland in the same role.

LILLIS, Mark
Midfielder/Striker
Born: *Manchester*
Playing career: *Huddersfield Town, Manchester City, Derby County, Aston Villa, Scunthorpe (1978-1992)*

A Huddersfield Town legend, he was sold to Manchester City for £130,000 but played there only for one season and then moved on to Derby and Villa. His playing career finished with Macclesfield in the mid 1990s. Since retirement, he has had a variety of managerial and coaching jobs with Halifax, Derby, Stockport and Macclesfield (both permanent and interim boss). Most recently, he was assistant manager of Indian Super League side Chennaiyin FC. His son Josh Lillis plays as a goalkeeper for Rochdale.

LINTON, Ivor
Midfielder
Born: *West Bromwich*
Playing career: *Aston Villa, Peterborough United, Birmingham City, (1976-1999)*

He played only two European games, both of them as a substitute and neither at Villa Park. But Ivor Linton can proudly boast a 100% record in Europe. Linton played in the 2-0 win at Fenerbahce in 1977's UEFA Cup run, and perhaps more pertinently, played his role on 'that' night in Rotterdam five years on. After 30 appearances in claret and blue, Linton had spells with Peterborough United and Birmingham City before heading off to Finland, where he played and worked. He now works as an electrician, having studied the profession on a day release course during his time with Villa and completed the course while in Finland.

LITTLE, Alan
Midfielder
Born: *Horden*
Playing career: *Aston Villa, Southend United, Barnsley, Doncaster Rovers, Torquay United, Halifax Town, Hartlepool. (1974-1985).*

Little spent 20 years as a professional footballer with seven different clubs. He began as a trainee at Aston Villa and went on to enjoy a career that lasted over two decades and took in 410 appearances in total, most of them in the lower divisions. He went into coaching having ginished his playing days at Hartlepool. Then went on to spend six seasons as the manager of York City and also managed Southend United. Little has also served as chief scout at Hull City.

LITTLE, Brian
Striker
Born: *Newcastle upon Tyne*
Playing career: *Aston Villa (1971-1979).*

Trawl through Villa's 145-year history and you probably won't find anyone else who has served the them in so many different roles, whether it be on the pitch, in the dugout, in the boardroom, or even in the club shop. A one club man, Little spent his entire decade-long career in the claret and blue of Villa, becoming a fans' favourite and club legend in the process. Throughout his lifelong long association with Villa, he has had roles as player, manager, youth team coach, kit man and board member. Little is remembered as the last Villa manager to win a trophy during his time in charge when he led them to League Cup glory in 1995-96. He made one appearance for the senior England side in 1975. Still strongly linked with Villa, he holds an advisory role on the board and is also the Jersey FA Director of Football.

LIVINGSTONE, Glen
Goalkeeper
Born: *Birmingham*
Playing career: *Aston Villa, Omagh Town, Cheltenham Town, York City (-)*
Started his career at Aston Villa where he featured mainly in the Youth and Reserve teams and never made a first team appearance. He had a loan spells at Omagh Town and Cheltenham Town before joining York City on non-contract terms, but he made no appearances with the club. He later transferred to Walsall in March 1992 where he made three appearances for them before leaving them and signing for Barry Town. Livingstone played for England at under 18 and under 19 level. Having hung up his boots, Livingstone worked as a delivery driver.

LOACH, Arthur
Forward
Born: *West Bromwich* Died: 1958
Playing career: *WBA, Aston Villa, Rhyl (1882-1896)*
Loach joined his hometown club West Bromwich Albion in 1882, six years before the inception of the Premier League. Loach became of one of Albion's first ever professional players when the FA introduced minimum wage. The forward feature in the 1886 FA Cup final for the side from The Hawthorns. Spent two years at Villa and remained there until joining Rhyl in August 1888. Loach retired from football in 1896 and went on to run a hotel in Rhyl.

LOCHHEAD, Andy
Striker
Born: *Milngavie, Stirlingshire, Scotland*
Playing career: *Burnley, Leicester City, Aston Villa, Oldham Athletic, Denver Dynamos (1960-1974)*
If there was one man more responsible than most for dragging Villa out of the old Third Division it was Andy Lochhead, whose 25 goals during the 1971-72 campaign were priceless. Having made his name with the other clarets of Burnley, he was signed from Leicester City and soon became a true claret and blue legend. His scoring feats are also fondly remembered at Burnley and Leicester, not to mention NASL side Denver Dynamo where he scored the first ever goal at their Mile High Stadium. In retirement, Lochhead now works in corporate hospitality at Turf Moor.

LOCKETT, Arthur
Outside-left
Born: *Alsager* Died: 1957
Playing career: *Alsager's Bank, Audley, Cross Heath, Audley, Crewe Alexandra, Stoke, Aston Villa, Preston North End, Watford, Mardy (1900-1907)*
Lockett made his Football League debut at Aston Villa in September 1900. He played 16 times during the 1900-01 season as Stoke fought a successful battle against relegation. Lockett established himself in the first team the next season which saw Stoke again in relegation trouble and for the second season running they survived on the final day. Won a solitary cap for England in 1903. Lockett joined Aston Villa for £400 in April 1903 where he spent two seasons and scored five goals in 41 appearances before joining Preston North End in April 1905. Later played for Watford and Mardy before he moved into coaching and he was also employed as a factory worker.

LOGAN, James
Born: *1870* Died: 1896
Playing career: *Ayr, Sunderland, Aston Villa, Notts County,Dundee, Newcastle United (1891-1896)*
No relation to his namesake (below), the 'other' James Logan started his career with Ayr. He then moved to Sunderland and on to Aston Villa, for a transfer fee of £30. Logan, a defender, turned out ten times for the club in the 1892/1893 season and scored seven goals. He won the FA Cup with Notts County and scored a hat-trick in the 1894 final as they beat Bolton 4-1. Played twice for the full Scotland team. He died at the young age of 25 having developed pneumonia.

Andy Lochhead

LOGAN, James
Defender
Born: *Barrhead, Scotland* Died: 1958
Playing career: *Aston Villa, Rangers (1905-1917)*
Logan joined First Division Aston Villa in July 1905. Described as "a sure kick and a player of great resource", he scored four goals in 158 appearances before joining Glasgow Rangers in September 1912 after seven years at Villa Park. He also played for Scotland in an unofficial wartime international in 1916 before finishing his professional career with Arthurlie. Logan later worked as a gardener and hotelier.

LOWE, Eddie
Wing-half
Born: *Halesowen* Died: 2009
Playing career: *Aston Villa, Fulham, Notts County (1946-1965)*
Lowe played for Aston Villa and Fulham, making the second-all-time club record

appearances for Fulham of 511, behind Johnny Haynes, between 1950 and 1963. Lowe played 104 games in claret and blue (1946/50). Strong in the tackle and energetic in attack, Lowe was also an England international - with three caps - and later, the manager for Notts County. In his time at Villa Park, after his initial success and the international caps, his form faded. Lowe died in 2009 in Nottingham aged 83.

LUCAS, Paul
Midfielder
Born: *1936* Died: 1992
Playing career: *Aston Villa, Gillingham (1956-1958)*
Lucas' time at the Villa did not work out, and after an unsuccessful career at Villa Park (five apps, no goals and a sending off), he moved on to Gillingham. After retiring, Lucas moved to Essex and became a secondary school teacher.

LUCAS, Tommy
Full-back
Born: *St Helens, Lancashire* Died: 1953
Playing career: *Aston Villa, Liverpool, Arsenal, Windsor Park, Belfast, Ashford Town (1916-1933)*
A full back who only ever played for the reserves before Liverpool came calling. He was capped three times by England and also represented the Football League on four occasions. He also coached Aylesbury United and served in the RAF during WW2.

LYNN, Stan
Right-back
Born: *Bolton* Died: 2002
Playing career: *Accrington Stanley, Aston Villa, Birmingham City (1946-1965).*
Nicknamed "Stan the Wham" due to his powerful right foot, "Boomin' Boots" quickly established himself as a Villa stalwart and fans favourite upon signing in 1950. A tough tackling right-back, he joined Villa for £10,000 from Accrington in 1935. With him as a mainstay at the back, the claret and blue won a seventh FA Cup in 1957, also going on to win the Second Division title and the League Cup. Combining a part-time career with Stourbridge with regular appearances for the Villa Old Boys team, Lynn also worked at Lucas car dealers in Birmingham. In later life he suffered from Alzheimer's and died in 2002 aged 73.

LYONS, Tom

Full-back
Born: *Hednesford*   Died: 1938
Playing career: *Hednesford Town, Bridgtown Amateurs, Aston Villa, Port Vale, Walsall (1907-1922)*

Lyons was a member of the team which won the FA Cup in 1913 and by the time World War One intervened, he had made 238 appearances for Villa. Later became player-coach at Walaall making a single Saddlers appearance in February 1923 when already 37 years old. Lyons played as a wicket-keeper for Staffordshire in the 1913 Minor Counties Cricket. Died in 1938.

MACEWAN, Jimmy

Winger
Died: 2017
Playing career: *Aston Villa, Walsall. (1947-1966).*

Described by Villa's historian as a "craggy and hungry looking outside right", MacEwan was sold to Aston Villa for £6,660 (1959), a fee that a few years ago was valued at £640,000 in the current price market. He went on to play 181 times for Aston Villa scoring 32 goals. In 1966, he left Villa to sign for Walsall and after one season playing, he remained on the coaching staff until 1973. He continued playing for the Villa Old Stars well into his 50's until he was forced to stop due to knee replacement operations. MacEwan worked at Ansell's Brewery in Birmingham, and also for social services. MacEwan died 88 in 2017 from heart failure.

MACKAY, Norman

Right-half/Inside right
Born: *Edinburgh, Scotland*
Playing career: *Edinburgh Royal, Broxburn United, Hibernian, Blackburn Rovers, Aston Villa, Lovells Athletic, Yoker Athletic, Plymouth Argyle, Southend United, Clydebank (1920-1935)*

Born in Edinburgh, Mackay began his career in his native Scotland, playing for Edinburgh Royal and Broxburn before joining Blackburn Rovers in 1921, although he did not make a League appearance. He then returned to Scotland to sign for Hibernian before moving south again to join Aston Villa. After just two first team starts at Villa Park, he dropped into non-league football with Lovell's Athletic, whilst also having a trial with Clydebank and playing junior football with Yoker Athletic. When he was signed by Argyle in 1927 for a fee of £200, he was combining playing for Lovell's with a job selling the toffees that the company produced. A hat-trick on his debut against Coventry was the perfect start, but proved to be a false dawn. He was never really a goal-scorer, but developed into an energetic, tough tackling half-back, and became a key part of the 1929-30 Division Three (South) winning side. After nearly seven years with Argyle, he joined Southend United in 1934, for whom he played 32 times, before moving back north of the border to play for his last club, Clydebank.

1982 European Cup winners reunion

MacLACHLAN, Bert
Defender
Born: *Kirkcudbright, Scotland* Died: 1956
Playing career: *Aston Villa, Aberdeen, Heart of Midlothian (1913-1927)*
Dumfries & Galloway born wing half MacLachlan joined First Division Aston Villa from St Cuthbert Wanderers in 1913, but played only three games for the club. Released, he moved to Aberdeen in the summer of 1914, where he was appointed club captain in 1919. He represented The Scottish League against The Football League in March 1920 in a 4-0 defeat at Celtic Park. After retiring he worked in agriculture north of the border. McLachlan died in 1956.

MacLEOD, John
Winger
Born: *Edinburgh, Scotland*
Playing career: *Edinburgh Thistle, Armadale Thistle, Hibernian, Arsenal, Aston Villa, KV Mechelen, Raith Rovers, Newtongrange Star (1954-1975)*
MacLeod's true claim to fame came in the red of Arsenal when he scored the Gunners first ever goal in a European tie. He netted in the Inter-Cities Fairs Cup back in September 1963 against Staevnet, a year before he signed for the Villa for a fee of £35,000. A talented winger, he earned four caps for Scotland and also represented the Scottish League XI. MacLeod plied his trade for four seasons in claret and blue, making 123 league appearances, before moving abroad to play for KV Mechelen. He retired in 1972 after finishing his career with Raith Rovers and Newtongrange Star. MacLeod worked as a fisherman after retiring and continues to live in Edinburgh.

MAIL, David
Central defender
Born: *Bristol*
Playing career: *Aston Villa, Blackburn Rovers, Hull City (1980-1994)*
Mail played for Aston Villa between 1978 and 1982, without making a senior appearance for them although he did play in the FA Young Cup winning team in 1980. He later made 356 appearances in the Football League for Blackburn Rovers and Hull City, before playing non-league football for Brigg Town whom he went on to coach. Mail is now earning a living by driving a lorry and managing youth teams in the Hull area.

MAKOUN, Jean
Midfielder
Born: *Yaounde, Cameroon*
Playing career: *Jeunesse Star, Tonnerre Yaounde, Lille, Lyon, Aston Villa, Olympiacos (loan), Stade Rennais, Antalyaspor (1997-2015)*
Began his career with Cotonsport Garoua, he enjoyed an impressive career in France, attracting the attention of several English clubs. Having signed for £6.2m, he struggled to hold down a first team place at left after two season having played nine times for the claret and blue. Joined Olympiakos and went on to finish his club career in France and then Turkey. Played in three AFCON tournaments and the 2010 World Cup finals for Cameroon - a 68 cap, five goal international career.

MALONEY, Shaun
Attacking Midfielder/Winger
Born: *Miri, Malaysia*
Playing career: *Celtic, Aston Villa, Celtic, Wigan Athletic, Chicago Fire, Hull City (1996-2015)*
Maloney spent the bulk of his career with Glasgow giants Celtic where he won five league titles, five Scottish Cups and three League Cups. Maloney also won the FA Cup with Wigan in 2013. He now cuts a somewhat unlikely figure as Roberto Martinez's number two with the Belgium national team. He had a loan spell with Villa in 2007-08, but despite being short of his best form he still played 30 games and scored five goals. Capped 47 times by Scotland, he worked for Celtic's youth teams having hung up his boots before leaving that job to focus on his role with Belgium.

MANDLEY, Jack
Right-winger
Born: *Hanley* Died: 1988
Playing career: *Hanley Roman Catholic School, Cross Street Mission, Boothen Vics, Port Vale, Aston Villa, Altrincham (1926-1934)*
He spent just over four years at Villa Park, making 106 First Division and six cup appearances, scoring one cup goal and 25 league goals. The "Villans" finished fourth in 1929–30, with Mandley scoring once in eleven appearances. Mandley helped Villa to finish second in the First Division in 1930–31 and 1932–33 and also won the Third Division (North) whilst at Port Vale in 1929/30.

MANN, Frank

Striker
Born: *Nottingham* Died: 1966
Playing career: *Aston Villa, Huddersfield Town, Manchester City (1912-1930)*
Mann joined First Division Aston Villa in 1911-12. but was qucikly released. He had to wait until later in his career before tasting real success. He played both sides of World War One for Huddersfield, his 17 goals in 1919-20 helping them gain promotion and played in the 1920 FA Cup Final. Mann had several jobs later in life including a warehouse operative, a bus driver and a mechanic.

MARJERAM, Arthur

Left-back
Born: *Brighton* Died: 1911
Playing career: *Aston Villa, Swanscombe, Thames Ironworks (1898-)*
Marjeram started as an amateur with Villa before playing in the first Thames Ironworks professional side, the club that later became West Ham United. Died in 1911.

Marshall, Andy

Goalkeeper
Born: *Bury, Greater Manchester*
Playing career: *Norwich City, Ipswich T, Millwall, Coventry C, Aston Villa, Millwall (1992-2014)*
He has previously played for the England Under-21s, Norwich City, Bournemouth, Gillingham, Ipswich Town, Millwall, Coventry City before joining Villa, but never never made a senior appearance for the Villains. After retirement, he returned to Villa as goalkeeping coach and also had a five-day stint as the club's interim manager alongside namesake Scott Marshall in 2015 following the departure of Paul Lambert.

MARSHALL, Colin

Midfielder
Born: *Glasgow, Scotland*
Playing career: *Aston Villa, St Johnstone, Falkirk, Stranraer, Dundee, Amicale FC (2000-2016)*
A much travelled midfielder, Marshall was a member of Aston Villa's FA Youth Cup winning team in 2002. He failed to make the grade but did make the first team bench twice. He also played overseas in Spain, Iceland, Japan and Vanuatu, where Marshall spent three months with Amicale FC. Since retiring he has gone into coaching.

MARTIN, Con

Goalkeeper/Defender/Midfielder/Forward
Born: *Rush, Dublin, Ireland* Died: 2013
Playing career: *Dublin GAA (Gaelic football), Drumcondra, Glentoran, Leeds United, Aston Villa, Waterford, Dundalk (1941-1960)*
He was rated at the time as one of the best centre-halves in the country and he enhanced his reputation at Villa Park. There was a time when players were permitted to represent both Northern and the Republic of Ireland - and in 1949 Martin became the first player to turn out for both in the same year. He played Gaelic football with Dublin before switching codes and embarking on a successful soccer career, Although he played mainly as a centre-half, the ball-handling skills he developed playing Gaelic football also made him a very useful goalkeeper. So much so that he played almost an entire season between the sticks for Villa when goalkeeper Joe Rutherford was injured and there was no cover. Left Villa to sign for Waterford before he became joint player/manager at Dundalk, taking sole charge the following season. He was also boss of Shelbourne and assistant manager at Cork Hibernians.

MARTIN, Jackie

Inside right
Born: *Hamstead, Birmingham* Died: 1996
Playing career: *Aston Villa (1934-1949)*
A war-time guest for Spurs, Jackie Martin plied his trade for Aston Villa in peace time. His first club was Hednesford Town, a non-league club close to his home town, where he made good progress and was snapped up on amateur forms by Villa in October 1934. He signed as an amateur, as he had a good job as a teacher in the town where he started his football career, but decided he could carry on his civilian trade as well as being a professional footballer. Scored at almost a goal every two and half games, getting called up by England a couple of times before the war interrupted league football and he went off to serve with the Army. When football resumed after the war, Jackie returned to Aston Villa and played out the remainder of his career there until his retirement in 1949, when he went back to teaching, although later he managed Hednesford Town. Later worked as a railway signalman.

MARTIN, Johnny
Winger
Born: *Ashington* Died: 2013
Playing career: *Aston Villa, Colchester United, Workington, Southport, Wigan Athletic (1964-1976)*
Born in Ashington, Northumberland, in 1946, he was scouted by a number of top teams, including his boyhood side Newcastle United, but ended up signing his first professional deal with Aston Villa. Martin said that not joining Newcastle "broke his heart." He played one game in claret and blue before moving on to Colchester and then Workington. He spent five seasons at Borough Park before leaving, this time to join Southport. After retiring, he went on to work in a supermarket. Martin also lived in Spain for 12 years and started out selling wallets and purses on a Spanish market.

MARTIN, Ray
Full-back
Born: *Wolverhampton*
Playing career: *Aston Villa, Birmingham City, Portland Timbers, Minnesota Kicks (1960-1979)*
Having turned out for Villa as a youth player, he spent most of his professional career in England with Birmingham City, where he played 333 games in the Football League, became the club captain, and won the Player of the Year award two years running, in 1969–70 and 1970–71. He later moved to the United States, initially playing for Portland Timbers and Minnesota Kicks in the North American Soccer League, and then coaching at Oregon State University.

MASSIE, Alex
Wing-half
Born: *Possilpark, Scotland* Died: 1977
Playing career: *Shawfield Juniors, Petershill, Benburb, Ashfield, Ayr United, Bury, Bethlehem Steel, Dolphin, Heart of Midlothian, Aston Villa (1927-1939)*
Right half Massie began his career in the amateur Scottish leagues. His performances at right half, and occasionally at inside right won him international recognition. Massie went on to be capped 18 times for Scotland and also represented the Scottish League on six occasions. Massie moved to Aston Villa in December 1935 after 24 goals in 204 appearances for Hearts. He retired from playing at end of the 1944-45 wartime season, and was appointed manager of Aston Villa soon afterwards. He went on to manage Torquay United, Hereford United, Hertford Town and Welwyn Garden City.

MATTHEWS, Billy
Forward
Born: *Derby* Died: 1916
Playing career: *Ripley Athletic, Aston Villa, Notts County, Derby County, Newport County (1903-1913)*
He played for Ripley Athletic, Aston Villa, Notts County, Derby County and Newport County. While a regular goalscorer when given the chance, he was very much a fringe player at Villa Park. In December 1906 Notts County paid a then club record fee for his services after Matthews had scored 12 goals in 26 appearances for The Villains, In later life he worked for the tourist board and as a school caretaker.

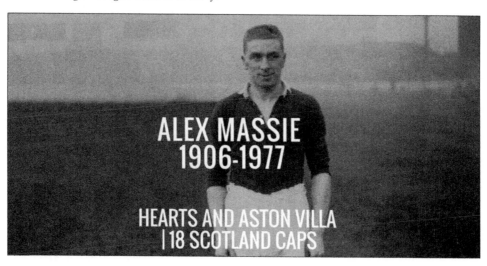

ALEX MASSIE
1906-1977

HEARTS AND ASTON VILLA
| 18 SCOTLAND CAPS

McALINDEN, Bobby
Winger
Born: *Salford*
Playing career: *Aston Villa, Manchester City, Port Vale, Glentoran, Durban City, Los Angeles Aztecs, Bournemouth (loan), Memphis Rogues, San Jose Earthquakes(indoor) (1961-1981)*

Between the age of 13 and 15 he played for Salford Boys. After interest from a number of League clubs, he joined Aston Villa, but homesickness meant he soon returned to the north west. A successful trial for Manchester City followed his spell at Villa Park. McAlinden was friends with George Best through a mutual interest in gambling. When Best joined the Los Angeles Aztecs of the North American Soccer League in 1975, he recommended McAlinden to Aztecs manager John Chaffetz. Off the field, McAlinden, Best and three others bought a bar in Los Angeles. McAlinden eventually bought the others out, and owned the bar for 20 years. He also turned out for Bournemouth and the San Jose Earthquakes.

McAULAY, William
Inside-left
Born: *Newton, South Lanarkshire* Died: 1935
Playing career: *Celtic , Sheffield Wednesday, Dundee , Walsall Town Swifts, Aston Villa, Portsmouth, Middlesbrough, Aberdeen, Arthurlie, Falkirk, Hibernian, Alloa Athletic (1898-1913)*

Most known for his time in the Granite City with Aberdeen, where he scored 20 goals in 63 league appearances from inside left. McAulay's claret and blue career was brief, playing only four times. He transferred to Hibernian in 1907. McAulay died in 1935.

McAVENNIE, Frank
Striker
Born: *Glasgow, Scotland*
Playing career: *Johnstone Burgh, St Mirren, West Ham United, Celtic, West Ham United, Aston Villa, Cliftonville, South China, Celtic, Swindon Town (loan), Falkirk, St Mirren (1979-1995)*

A striker who is best remembered in England for his two spells at West Ham United between 1985-87 & 1989-92. He played a total of 153 league games for them scoring 49 goals. He won five full caps for Scotland between 1985-88 scoring one goal. After his playing career finished in 1995 he did a bit of coaching. After this things spiralled downwards in a drug fuelled cycle of crime, scandal and reckless misbehaviour. McAvennie also received a four month suspended sentence in 2008 for an incident in which he head-butted a man on the Isle of Man. He ended up penniless, unemployed and living in Gateshead. Thankfully he managed to alter some things in his lifestyle getting married for the second time in 2001. However the marriage ended in 2013 when he decided to return to his birthplace Glasgow. He now owns a football agency and is a well respected after dinner speaker. He was recently described as 'Scottish football's ultimate lovable rogue'. Read more at performingartistes.co.uk/artistes/frank-mcavennie

Frank McAvennie

McCANN, Gavin
Midfielder
Born: *Blackpool*
Playing career: *Everton, Sunderland, Aston Villa, Bolton Wanderers (1995-2011)*

He has one England cap to his name, playing against Spain at Villa Park in 2001 and is the current Under-18s assistant manager at Bolton Wanderers. He signed for Everton where he was a product of their academy. In 1998, he moved to Sunderland where he was a member of the side which won the Division One title and promotion to the Premiership 1999. He signed for Aston Villa in 2003, where he had numerous injury setbacks but went on to play over 100 times for the club. Moved on to Bolton and became a coach at Hyde and the Lytham St Anne's football academy in later life.

McCLAIR, Brian
Forward /Midfielder
Born: *Bellshill, Lanarkshire, Scotland*
Playing career: *Aston Villa, Motherwell, Celtic, Manchester United, Motherwell (1980-1998)*

It is easy to forget that the free goalscoring Scotsman actually started his career at Villa. He ventured south as a 17 year old in 1980 but, despite showing promise, failed to break into the first team squad which won the League Championship. His opportunity did come when Motherwell manager Jock Wallace snapped him up and converted him from midfield to a more attacking role. In turn, this lead to a successful spell with Celtic and then a £400,000 move to Manchester United, which saw him win 14 trophies and most of his 30 international caps. Became assistant manager to Brian Kidd at Blackburn Rovers in 1998 but they were both dismissed at the end of the season following relegation. mcClair then return to Old Trafford where he held a number of coaching positions.

McCLURE, Alec
Centre-half
Born: *Workington* Died: 1973
Playing career: *Grangetown Juniors, Birmingham, Aston Villa, Stoke, Coventry City, Walsall (1912-1928)*

McClure joined Second Division Birmingham in 1911, playing both sides of World War One for Birmingham before establishing himself as club captain and linchpin of the first team's defence. He played for the Football League in a 1-0 victory over the Irish Football League in Belfast in October 1921. Having lost his place in the Birmingham line-up, he joined fierce derby rivals Aston Villa in February 1924 but his stay at Villa Park was relatively brief, signing for Stoke City in September 1924 after only 7 appearances in claret and blue. On retiring from playing he worked for short periods as trainer at various clubs, including trainer of Birmingham's juniors, and in 1932 he was appointed assistant manager of the club under Leslie Knighton and later under George Liddell before leaving football. After retiring, he worked for Rudge motorcycles and went on to own and manage a successful haulage business in the Midlands. During the First World War McClure served in the Royal Navy and was involved in the Zeebrugge Raid.

McDONALD, Bobby
Left-back
Born: *Aberdeen, Scotland*
Playing career: *Aston Villa, Coventry City, Manchester City, Oxford United, Leeds United, Wolverhampton Wanderers, V.S. Rugby (1972-1988)*

A defender of great poise and positional sense, McDonald boasted an unusually prolific knack in front of goal considering he was a left-back. He scored 43 goals during his professional career, including three for Villa. Won the League Cup in 1975 and also played a key role in the claret and blue's promotion into Division One. Signed for Coventry for a £40,000 fee and became a mainstay in one of the Sky Blues best ever sides. Moved on to Oxford where McDonald helped his new club to the Third Division and Second Division titles in successive years, and later had spells at Leeds, Wolves and a host of non-League sides. Today, McDonald coaches in Scotland and is a youth coach with Aberdeen FC helping guide youngsters in the Glasgow area.

THE NO. 1 BESTSELLER

PAUL McGRATH

'Heartbreaking...
poignant'
Daily Telegraph

Back from
the Brink

McELENY, Charlie

Centre-half
Born: *County Donegal, Ireland* Died: 1908
Playing career: *Burnley, Celtic, New Brighton Tower, Aston Villa, Swindon, Brentford, Morton (1893-1901)*
McEleny signed for Villa in 1899 from capital club Celtic, as one of the club's first ever professional players. He played only once for the claret and blue before moving on to Southern League Swindon Town. A strong and powerful centre half, he played 48 times for them before returning to Scotland via Brentford. McEleny also featured for Burnley and New Brighton Tower. On quitting football he worked as a painter/decorator. McEleny died in August 1908 aged 35 at Smithston in Greenock.

McGRATH, John

Midfielder
Born: *Limerick, Ireland*
Playing career: *Aston Villa, Dagenham & Redbridge (loan), Doncaster Rovers, Shrewsbury Town (loan), Kidderminster Harriers, Alfreton Town (1996-2013)*
He joined Villa in 1999 following a two-week trial. After making only two appearances he went out on loan to Football Conference side Dagenham & Redbridge in November 2002 then played for many lower and non league clubs both in England and in his native Ireland. He represented his country the Republic of Ireland five times at Under 21 level and has been player/manager of Northern Premier League side Mickleover Sports in 2016.

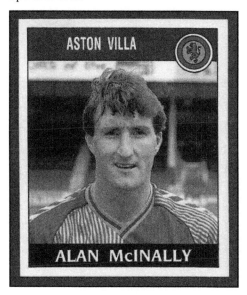

ASTON VILLA

ALAN McINALLY

McGRATH, Paul

Centre-back
Born: *Ealing*
Playing career: *Manchester United, Aston Villa, Derby County, Sheffield United (loan), Sheffield United (1981-1998)*
Spotted by Ron Atkinson and quickly snapped up for only £30,000 from Dublin side, St Patrick's. Had it not been for injuries and personal problems, McGrath would surely have added to his haul of 83 Republic of Ireland caps and United appearances. He featured in three major tournament finals for ROI, Italia 90, USA 94 and Euro 1988, which was the team's first ever international finals. Won the FA Cup during his time at United and then went to Aston Villa to continue his career. McGrath now lives in Monageer, County Wexford, in his native Republic of Ireland. His autobiography that dealt with his alcoholism as a player, named "Back from the Brink", was the most successful Irish sports book ever.

McINALLY, Alan

Striker
Born: *Ayr, Scotland*
Playing career: *Ayr United, Celtic, Aston Villa, Bayern Munich, Kilmarnock (1980-1994)*
McInally won trophies in Scotland and England before making the move into Central Europe with German giants Bayern Munich. McInally is now a regular fixture on Sky Sports 'Soccer Saturday' show from which he is able to pontificate on the game using his continental experience – a rarity among British players-turned-pundits. McInally's career spanned around 14 years although he only made less than 300 competitive appearances, despite this the striker was popular amongst fans of clubs throughout his career including Celtic and Villa. As his contract at Celtic came to an end, Aston Villa bid (pre-Bosman era) £250,000 for the striker and he began his career at Villa Park in July 1987. His first season in the claret and blue of Villa saw them promoted to the top-tier of English football with the new No. 9 grabbing 4 league goals in 18 appearances. McInally is seen as a hero of the Holte End during a difficult period for the club, the faith shown in him by the fans was repaid in the 1988/89 season when the club were able to fend off relegation and keep their top division status.

McKNIGHT, Tom
Forward
Born: *Lichfield* Died: 1930
Playing career: *Aston Villa (1890-1891)*
Joined Villa initially on a trial basis, McKnight made ten appearances for the club in the 1890/91 season. The club finished ninth in Division One with McKnight scoring one goal. There is no record of him ever having played for any other club although he did hold a brief coaching role at Walsall before he drifted out of the game to work in the manufacturing trade.

McLEOD, William
Full-back
Born: *Glasgow, Scotland* Died: 1943
Playing career: *Cowlairs, Aston Villa, Queen's Park*
A full-back small in size but big in stature, McLeod played his club football for Cowlairs and Queen's Park at amateur level and Aston Villa as a professional. He played two games for the Midlands club as a guest in 1882. McLeod made one appearance for Scotland against England in 1886. He was later active as a referee and also worked for the Scottish FA. He died in his native Glasgow in 1943 aged 83 after a short illness.

Alan McLoughlin

McLOUGHLIN, Alan
Midfielder
Born: *Manchester*
Playing career: *Manchester United, Swindon Town, Torquay United (loan), Southampton, Aston Villa (loan), Portsmouth, Wigan Athletic, Rochdale, Forest Green Rovers (1985-2003)*
A former class-mate of Noel Gallagher, McLoughlin was a Manchester United apprentice, who despite never quite managing to break into the first team at Old Trafford, did later carve out a very successful career at both club and international level. Controversially joined Portsmouth from arch rivals Southampton in February 1992 for £400,000 following a short loan stint at Villa which did not see him feature for the first team. As well as being a familiar voice on local radio, he has also scouted for Nottingham Forest and run a football clinic and summer soccer schools. McLoughlin won 42 Republic of Ireland caps.

McLUCKIE, Jasper
Centre-forward
Born: *Glasgow, Scotland* Died: 1924
Playing career: *Jordanhill, Bury, Aston Villa, Plymouth Argyle, Dundee (1898-1905)*
In 1901 he signed for Aston Villa, where he continued to build a reputation as a fine centre-forward, appearing 62 times and netting and impressive 46 times over a three-year period. McLuckie's next move was to Home Park in May 1904, where he was a consistent performer throughout his only season with Argyle. He returned to Scotland to join Dundee in 1905 and then played for Third Lanark before moving to Hamilton Academical. By the time he arrived at Hamilton's Douglas Park he was in the twilight of his career, but played a key role as an example to the club's younger players. He made eight Scottish League and Cup appearances for the club, scoring the first of his two goals on debut against Morton in December 1908. By 1917 McLuckie had become a Sergeant with the Canadian Army, and following his discharge he resided, ironically, in another Hamilton - Ontario's variant. From there he moved to New York, where illness overtook him and an operation became necessary. This proved unsuccessful and sadly he passed away in hospital in 1923 at the age of 45

McLUCKIE, Jimmy

Wing-half

Born: *Stonehouse, Scotland* Died: 1986
Playing career: *Manchester City, Aston Villa, Ipswich Town (1933-1945)*

He began his career at Manchester City and then moved to Aston Villa in 1934. After only 15 appearances in two years at the club, he then signed for Ipswich. He was rewarded by becoming the first captain of Ipswich's full-time professional era and went on to play 100 games in east Anglia. Retiring in 1945, McLuckie worked as a reserve-team coach (enjoying a late emergency appearance after winger Geoff Fox was injured in the dressing room before an FA Cup match), then became manager of Clacton Town. He later worked for the Football Association before his death in 1986.

McMAHON, Pat

Midfielder

Born: *Croy, North Lanarkshire, Scotland*
Playing career: *Celtic, Aston Villa, Portland Timbers, Colorado Caribous, Atlanta Chiefs (indoor), Portland Timbers (1967-1982)*

The midfielder moved to Aston Villa in 1969 under ex-Celt Tommy Docherty who managed to get him on a free. However, his subsequent career with Aston Villa was mostly low-key, and likely indicates that the other youth players at Celtic at the time (which included the highly regarded Quality Street Gang) were better prospects, so in retrospect the Celtic coaches made the right decision to move him on for the benefit of the first team. He later moved to the US and after spells as a player with Portland Timbers and Colorado Caribous, he became a coach/assistant manager with the Atlanta Chiefs. McMahon still lives in America, working as a partner in a company supplying aluminum to industry.

McMAHON, Steve

Midfielder

Born: *Halewood, Liverpool*
Playing career: *Everton, Aston Villa, Liverpool, Manchester City, Swindon Town, (1979-1998).*

McMahon signed for Villa in 1983 for £175,000 and quickly established himself at the heart of midfield as a spiky and tenacious player. As well as Villa, he played for Everton, Manchester City and Swindon Town, where he was to become coach.

STEVE McMAHON
ASTON VILLA

After winning promotion with the Wiltshire side, he repeated the same feat at his next managerial stop - Blackpool. He later had a short-lived spell as manager of Perth Glory in Australia before returning home to sign a contract with ESPN to become a TV pundit. The former England international is also involved with Ormskirk based 'Bootroom Academies' who offer coaching and training courses to develop football skills in boys and girls aged 5-13 years.

McMORRAN, Jimmy

Winger

Born: *1942*
Playing career: *Aston Villa, Walsall*

Former Villa, Walsall and Swansea winger McMorran made 14 appearances for the claret and blue, scoring once, in four seasons. He went on to manage Darlaston in three different spells, including winning the FA Vase as boss in 1991/92. Also worked as a PE teacher in Essex after leaving the game.

"DID YOU KNOW?"

"Villa were the first British club to give up a shirt sponsorship fee and promoted Axorns Children's Hospice charity beween 2008/2010 instead."

McNAUGHT, Ken

Centre-back
Born: *Kirkcaldy, Scotland*
Playing career: *Everton, Aston Villa, WBA, Manchester City, Sheffield United. (1974-1985)*
Became Dunfermline coach then worked in the Pro Shop at the famous Gelneagles Golf Course and then worked in a mine in Western Australia. Having returned from 'Oz' Ken McNaught now lives is Dickens Heath, Solihull. McNaught's links with Aston Villa, where he achieved so much success, continue with involvement in corporate hospitality on match days, in addition to local radio, television work and playing in charity matches for the Villa Old Stars. His career hit its zenith during McNaught's six seasons in claret and blue as he was influential in the team winning the League, European Cup and European Super Cup (in which he scored). McNaught and his compatriot John McGovern are the only Scottish men to win the European Cup and never be rewarded with a senior cap.

McPARLAND, Peter

Striker
Born: *Newry, County Down, Northern Ireland*
Playing career: *Dundalk, Aston Villa, Wolverhampton Wanderers, Plymouth Argyle, Worcester City, Toronto Inter-Roma, Peterborough United, Worcester City, Atlanta Chiefs, Glentoran (1951-1971)*
McParland holds a unique place in English football history as the first player in the game to score in and win both English major domestic knockout Finals.

One of the club's greatest post-war goalscorers, he became best known for a controversial incident in the FA Cup final of 1957 when he shoulder-barged United keeper Ray Wood leaving him unconscious and with a broken cheekbone. He was manager of Glentoran and the Hong Kong national team and also scored five goals ifor Norther Ireland in the 1958 World Cup as his country reached the quarter finals - making him the highest scoring Northern Irish player in World Cup finals history.

MELLBERG, Olof

Centre-back
Born: *Gullspang, Sweden*
Playing career: *Gullspangs IF, Degerfors IF, AIK, Racing Santander, Aston Villa, Juventus, Olympiacos, Villarreal, Copenhagen (1994-2014)*
As well as spells with Juventus and Greek side Olympiacos, Mellberg turned out 232 times for Villa as a versatile defender. He played for Sweden in two World Cups and four European Championships and is a former captain of the national team. Mellberg ended his international career with 117 caps and eight goals to his name. He is the current manager of Danish First Division side Fremad Amager. Also had a spell as boss of IF Bromma in his native homeland.

"DID YOU KNOW?"

"Brad Friedel was 40 years 4 days when he broke the record for oldest player in 2011."

Ken McNaught

MERSON, Paul

Winger/Attacking Midfielder/Second Striker
Born: *Harlesden*
Playing career: *Arsenal, Brentford, Middlesbrough, Aston Villa, Portsmouth, Walsall (1985-2006)*

Although 'Merse' may be better known to the outside world for his time with Arsenal, he has stated that his time at Villa was the best of his career. Having scored on his debut following a £6.75 million move from the Gunners, he went on to make over 100 appearances including the FA Cup final in 2000. The likeable Londoner then moved down to the south coast to play for Portsmouth and was a key reason for their promotion back to the Premiership despite being well into his 30's by then. He later played one game for Tamworth and managed Walsall for two seasons between 2004 and 2006. Merson is now a regular pundit on Sky Sports, and can be seen on Gillette Soccer Saturday. He has also turned out for the England Legends side.

MILLINGTON, Charlie

Outside-right
Born: *Lincoln* Died: 1945
Playing career: *Grantham Town, Ripley Athletic, Aston Villa, Fulham, Birmingham (1901-1920)*

Known for his pace, Millington joined Villa in the 1905 close season and the following campaign he played regularly, scoring seven goals in 29 appearances. Moving on to Fulham and Birmingham and finished his career as player/coach of Stourbridge. After retirement he worked as a taxi driver.

MILNE, Vic

Defender
Born: *Aberdeen, Scotland* Died: 1971
Playing career: *Aberdeen, Aston Villa (1920-1929)*

Dr Vic Milne played junior football for Aberdeen Boys Brigade and Aberdeen City Boys, before playing for junior club Strath in 1914 and Aberdeen University in 1915. The son of Aberdeen's first Chairman, Baillie Milne, he joined Scottish First Division Aberdeen in 1920. He became a regular in the Dons first eleven over the next three seasons, scoring seven goals in 122 appearances, before he signed for Aston Villa in May 1923, retaining his amateur status. In his first season at Villa, he played in 1924 FA Cup Final at Wembley, where they were beaten 2-0 by Newcastle United. His only goal for Villa came in a 2-1 win against Notts County at Villa Park in September 1925. He played his last match for Villa in April 1929 at Leicester City and retired from playing in May 1929. Having qualified as a Doctor of Medicine while still playing for Aberdeen, he served Aston Villa as their club doctor from 1930 to 1933.

MILOSEVIC, Savo

Striker
Born: *Bijeljina, SFR Yugoslavia*
Playing career: *Partizan Belgrade, Aston Villa, Real Zaragoza, Parma, Espanyol, Celta Vigo, Osasuna, Rubin Kazan (1992-2008)*

Villa manager Brian Little signed Milosevic for the claret and blue in 1995 for a then club record £3.5m from FK Partizan. The Serbian spent three years in England and was quickly coined "Miss-a-lot-evic" owing to frequent barren runs in front of goal. Despite this criticism, Milosevic was fairly prolific and scored in the 1996 League Cup final. Over the course of his almost two decade long professional playing career, Milošević boasted an impressive strike rate of over 300 goals in nearly 700 games . He played 102 times for Yugoslavia (now Serbia), and appeared in three major tournaments for his country - the 1998 FIFA World Cup, Euro 2000 and 2006 World Cup in Germany. He is currently the manager of Serbian giants FK Partizan, the club he served with distinction as a player.

MITCHELL, Andy

Defender
Born: *Rotherham*
Playing career: *Aston Villa, Chesterfield, Boston United, Belper Town (1993-1998)*

He played in the Chesterfield side that had a shock run to the FA Cup semi finals in 1997. Never featured for the Villa first team before he moved on to the Spireites. He also turned out once for Boston United and played for Belper whom he later coached.

MITCHELL, Archie

Centre-half
Born: *Smethwick* Died: 1949
Playing career: *Oldbury St John's, Aston Villa, QPR, Brentford (1905-1922)*

Mitchell, a centre half, had been with Aston Villa as a 20 year old in 1905 without making a first team appearance, albeit he won England junior international honours. Joined Southern League Queen's Park Rangers in the summer of 1907. A further Southern League Division One title was won in 1911-12, with the Charity Shield being lost 2-1 to Football League Division One champions Blackburn Rovers. He appeared seven times for The Southern League XI, and once, in 1921, for The Football League. He remained with Queens Park Rangers through to 1921 before signing for Watford. He moved to Brentford as player-manager before hanging up his boots and continuing as Brentford boss. He subsequently became QPR manager between 1931 and 1933. He worked as a schoolteacher after he left football.

MOONEY, Tommy

Striker
Born: *Middlesbrough*
Playing career: *Aston Villa, Scarborough, Southend United, Watford, Birmingham City, Stoke City (loan), Sheffield United (loan), Derby County (loan), Swindon Town, Oxford United, Wycombe Wanderers, Walsall, UD Marbella (1989-2009)*

Middlesbrough-born Mooney began his professional career at Aston Villa, but was released in 1990 by Graham Taylor without ever playing for the first team. Mooney has scored in each of England's four professional divisions, and went on to have a journeyman career for 13 different teams having left Villa. As of 2018, he returned to Villa Park to work as a coach where his son is a member of the Academy.

A striker by trade, his committed style of play made him a firm favourite with football fans, and he made an impact at Scarborough, Watford and Birmingham City.

MOORE, Isaac

Left-half/Forward
Born: *Dundee, Scotland* Died: 1954
Playing career: *Dundee Our Boys, Lincoln City, Aston Villa, Newcastle West End, Lincoln City, Burton Wanderers, Swindon Town (1889-1896)*

Moore's solitary season in the Midlands proved merely a footnote on his whistlestop tour of England's lower leagues. He plied his trade as a left-half and forward, and scored three goals from six appearances. Moore had two spells at Lincoln, during the second of which he was the club's top scorer with 16 in league and cup. Moore also turned out for Newcastle West End, Burton Wanderers and Swindon. After retirement, Moore worked in a cotton factory. His grandson, Thomas Moore, also played for the claret and blue.

MOORE, Stefan

Forward
Born: *Birmingham*
Playing career: *Romulus, Aston Villa, Chesterfield (loan), Millwall (loan), Leicester City (loan), QPR, Port Vale (loan), Walsall, Kidderminster Harriers, Silhill, Halesowen Town, St Neots Town, Leamington, Brackley Town (dual registration), Brackley Town, Leamington, Solihull Moors (1998-2014)*

Once lauded as one of the most promising, young English players in the Premier League, the former Villa yougster Stefan Moore has almost fallen off the face off the football world. He nows plays his football for Highgate United in the Midland League Premier Division. From a player who promised so much in his youth, it has been a quite spectacular fall from grace. Moore first appeared on football fans' radars when he scored a hat-trick and captained Aston Villa to a FA Youth Cup Final win in 2002. Both Moore and his brother Luke, appeared to be destined for great things. Moore went on to make fourteen more appearances in that season before a knee injury curtailed his progress. On his return from injury, Moore struggled to establish himself in the Villa side and had loan spells at Millwall and Leicester City. With first team football out of his reach at Villa, Moore moved on a free transfer to QPR in 2005.

MORALEE, Matt
Inside-forward
Born: *Barnburgh, Yorkshire* Died: 1991
Playing career: *Ormsby United, Denaby United, Gainsborough Trinity, Grimsby Town, Aston Villa, Leicester City (1934-1939)*

Moralee arrived at Division 1 side Aston Villa in October 1936 where he played in 12 games scoring one goal. In November 1937, he moved to Leicester City who had just been promoted to Division 1. Scoring six goals, he played in 43 league and cup matches for them before the outbreak of the war. He was the son of The Wednesday and Doncaster Rovers player, also called Matt Moralee.

MORGAN, Sammy
Forward
Born: *Belfast, Northern Ireland*
Playing career: *Port Vale, Aston Villa, Brighton & Hove Albion, Cambridge United, Sparta Rotterdam, FC Groningen, Gorleston (1970-1980)*

Morgan began his footballing career in Norfolk with Gorleston FC before playing professionally with Port Vale, Aston Villa, Brighton and Cambridge. He was also academy director of Ipswich Town FC and spent two years in Holland playing for Sparta Rotterdam and Groningen FC.

He earned 18 caps at international level for Northern Ireland and went on to manage Gorleston. Now aged 72, Morgan still works in football as head of youth at Ipswich Town. He was diagnosed with stomach cancer in 2014 but after two operations he's happily recovered.

MORLEY, Tony
Winger
Born: *Ormskirk*
Playing career: *Preston North End, Burnley, Aston Villa, West Bromwich Albion, Birmingham City, West Bromwich Albion, Burnley. (1972-1988).*

He played in the Football League for Preston North End, Burnley, Aston Villa, West Bromwich Albion and Birmingham City, as well as playing for other teams abroad. A skilful, nippy winger regarded as a flawed geniud, Morley also won six caps for England. Morley was a key man for Villa during their glory years in the early 1980s, winning the First Division title in 1980/81, the European Cup and the Super Cup. Morley is now a regular on the 'Villa Old Stars' circuit. He also provides commentary for radio broadcasts on Aston Villa's website and works coaching kids in the West Midlands.

Tony Morley (on the right)

MORRIS, Sam
Wing-half
Born: *Handsworth* Died: 1969
Playing career: *Aston Villa, QPR, Birmingham, Bristol Rovers, Brentford, Maidstone United (1906-1921)*

A wing-half (midfielder in today's parlance), signed for Villa having plied his trade in the local amateur leagues. However he never made an appearance for the club in the 1906/07 season and soon departed the club. Turned out for QPR, Birmingham, Bristol Rovers and guested for Clapton Orient and Brentford during WW1. He dropped into non league football with Maidstone United. Morris served as a private with the Duke of Cambridge Middlesex Regiment during the war. Morris died in Paddington, London in December 1969, aged eighty-three.

MORT, Thomas
Defender
Born: *Kearsley* Died: 1967
Playing career: *Kearsley St. Stephens, Newton Lads Club, Lancashire Fusiliers (wartime), Altrincham, Rochdale, Aston Villa (1922-1935)*

Villa stepped in for Lancashire born left back Tom Mort's signature in April 1922 for a £1,300 transfer fee. Mort stayed at Aston Villa for the next 13 seasons, and along with Tommy Smart was part of a defensive tandem known for Villa as "Death and Glory." Although never an ever present, he scored twice in 368 appearances through to his eventual retirement in May 1935, having played his final match for Villa in January that year. He was capped 3 times for England. In retirement, Mort continued to work at Villa as a coach and board member. He died in 1967.

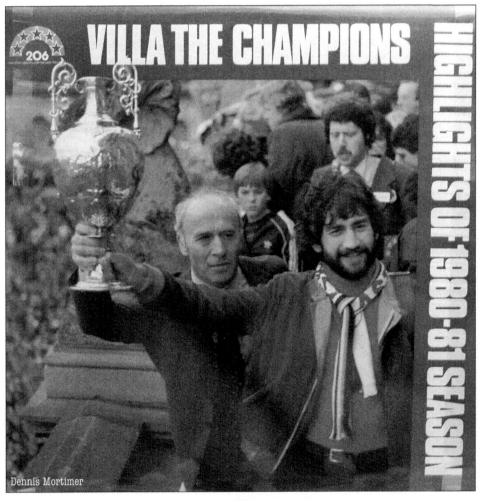

Dennis Mortimer

MORTIMER, Dennis
Midfielder
Born: *Liverpool*
Playing career: *Coventry City, Aston Villa, Sheffield United (loan), Brighton & Hove Albion, Birmingham City, Redditch United (1969-1987)*

Mortimer was captain of the team which achieved a feat that even the most ardent Villa supporter could not have envisaged when winning the European Cup in 1982. He was also skipper and driving force of the side who, 12 months earlier, had become Football League champions for the first time since 1910. Those achievements alone make him one of the greatest players in Villa history, although he served the club for rather longer than two glorious seasons, having made more than 400 appearances during a decade in claret and blue.
Signed from Coventry City for £175,000 on Christmas Eve 1975, the forceful midfield made an immediate impact on his debut against West Ham on Boxing Day, helping Villa to a 4-1 victory over West Ham. Mortimer left Villa to join Brighton in 1985 and by the time he retired two years later he had amassed more than 700 appearances for his various clubs.

MORTIMER, Paul
Midfielder
Born: *Kensington*
Playing career: *Farnborough Town, Aston Villa, Crystal Palace, Brentford (loan), Charlton Athletic, Bristol City (1986-2001)*

After his playing career, Mortimer held coaching roles with Wimbledon, Arsenal, Torquay United and Brentford, the latter two appointments being as first team coach under Leroy Rosenior, with whom he played at Fulham and Bristol City He served as coach of the Sierra Leone national team for two matches in 2007, again under Rosenior. Later in 2007, Mortimer returned to Charlton Athletic to coach the club's women's team. Since 2009 he has been working for "Show Racism the Red Card" as a coach and educational worker in schools across the southand south east.

MORTON, Harry
Goalkeeper
Born: *Chadderton, Lancashire* Died: 1974
Playing career: *Villa, Everton, Burnley (1930-1940)*

Morton worked his way up from local amateur leagues and embarked on national service before he was spotted by Villa playing in Germany. After a trial with Villa, he joined the club and soon became first choice stopper and helped Villa to second place in the league and the FA Cup semi finals. Although consistently impressive, he never earned a call up for England. Morton moved to Everton and made 27 appearances in two seasons before his career was ended by the outbreak of WW2 shortly after his move to Burnley. After retiring, he held a series of manual labour jobs before he died aged 65 in 1974.

MOSELEY, Graham
Goalkeeper
Born: *Manchester*
Playing career: *Blackburn Rovers, Derby County, Aston Villa (loan), Walsall (loan), Brighton & Hove Albion, Cardiff City (1971-1988)*

Beginning as an apprentice at Blackburn Rovers, Moseley also played for Derby County, Aston Villa, Walsall, Brighton & Hove Albion and Cardiff City. He played in both games of the 1983 FA Cup final for Brighton against the team he supported, Manchester Utd and made three appearances for Villa when on loan from Derby. Moseley, a goalkeeper, has since sold caravans and owns properties in Brighton. He now works as a delivery driver for the post office in Chepstow, Wales.

MOSS, Amos
Defender
Born: *Birmingham* Died: 2004
Playing career: *Aston Villa (1945-1956)*

He played over 100 times for Villa as a defender, scoring five goals. A one club man, he represented the claret and blue for eleven years before retiring to run a sports centre in Walsall. His father Frank also played for Aston Villa and England between 1910 and 1914. Upon retirement, Moss worked as a receptionist for an electrical company in Walsall. He died in 2004 aged 34. His brother Frank was also a professional footballer who donned the famous claret and blue.

MOSS, Arthur

Half-back
Born: *Crewe* Died: 1964
Playing career: *Crewe Central, Willaston White Star, Crewe Alexandra, Whitchurch, Aston Villa, Bristol City, Runcorn (1909-1924)*

A half back, he made over 220 Football League appearances in the years before and after the First World War. Moss was initially trained as a joiner, but later worked at the Crewe locomotive works for the London and North Western Railway as a locomotive fitter. He also played football and was taken on by Crewe Alexandra in the Birmingham & District League. Later, he played for Aston Villa F.C. and then Bristol City. After retiring from professional football, he continued to work as a fitter at the Crewe locomotive works, which was now owned by the London, Midland and Scottish Railway. After retirement he moved to Pembrokeshire, and then Wiltshire, where he died in 1964.

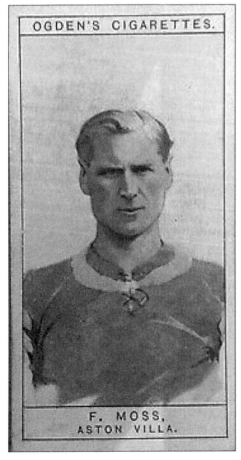

OGDEN'S CIGARETTES.

F. MOSS,
ASTON VILLA.

MOSS, Frank

Defender
Born: *Aston* Died: 1997
Playing career: *Wolverhampton Wanderers, Sheffield Wednesday, Aston Villa (1935-1954)*

Birmingham-born Moss began his career at local outfit Aston Manor before joining Southern League side Walsall in 1912. Two years later, Moss made the short hop across town to Aston Villa before his career was put on hold when official competition was suspended for the duration of the war. By the end of the 1919/20 season, Moss had made 18 appearances in all competitions and was part of the side that beat Huddersfield Town 1-0 to lift a record-breaking sixth FA Cup on 24 April 1920. He also earned six caps for England. When Moss finally left Villa Park to join Cardiff City in January 1929, he had played 281 games in all competitions and scored eight goals. He had also become one of the most popular and highly-respected captains in the club's history. An ageing Moss would play five times for Cardiff during the latter part of the 1929/30 season, before finally calling time on his career after spells at local amateur clubs Bromsgrove Rovers and Worcester City. He enlisted in the war effort and also ran a holstery in Worcester. Moss died in 1965 aged 70.

MOUNTFIELD, Derek

Defender
Born: *Liverpool*
Playing career: *Tranmere Rovers, Everton, Aston Villa, Wolverhampton Wanderers, Carlisle United, Northampton Town, Walsall, Scarborough. (1980-1999)*

After appearing in just nine out of 40 First Division games for Everton in 1987–88, a £400,000 fee took him to newly promoted Aston Villa in June 1988. He was a regular in the Villa defence for the next three years, helping secure their First Division survival in 1988–8 but fell out of favour under Ron Atkinson and moved on to Everton. Having retired, Mountfield went on to manage former club Scarborough and then York City. He is a member of the PE staff at Pensby High School, a Specialist Sports College on the Wirral, an ambassador for the North West Special Olympics and also works for the Everton former players' foundation. (https://twitter.com/degsymount)

Derek Mountfield

MULDOON, Tommy
Midfielder/Defender
Born: *Athlone, Ireland* Died: 1989
Playing career: *Athlone Town, Aston Villa, Tottenham Hotspur, Walsall (1919-1931)*
A defender/midfielder, Muldoon started out playing in the League of Ireland for Athlone Town, winning the FAI Cup in his final season. Played for Ireland in the 1924 Paris Olympics, earning five caps in total. He signed for Aston Villa the same year and went on to play 34 games for the club across a three year stint in the Midlands. Muldoon moved on to Spurs and Walsall where he played 50 games and served with the Prince of Wales Leinster Regiment in British India.

MULRANEY, Jock
Outside-right
Born: *Wishaw, Scotland* Died: 2001
Playing career: *Celtic, Dartford, Ipswich Town, Birmingham City, Shrewsbury Town, Kidderminster Harriers, Aston Villa, Cradley Heath (1933-1952)*
A diminutive winger with considerable pace and trickery, Mulraney's stint with Villa came towards the end of his football career. Unable to break through into the senior team at Celtic, he played for several Football League clubs and at non league level both north of the border and in England. He served in the RAF during WW2 as a PT instructor, then becoming a flight sergeant. Mulraney later tried his hand at management, with Birmingham & District League side Cradley Heath as player/boss, then with divisional rivals Brierley Hill Alliance. Died 2001.

MURRAY, Jimmy
Forward
Born: *Benwhat, Scotland*
Died: 1933
Playing career: *St Augustine's, Benwhat Heatherbell, Ayr, Aston Villa, Small Heath, Watford, Kettering, Wellingborough, Kings Heath Albion (1897-1905)*
Described as "fast, with good ball control and can shoot excellently", Murray began his career in the lower leagues in Scotland. In 1901 he joined the reigning champions Aston Villa but was on the move again after only one appearance. He didn't go far however, joining fierce derby rivals Small Heath (now Birmingham City) after seven months at Villa. Later played for Southern League Watford and ended his career with Kettering and Wellingborough. He also turned out for the Scotland Juniors international team. He died in Glasgow in 1933 at the age of 53.

MURRAY, Scott
Winger
Born: *Aberdeen, Scotland*
Playing career: *Fraserburgh, Aston Villa, Bristol City, Reading, Bristol City, Cheltenham Town (loan), Yeovil Town, Bath City (1990-2012)*
Currently the kit man at former club Bristol City. During his three years at Villa Park, Murray failed to make a big impression and made only four league appearances in that time. He was signed by Bristol City from Aston Villa in December 1997 and was City's top scorer in the 2002–03 season. Went on to play for Reading, City for a second time, Cheltenham Town, Yeovil and Bath. Also worked as a coach at Ashton Gate and earned a solitary cap for the Scotland B team in 2004.

MWILA, Freddie

Midfielder

Born: *Kasama, Northern Rhodesia*
Playing career: *Wusakile Youth Club, Rhokana United, Atlanta Chiefs, Aston Villa F.C., Rhokana United, Atlanta Chiefs, Rhokana United, Atlanta Apollos, Ndola United (1960-1977)*

The first Zambian to play for Aston Villa, Mwila featured only once for the first team during his time at Villa Park. He also played for Rhokana United and Atlanta Chiefs before becoming a manager. His management career was longer than his playing one, taking charge of 12 different sides including his native Zambia - whom he also represented as a player - and Botswana national teams. Mwila lives in Lusaka, where he got involved with farming. He had six children, several of whom have inherited his football ability.

MYERSCOUGH, Bill

Inside-forward

Born: *Bolton*
Died: 1977
Playing career: *Ashfield, Walsall, Aston Villa, Rotherham United, Coventry City, Chester, Wrexham, Macclesfield Town (1954-1967)*

A late bloomer, Myerscough did not enter the world of professional football until the relatively veteran age of 24. A 5ft 9 neat and tidy centre forward, he played in and won the 1957 FA Cup final with Villa. Spent four years in claret and blue with that cup win the undoubted high point.

His career took in Rotherham United, Coventry, Chester, Wrexham and Macclesfield, boasting an impressive goals to games ratio throughout. Myerscough retired in 1969 and went on to become a pub owner and shop keeper.

MYHILL, Boaz

Goalkeeper

Born: *Modesto, California, United States*
Playing career: *Aston Villa, Stoke City (loan), Bristol City (loan), Bradford City (loan), Macclesfield Town (loan), Stockport County (loan), Hull City, West Bromwich Albion, Birmingham City (loan) (1994-2012)*

US-born Myhill joined Aston Villa at the age of 12 and signed his first professional contract with Villa six years later. After a series of loan moves, he represented Bradford City, Macclesfield, Stockport, Hull, West Brom - where he vied with long term friend and rival Ben Foster for the gloves - and Birmingham. He also earned 19 caps for Wales. As of 2019, the former custodian works back at his former employers, plying trade at the Hawthorns as WBA's lead goalkeeping coach.

"DID YOU KNOW?"

"In 1897, Villa became only the second side to achieve the league and cup double."

NEAL, John
Defender
Born: *Seaham, County Durham*
Died: 2014
Playing career: *Hull City, Swindon Town, Aston Villa, Southend United. (1949-1965).*

A defender, he had seven seasons in the Football League with Hull City and then joined King's Lynn before moving to Swindon. A tough tackling full-back, Neal's career hit a zenith when he signed for Aston Villa in 1959, with whom he won the Football League Second Division championship and promotion to the Football League First Division. He was part of the team to win the inaugural Football League Cup a year later. He joined Southend United in November 1962. He was appointed manager at Wrexham in 1968 and went on to become boss of Middlesbrough and then Chelsea, for whom he also later worked as a scout. He died in 2014 after a battle with dementia.

NELSON, Fernando
Right-back
Born: *Porto, Portugal*
Playing career: *Salgueiros, Sporting Lisbon, Aston Villa, FC Porto, Vitoria Setubal, Rio Tinto (1990-2005)*

Fernando Nelson de Jesus Vieira Alves told Villa fans to "just call me Nelson" when Brian Little bought him from Sporting Lisbon. Stayed in the Midlands from 1996 to 1999 before heading home for four campaigns with Porto and then moving to Vitoria de Setubal. Capped ten times by the Portugal senior side. Despite his unfamiliar surroundings, Nelson enjoyed two impressive Premier League campaigns in the Midlands and played 75 games across all competitions, later returning to his native homeland. He went on to become president of his last club Rio Tinto and also worked in the political spectrum.

NIBLO, Tom
Left winger/forward
Born: *Dunfermline, Scotland* Died: 1933
Playing career: *Newcastle United, Aston Villa, Nottingham Forest, Watford, Newcastle United, Middlesbrough (loan), Aberdeen (1898-1908)*

A versatile centre forward who could play in all five attacking roles, Niblo joined Villa from Newcastle in 1902. He served in the British Armed Forces during the First World War and also had a brief stint as player/manager of Hebburn Argyle. Died in 1933.

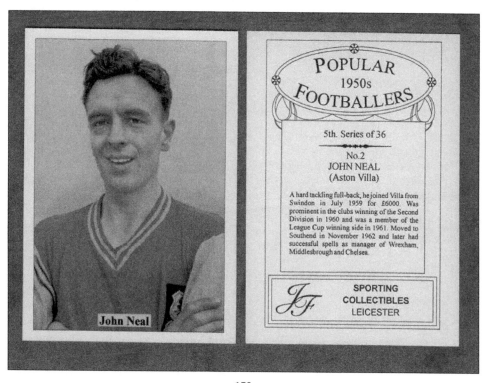

John Neal

POPULAR 1950s FOOTBALLERS

5th. Series of 36

No.2
JOHN NEAL
(Aston Villa)

A hard tackling full-back, he joined Villa from Swindon in July 1959 for £6000. Was prominent in the clubs winning of the Second Division in 1960 and was a member of the League Cup winning side in 1961. Moved to Southend in November 1962 and later had successful spells as manager of Wrexham, Middlesbrough and Chelsea.

SPORTING COLLECTIBLES LEICESTER

NIBLOE, Joe
Full-back
Born: *Corkerhill, Scotland*
Died: 1976
Playing career: *Shawfield Juniors, Rutherglen Glencairn, Glencairn Green, Kilmarnock, Aston Villa, Sheffield Wednesday (1924-1939)*
One of only three players to have won the FA Cup in both England and Scotland - for Kilmarnock and then later Sheffield Wednesday. He earned eleven Scotland caps and also played twice for the Scottish League. He signed for Villa for £1800 and played for two seasons before moving to Hillsborough. Won the FA Cup in 1935 and retired from playing upon the outbreak of WW2, working in a Stockbridge munitions factory and steelworks during the conflict. Nibloe died aged 72 in Doncaster.

NICHOLL, Chris
Centre-back
Born: *Wilmslow*
Playing career: *Burnley, Halifax Town, Luton Town, Aston Villa, Southampton, Grimsby T. (1965-1984).*
Captained Villa to victory in the 1977 League Cup final against Everton, secured at the second attempt after a replay. 210 league appearances, eleven goals. He earned 51 caps for Northern Ireland, and later went on to manage Southampton and Walsall. He also served as assistant boss alongside Laurie McMenemy for Northern Ireland and also was number two at Grimsby. Played in the 1979 League Cup final for Saints and is infamous for creating a piece of unwanted history when he scored all four goals in a 2-2 draw between Villa and Leicester in 1976. Now living in Walsall, this former favourite is suffering from dementia and needs assisted living. He has previously stated that regular heading of the ball during his career had contributed to its onset.

NICHOLSON, Joe
Wing-half/Centre-forward
Born: *Ryhope*
Died: 1974
Playing career: *Clapton Orient, Cardiff City, Aston Villa (1919-1927)*
Sunderland born wing half Joe Nicholson joined Second Division Clapton Orient in 1919 from Ryhope Colliery making his Football League debut that September at Fulham.

He scored four goals in 147 games for Clapton Orient before transferring to First Division Cardiff City in 1924, where he soon established himself in the first eleven and played in their 1925 losing FA Cup Final team, narrowly beaten at Wembley 1-0 by Sheffield United. He scored an impressive 14 goals in 55 games for Cardiff and after two seasons in Wales he joined Aston Villa in the summer of 1926. However he played only one game for Aston Villa, a 4-0 defeat at Newcastle United on the opening day of the 1926-27 season, before joining non league Bangor City. He subsequently played for Spennymoor United in non league.

NICOLAS, Alexis
Midfielder
Born: *Westminster*
Playing career: *Aston Villa, Chelsea, Brighton & Hove Albion (loan), Brighton & Hove Albion, St Albans (2002-2007)*
Nicolas began his youth career with Aston Villa having been scouted for London Boys by the club,. A path to the first team failed to come to fruition, and he instead joined Chelsea. Played twice as the Roman Abramovic revolution gathered pace and was eventually loaned to Brighton. He signed permanently and stayed with the Albion for two years before Nicolas dropped into non league with St Albans City and Hadley. He was also a Cyprus Under 21 international. He currently works in commercial real estate investment. Nicolas has since set up his own investment company.

NIELSEN, Kent
Centre-back
Born: *Frederiksberg, Denmark*
Playing career: *Brondby IF, Aston Villa, AGF Aarhus (1980-1994)*
Currently manager of Silkeborg IF, Nielsen played for Bronshoj BK, Brondby and AGF Aarhus in his homeland as well as a two year spell at Villa where he turned out 79 times and scored four goals having signed for £500,000 under Graham Taylor in 1989. Won Euro 1992 with Denmark, for whom he earned 54 caps. Since retirement as a player, he has managed AGF Aarhus, Horsens,Brondby, Aalborg, Odense and Silkeborg.

CHRIS NICHOLL
Aston Villa

NILIS, Luc

Striker

Born: *Hasselt, Belgium*
Playing career: *Winterslag, Anderlecht,PSV Eindhoven, Aston Villa (1973-2000)*

He enjoyed a successful career in his native Belgium and, in particular, in the Netherlands with PSV Eindhoven. However, his playing days came to an end in the 2000–01 season after breaking his leg whilst with Villa. Scored on his Villa debut in an Intertoto Cup tie. Nilis currently works as striker coach at former club PSV Eindhoven - where he has also served as assistant boss and scout.

NORTON, Dave

Midfielder

Born: *Cannock*
Playing career: *Aston Villa, Notts County, Rochdale (loan), Hull City (loan), Hull City, Northampton Town, Hereford United (1981-2002)*

His career started at Aston Villa, where he began as an apprentice on leaving school in the summer of 1981, turning professional two years later. He played 44 games in five years in the Midlands, before he embarked on an extensive career in lower and non league football. Forced to retire through injury, Norton became joint manager alongside another former Villa man Nigel Spink at Forest Green Rovers. He was also boss of Gainsborough Trinity and assistant at Tamworth before he had a spell at Grantham. He later became an accountant.

O'CONNOR, James

Defender

Born: *Birmingham*
Playing career: *Aston Villa, Bournemouth (loan), Bournemouth, Doncaster Rovers, Derby County, Bristol City (loan), Walsall (1997-2014)*

An FA Youth Cup winner with the Aston Villa youth team, he had a loan spell at Port Vale before making rising to prominence with Bournemouth in the 2005–06 season. Comfortable anywhere in defence, O'Connor possesses vision, stamina and the ability to play out from the back. He was an organised and disciplined defender with a wealth of experience. Birmingham born, O'Connor has played his entire career to date in the second and third tier, and made 40 appearances in League One during the 2016/17 season.

Never played for Villa's first team despite his exploits at youth team level. Finished his playing career with Kidderminster Harriers, a club he also took of for two games as caretaker manager at the end of 2018/19.

O'DONNELL, Frank

Forward

Born: *Buckhaven, Scotland* **Died:** 1952
Playing career: *Wellesley Juniors, Celtic, Preston North End, Blackpool, Aston Villa, Nottingham Forest, Raith Rovers, Buxton (1930-1947)*

O'Donnell joined Aston Villa for £11,000 in November 1938 from Blackpool, and he scored 14 goals in 31 appearances for Villa over the remainder of the season, however the outbreak of The Second World War restricted his Aston Villa career and he only made a further three appearances for them in the 1939-40 games before the season was abandoned. After the War he joined Second Division Nottingham Forest in 1946 and also had a brief spell with Raith Rovers in 1947 before retiring from playing professionally. He then managed Cheshire County League Buxton between 1947 and until his death at only 41 years old in 1952. He was the elder brother of Hugh O'Donnell, who played for Celtic, Preston (in the same teams) and Blackpool, and also Rochdale and Halifax Town after the Second World War. O'Donnell also played six times for Scotland.

O'NEILL, Alan

Inside-forward

Born: *Leadgate*
Playing career: *Sunderland, Aston Villa, Plymouth Argyle, Bournemouth, Cambridge United (1956-1966)*

Popular inside right O'Neill played in the Football League for Sunderland, Aston Villa, Plymouth Argyle and Bournemouth. He scored twice on his claret and blue debut against fierce local rivals Birmingham City in 1960 - the first after only 20 seconds - and in later life he worked as a scout and in matchday hospitality at Sunderland. He now lives in Bournemouth. His derby debut heroics proved to be the highlight of his time at Villa Park and he moved on to Argyle two years later. Despite being virtually ever-present during his first 12 months at Home Park, he lost his place in the team and was sold to Bournemouth, where he ended his professional career. O'Neill also went on to play for Cambridge United.

OAKES, Michael

Goalkeeper
Born: *Northwich*
Playing career: *Aston Villa, Bromsgrove Rovers (loan), Gloucester City (loan), Tranmere Rovers (loan), Wolves, Cardiff City (1991-2008)*

Having started in the youth system, an injury to Mark Bosnich gave Michael Oakes his chance to impress in the first team. Oakes is also a handy league cricketer, appearing as a wicket-keeper and batsman for clubs in the Saddleworth League. Re-joined Wrexham for a third spell as their goalkeeping coach in June 2019 having spent the previous season at Walsall. Oakes was also capped five times by England's Under 21 team but never earned a senior call up.

OBI, Tony

Striker
Born: *Birmingham*
Playing career: *Aston Villa, Bristol Rovers, Oxford United, KV Oostende, KSV Roeselare (1981-1998)*

Short in both name and stature, Obi was born in Marston Green, near Birmingham, and was signed by Aston Villa from Harborne Boys. He didn't manage a first team appearance for Villa but did win an England Youth cap as a substitute in 1983. He played for both Walsall and Argyle in loan spells from Villa Park in the 1984-85 season before finally moving permanently to Bristol Rovers and then Oxford United, before finally moving to Oostende in Belgium where he later became part-owner of a bar and restaurant.

OLNEY, Ben

Goalkeeper
Born: *Holborn* Died: 1943
Playing career: *Aston Villa (1927-1930)*

A goalkeeper, Olney played 97 times for Villa between 1927 and 1930, having signed from Derby. Olney left the club to join Bilston United as player/manager after three years in the Midlands. Capped twice by England in 1928, he also played for England A and the Football League XI. Olney returned to Derby to become licensee of the Castle and Falcon, and was later licensee of the Normanton Hotel. He was employed with Rolls Royce at the time of his death.

OLNEY, Ian

Striker
Born: *Luton*
Playing career: *Aston Villa, Oldham Athletic, Kidderminster Harriers, Forest Green (1988-2001)*

Before there was Peter Crouch there was this gangly and unique looking forward in Villa's early 90s line-up. He however, didn't have that 'great touch for a big man' and despite become Oldham's record signing in 1992, he quickly fell away from the game. Olney scored 16 goals in 188 games in claret and blue and failed to convince.Following his career ending, he began training to become an Independent Financial Advisor, and is now a partner in a Lichfield based Wealth & Tax Management Company called Pro-Synergy. (http://www.pro-synergy.co.uk)

"On our way to Wembley"

ORMONDROYD, Ian

Striker

Born: *Bradford*
Playing career: *Bradford C, Oldham A, Aston Villa, Derby C, Leicester City, Hull City, Bradford City, Oldham Athletic, Scunthorpe United. (1985-1997)*

A 6ft 5in striker - known for his height and stocky build - played for Bradford City, Oldham Athletic, Derby County, Leicester City, Hull City, Scunthorpe United and spent as couple of years at Villa Park between 1989 and 1991. 56 appearances resulted in 6 goals before moving to Derby County, where his strike rate more than doubled. This prompted Leicester to break their transfer record and pay £350,000 for his services in 1992. At the age of 33, Ormondroyd retired from football due to arthritis. Since then, he has returned to Bradford City as community officer and has also worked as a commentator for Pulse FM. (You can watch an interview with Ian talking about his time at Villa - https://www.youtube.com/watch?v=H1I_W3rMGho)

Brendan Ormsby

ORMSBY, Brendan

Defender

Born: *Birmingham*
Playing career: *Aston Villa, Leeds United, Shrewsbury Town (loan), Doncaster Rovers, Scarborough, Waterford United, Wigan Athletic (1978-1995)*

A central defender, Ormsby played for Aston Villa, Leeds United, Shrewsbury, Doncaster, Waterford United (player/manager), Scarborough and Wigan. He worked as a postman in Leeds after retiring from football. Ormsby is also the honorary president of the Scarborough Branch of the Leeds United Member's Club. Between 2000 and 2012, he also worked for the Press Association, providing live by the second action from Leeds United, Bradford City and Manchester City as part of the Football Live Project. Ormsby served as First Team Manager at Pontefract Collieries from 2012 but suffered a stroke in December 2013 which left him unable to speak. An event was held to raise funds to help him and his wife Wendy who had to become his carer. This was attended by attended by members of Villa's 1982 European Cup-winning squad including Gary Shaw, Nigel Spink, Gordon Cowans, Des Bremner and Pat Heard. Former Villa manager Ron Atkinson took part along with ex-players Chris Nicholl and Steve Staunton. There is a GoFundMe page at: https://www.gofundme.com/f/brendan-amp-wendy-ormsby

Yorkshire Legends

Ian Ormondroyd on breaking through at Bradford & his time at Villa

0:00 / 11:40

OVERTON, John

Defender

Born: *Rotherham*

Playing career: *Aston Villa, Halifax Town (loan), Gillingham, Frickley Athletic (1975-1981)*

He made 195 Football League appearances for Aston Villa, Halifax Town and Gillingham. He also served Frickley Athletic as player/manager after retirement. Played three games for Villa in the 1975/76 season as a midfielder. He converted to a centre back when he signed for Gillingham, to great success. A no nonsense, "up and at em" defender, Overton was named as Player of the Season in his debut campaign for the Kent club and made 205 appearances in five years.

OZALAN, Alpay

Centre-back

Born: *Turkey*

Playing career: *Altay, Besiktas, Fenerbahce, Aston Villa, Incheon United, 1. FC Koln (1992-2007)*

He signed for Villa off the back of a superb showing for Turkey at Euro 2000 and went on to feature 66 times for the club. An impressive debut season saw him become a popular fans favourite but his partnership with Olof Mellberg was cut short with injury. Represented his country 90 times at two European Championships and the 2002 World Cup, where Turkey finished third. Ozalan was selected in the team of the tournament for the latter. Since retirement he has worked as a politician and manager of Eskisehirspor and most recently Samsunspor in his homeland.

PACE, Derek

Striker

Born: *Bloxwich*

Playing career: *Walsall Schoolboys, Bloxwich Scouts, Bloxwich Wesley, Walsall Wood, Aston Villa, Sheffield United, Notts County, Walsall (1950-1966)*

Pace was signed by Aston Villa from Bloxwich Scouts in September 1949 and almost immediately was called up to do his two years National service in the Medical Corps where he obtained the nickname "Doc". Pace was rather on the small size for a centre forward, but was hardy and tough a player as one could hope to see, a real problem for defenders to cope with, but opportunities were limited with Villa, albeit scoring on his debut in March 1951.

He came out of the Army two years later. After not getting selected for the Villa's 1957 cup final side, in the following season he played in 12 games scoring 3 goals (he played in the Charity Shield side that lost to Manchester United) before he moved to Sheffield United in December 1957 after scoring 42 league and cup goals in 106 matches. After retiring from football Pace became a sales representative for Churchfield Springs Ltd of West Bromwich. He died in October 1989.

PALETHORPE, Jack

Centre-forward

Born: *Leicester* Died: 1984

Playing career: *Maidenhead United, Reading, Stoke City, Preston North End, Sheffield Wednesday, Aston Villa, Crystal Palace (1930-1939)*

Palethorpe played for Reading, Stoke City, Preston North End, Sheffield Wednesday, Aston Villa and Crystal Palace. He was a tall Centre forward who scored 106 League goals (113 including FA Cup) in a career which lasted from 1929 to 1938, making 177 League appearances (197 in all competitions). He won the FA Cup with Sheffield Wednesday in 1935. Throughout his career, centre-forward Palethorpe had a reputation for never staying at any of his clubs for any length of time, his longest stint at any one club was two seasons and 59 league appearances in Berkshire with Reading. After leaving football he worked for the Fairey Aviation Company as a parts manufacturer.

PALIN, Leigh

Midfielder

Born: *Worcester*

Playing career: *Aston Villa, Shrewsbury Town (loan), Nottingham Forest, Bradford City, Stoke City, Hull City, Rochdale (loan), Burnley, Partick Thistle, Tadcaster Albion (1983-1993)*

He started his career with Aston Villa but never played for the senior side. Following a short loan spell with Shrewsbury Town, he moved to Nottingham Forest, where he also failed to reach the first team. Also turned out for Bradford, Stoke City, Hull, Rochdale, Burnley and Patrick Thistle. Current manager of Walkington FC in the Hull Sunday League, Leigh is also MD of LP Engineering in Durham. Palin won England Youth caps as a youngster.

PARKER, Garry

Midfielder

Born: *Oxford*

Playing career: *Luton Town, Hull City, Nottingham Forest, Aston Villa, Leicester City (1983-2001)*

Parker played notably in the Premier League for Nottingham Forest, Aston Villa and Leicester City. Parker won the League Cup with Forest in 1989 and again in 1990. He was capped by England at under-21 and B international level. After retiring from playing he has been a coach at several clubs, often working under manager Neil Lennon. In 2001, he became caretaker manager of Leicester City following the sacking of Peter Taylor, after one game in charge (a 0-6 cup defeat against Leeds United) he was relieved of his position. Having been born in the area, he was delighted to be invited to join the backroom staff as performance analyst with hometown club Oxford United in August 2019.

PARKES, Harry

Full-back

Born: *Birmingham* Died: 2009

Playing career: *Aston Villa (1939-1955)*

Parkes was a one club man having only played for Aston Villa. He is widely regarded as one of the club's most popular players of all-time. Parkes appeared for the club 345 times scoring 4 goals; plus another 144 wartime games. He missed only 12 League games in seven seasons from 1947–1954. He also sat on Aston Villa's board of directors in the 1970s. He was in line for an England call-up in 1946, but an injury meant he could not play, and he never got another chance to play for his country. His only honour with Villa was winning the League War Cup in 1944. He retired from playing football in 1955 to concentrate on his sports shop in Corporation Street, Birmingham. At one time it supplied all the boots to the Villa team. The shop closed when Parkes retired in the mid-1990s.

"DID YOU KNOW?"

"Jozef Venglos became the first foreign manager to manage a top-flight club when he joined Villa in July 1990."

PATON, Daniel

Forward

Born: *Bonhill, Scotland*

Playing career: *Aston Villa, St Bernard's (1889-1890)*

Played at amateur level for Vale of Leven and St Bernard's, in between a brief spell at Aston Villa (three games, one goal). He was also capped once by Scotland in 1896. After retirement he worked on the railways and the docks at Gourock. His older brother Robert was also a Scottish international.

PEARSON, Joe

Wing-half

Born: *Hulme End, Staffordshire* Died: 1946

Playing career: *Aston Villa (1900-1908)*

Staffordshire born wing half Joe Pearson played for Saltley College and joined Villa in 1900, making his Football League debut at Sheffield Wednesday. Initially a fringe player, he became a regular in the Villa first team from January 1903 and won the FA Cup in 1905. He lost his place in the Villa line up at the beginning of March 1906, and only made three more appearances ibefore finishing his career, having scored seven goals in 118 games. After retirement he was a coach and then physio at Villa.

Mike Pejic enjoyed a successful career at Stoke City FC

Signal Sport pundit Mike Pejic has won a Gold medal for Great Britain at the Northern Ireland Taekwondo Championships.

PEJIC, Mike

Left-back
Born: *Chesterton, Staffordshire*
Playing career: *Stoke C, Everton, Villa (1966-1980)*
He is best remembered for his time at Stoke
City between 1968-76, winning the League
Cup with the Potters in 1972. He also won
four England caps in 1974. After his playing
career finished he set up his own business
supplying fish, fruit & veg at the market in
Liverpool. In 1984 he returned to the game
as manager of Leek Town before spending
time abroad as a coach in Kuwait and then
Malaysia. It was during his stay in Kuwait
that he discovered a new passion for martial
arts and this was to lead to winning a gold
medal for Great Britain at the Northern
Ireland Taekwando Championships... at the
age of 65!

PENRICE, Gary

Striker/Attacking Midfielder
Born: *Bristol*
Playing career: *Bristol Rovers, Watford, Aston Villa,
QPR, Watford, Bristol Rovers (1984-2000)*
Since retiring Penrice has worked closley
with friend and former team mate Ian
Holloway. This has seen him be on the
coaching staff at both Bristol Rovers and
QPR, as well as becoming chief scout for
Plymouth Argyle. He had a brief spell
as head of recruitment for Leicester City
before joining Stoke City as a European
scout. Three years working with a top talent
agency who dealt with the likes of Steven
Gerrard followed. Having set up a European
division for them, he set up Gary Penrice
International Recruitment Ltd. He currently
lives in South Gloucestershire.

PETROV, Stiliyan

Midfielder
Born: *Montana, Bulgaria*
Playing career: *Celtic, Aston Villa (1995-2013)*
Petrov joined Celtic from CSKA Sofia in
1999, and won ten trophies in his time at
Celtic Park, including four Scottish Premier
League titles. In 2006, he moved to Aston
Villa, along with his former manager Martin
O'Neill. Petrov became club captain at Villa
Park, and was an inductee to the Aston
Villa Hall of Fame in 2013. In addition he is
Bulgaria's all-time most-capped player with
105 appearances for the national side.

Gary Penrice • Aston Villa

In March 2012, Petrov was diagnosed
with acute leukaemia, suspending his
football career to have treatment which was
ultimately successful. He announced his
retirement from the game in May 2013, but
began searching for a new team three years
later. Having returned to Villa Park a couple
of times in coaching capacity, he has decided
to devote his time to his family. The Stiliyan
Petrov Foundation (SPF) was established
in 2013 with the purpose to revolutionise
the way leukaemia and cancer are treated.
The foundation seeks to develop a safer,
more practical and effective process for
treatment, relapses and prevention of these
illnesses. Fijnd out more at: http://www.
thestiliyanpetrovfoundation.com/

PETTY, Ben

Defender
Born: *Solihull*
Playing career: *Aston Villa, Stoke City, Hull City,
Stafford Rangers (loan), Moor Green (loan), Burton
Albion, Moor Green, Redditch United (1994-2007)*
Petty started his career off in the youth ranks
at Aston Villa. He failed to make the grade
and joined Stoke City, then drifted into non-
league football. He worked as a coach for
the Aston Villa Academy team until 2016,
when he joined Leicester City's under 23's.

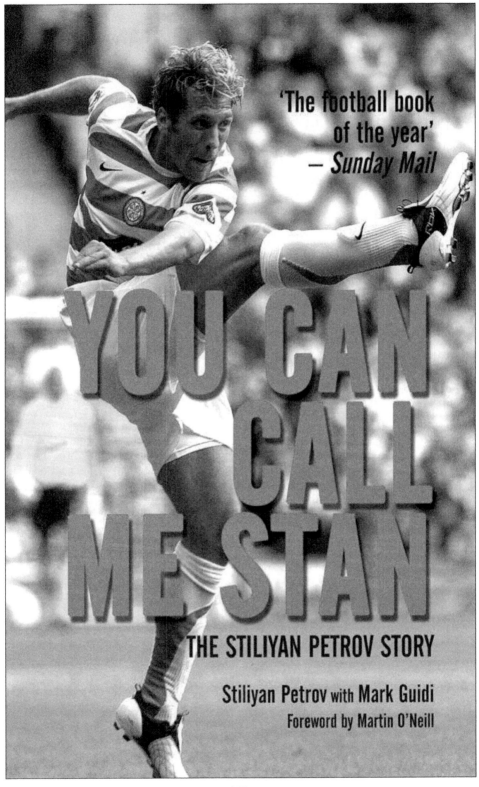

'The football book
of the year'
– *Sunday Mail*

YOU CAN CALL ME STAN

THE STILIYAN PETROV STORY

Stiliyan Petrov with Mark Guidi

Foreword by Martin O'Neill

P

PHILLIPS, Charlie
Forward
Born: *Victoria, Newport, Wales* Died: 1969
Playing career: *Wolves, Aston Villa, Birmingham, Chelmsford City (1929-1939)*
Cuthbert "Charlie" Phillips was capped twice at schoolboy level for Wales and began his football career with Ebbw Vale in 1925 before turning pro. After 65 goals in 202 appearances for Wolves, Phillips moved to Villa for a fee of £9,000 in January 1936. Despite being a Welsh international, he never really became a regular starter and moved on to Birmingham City two years later. He kept a pub after retirement, first in Wolverhampton and then in Lichfield - where he died aged 59 in 1969.

Kevin Phillips

PHILLIPS, John
Goalkeeper
Born: *Shrewsbury* Died: 31/3/2017
Playing career: *Shrewsbury Town, Aston Villa, Chelsea, Crewe Alexandra, Brighton., Charlton Athletic, Crystal Palace (1968-1983).*
The unenviable understudy, Phillips played a handful of matches for the claret and blue before he joined Chelsea for £25,000. Shrewsbury-born Phillips joined Aston Villa from his home town club in 1969 and signed for the Blues in 1971. Phillips won four caps for Wales and worked in the motor trade after retirement but died in 2017 at the age of 65 after a long illness. Both his father and grandfather played League football.

PHILLIPS, Kevin
Striker
Born: *Hitchin, Hertfordshire*
Playing career: *Watford, Sunderland, Southampton, Aston Villa, WBA, Birmingham City, Blackpool, Crystal Palace, Leicester City (1985-2014)*
Phillips was the Premier League top scorer in the 1999–2000 season with 30 goals for Sunderland, a tally which won him the European Golden Shoe. He remains the only Englishman to win the trophy. He joined Villa from the Black Cats for a fee of over £1 million in 2005 but his stay was blighted by injuries and he moved on to West Brom after only 23 appearances. Played eight times for England. Since retirement as a player, he has worked as assistant manager for Leicester, Derby and Stoke. Left the Potters in Jan 2019.

PHILLIPS, Leighton
Defender
Born: *Neath, Wales*
Playing career: *Cardiff City, Aston Villa, Swansea City, Charlton Athletic, Exeter City (1967-1983)*
Defender Leighton Phillips was something of an unsung Villa hero. The Wales international was also a versatile footballer, playing in eight different positions during the course of his 18-year career. Signed from Cardiff City for £100,000 in September 1974, Phillips won promotion in his first season at Villa Park. Although he missed the 1975 League Cup run because he was cup-tied, he was a member of the triumphant 1977 team. He played 58 times for Wales. Following his retirement, the Welshman returned 'home' to live in Neath and worked as a financial adviser.

PHOENIX, Arthur
Inside right/Right-half
Born: *Patricroft, Eccles* Died: 1979
Playing career: *Hadfield, Glossop, Birmingham, Aston Villa, Barnsley, Exeter City, Wigan Borough, Bath City, Torquay United, Mansfield Town, RC Paris, Sandbach Ramblers, Shelbourne, Colwyn Bay United, Brierley Hill Alliance, Ballymena United, Mossley (1922-1937)*

Often known as Ginger Phoenix, he was a defender who played in the Football League for Birmingham, Aston Villa, Barnsley, Exeter City, Wigan Borough, Torquay United and Mansfield Town, and in Division 1 of the French League for Racing Club de Paris. Phoenix - a much travelled, journeyman veteran, also played for clubs in Wales and Ireland and had an extensive career at non league level. He later went into coaching and also worked as a scout in the non league game.

PHYPERS, Ernie
Wing-half
Born: *Walthamstow* Died: 1960
Playing career: *Walthamstow Avenue, Aston Villa, Tottenham Hotspur, Northfleet United, Tottenham Hotspur, Doncaster Rovers (1932-1939)*

Phypers had signed for Villa as an amateur in 1932, but his registration was cancelled after four months with no professional deal offered. Phypers continued in the amateur, non league game with Walthamstow Avenue before joining Spurs. Made his Lilywhites debut in a North London derby. Phypers only significant run in the Tottenham team came between September '35 and March 1936, before he dropped back to the reserves. Two months later he moved to Doncaster where he played for a couple of years in wartime before calling it a day.

PINNER, Mike
Goalkeeper
Born: *Boston*
Playing career: *Aston Villa, Sheffield Wednesday, QPR, Manchester United, Chelsea, Swansea City, Leyton Orient, Lisburn Distillery (1952-1966)*

One of the leading amateur goalkeepers of his era, Pinner started his career at Villa and notched up over 100 appearances for League sides. He played in two Olympic Games and represented England amateur team. Combining his amateur playing career with his day job as a lawyer, he later became a property developer, living in London.

PIRES, Robert
Winger/Attacking midfielder
Born: *Reims, France*
Playing career: *Reims, Metz, Marseille, Arsenal, Villarreal, Aston Villa, FC Goa (1989-2015)*

A former France international, Pires earned 79 caps between 1996 and 2004 for his country, including winning both the 1998 FIFA World Cup and UEFA Euro 2000. Best known for his time with Arsenal, he played for Metz and Marseille in his native France and also had spells at Villarreal. A then 37-year old Pires played nine times for Villa in 2010/11, before he finished his career as player/coach of Goa. As of 2019, Pires is back in north London working with Unai Emery at Arsenal.

PLATT, David
Midfielder
Born: *Chadderton, Lancashire*
Playing career: *Manchester United, Crewe Alexandra, Aston Villa, Bari, Juventus, Sampdoria, Arsenal, Nottingham Forest (1982-2001)*

Platty built his reputation at Crewe Alexandra having been released from Manchester United by Ron Atkinson. In 1988, he signed for Aston Villa for £200,000, and in his first season at Villa Park he helped the club achieve promotion to the First Division, one season after they had been relegated. He managed Sampdoria, Nottingham Forest, Pune and the England Under-21 side. Platt served as first team coach at Manchester City between 2010 and 2013. Learning Italian helped his aclimatisation as a player but has also come in handy in recent years, no doubt helping him to secure a role as club consultant for Serie B side U.S. Citta di Palermo in December 2018.

POOLE, Kevin
Goalkeeper
Born: *Bromsgrove*
Playing career: *Aston Villa, Northampton Town, Middlesbrough, Hartlepool , Leicester C, Birmingham C, Bolton W, Derby C, Burton A (1981-2010)*

Poole, who numbers Aston Villa, Leicester City and Derby County among nine clubs he played for, was the Football League's oldest registered player when he retired aged 48 at the end of the 2011-12 season.

A veteran of more than 500 senior career appearances in the Premier League, EFL and non-league, Poole is one of the most recognised and widely-respected coaches in the Midlands. After hanging up his gloves, the Bromsgrove-born shot-stopper transitioned into coaching with Burton Albion, holding similar roles at the Blues and Derby County.At Aggborough, Poole will work not only with the club's goalkeepers but will also bring tremendous knowledge to the first-team camp in general. He had an interim spell as manager of Burton in 2012, when he retired from playing at the age of 48; however, he later re-registered himself as a player on two occasions due to goalkeeping crises at the club, making Poole one of the few players in English football ever to be registered to a professional club at the age of 50. He is currently goalkeeping coach at Derby.

POSTMA, Stefan
Goalkeeper
Born: *Utrecht, Netherlands*
Playing career: *Utrecht, De Graafschap, Aston Villa, Wolverhampton Wanderers (loan), Wolverhampton Wanderers, ADO Den Haag, De Graafschap, Ermis Aradippou, AGOVV Apeldoorn (1995-2011)*

Postma was signed by Villa for £1.5 by Martin O'Neill in 2002 but was only ever second choice. The Dutch shot stopper played 13 times for the claret and blue in four undistinguished years in the Midlands and later moved on to rivals Wolves. He then returned to his homeland where he played in the Eredivisie before hanging up his gloves. Postma was embroiled in a sex tape controversy in 2006 when his ex-girlfriend posted a video on youTube of him performing a, shall we say, reversal of normal positions. He is currently goalkeeping coach at his last club, AGOVV Apeldoorn.

POTTER, Fred

Goalkeeper
Born: *Cradley Heath*
Playing career: *Aston Villa*
Originally an inside forward, he played for local side Cradley Heath before he signed for Villa in 1959 as a goalkeeper. He made three appearances in claret and blue and then went to Doncaster and Hereford United, making over 100 appearances for the former. Potter played seven times for Villa's first team. But once Nigel Simms and Kevin Keelan had recovered, Fred found himself back in the Thirds and was released by Villa 12 months later. Potter is best known for his part in Hereford's famous giant-killing exploits over Newcastle in the 1972 FA Cup. After retirement, he worked as a goalkeeper coach at Doncaster and also for the professional players union. Now aged 79, he suffers with Parkinson's disease.

POUNTNEY, Dave

Winger/Midfielder/Defender
Born: *Baschurch, Shropshire*
Playing career: *Myddle, Shrewsbury Town, Aston Villa, Chester, Oswestry Town (1957-1979)*
A real "local hero", Dave Pountney made his debut for Shrewsbury Town in September 1957 and between 1957 and 1964 made a total of 271 appearances. In October 1963 he created history by becoming the first Shropshire born player to leave the club for a fee, joining Aston Villa for £20,000. He became a firm favourite and first team regular at Villa Park and later rejoined Shrewsbury Town, giving a further three years service. Pountney remains a well known part of the town as a successful businessman where he runs an electrical parts store. When it comes to promoting football at grass roots level, he has made an incredible contribution over the years, both coaching and running football Academies for kids in the Shropshire area.

POWELL, Ivor

Wing-half
Born: *Bargoed, Wales* Died: 2012
Playing career: *Bargoed, Barnet, QPR, Aston Villa, Port Vale, Barry Town, Bradford City (1937-1954)*
On leaving QPR for Aston Villa at the end of 1948, Powell set a record transfer fee for a half-back of £17,500. During his three years in the First Division, he made 86 appearances and was made captain in the 1949-50 season. He was one of the best British players of the era, a tactically astute, tough-tackling defender who motivated the players around him – qualities that would later make him a successful coach.Served as a PT instructor during World War 2. Powell entered the Guinness Book of Records as the world's oldest working coach on his 90th birthday after 55 years as a coach. Powell died in 2012 aged 96.

PRICE, Chris

Full-back
Born: *Hereford*
Playing career: *Hereford United, Blackburn Rovers, Aston Villa, Blackburn Rovers, Portsmouth, Dallas Sidekicks, Cinderford Town (1977-1996)*
Price was a vastly experienced full back with over 500 league appearances to his name inlcuding over 100 in claret and blue following a £150,000 transfer from Blackburn Rovers in 1968. Price managed Newport AFC and Cinderford Town before moving to Spain in 2003 where he was involved with Charlton Athletic's European Soccer School in Torrevieja. He later emigrated to Australia. Price almost died in 2011 when he was swept out to sea in Queensland and went into cardiac arrest. Luckily he was saved he was resuscitated by local lifeguards and made a full recovery.

PRICE, Haydn

Wing-half/Centre-forward
Born: *Maerdy, Wales* Died: 1964
Playing career: *Mardy Corinthians, Mardy Corinthians, Aston Villa, Burton United, Wrexham, Leeds City, Shrewsbury Town, Walsall, (1902-1919)*
Price began with his hometown team Aberdare as an amateur in 1902 before landing his move to First Division Villa two seasons later. However, things did not work out as he only sporadically featured for the reserves and never played for the senior side. Described as a "strong sprinter with good distributive ability but inaccurate shooting", Price was an extremely versatile player who could play at wing half, left wing or as a central forward. Price played five times for Wales and guested for Spurs in wartime. Price went on to manage Walsall, he had two spells as boss of Mid Rhondda and also had a brief spell as Grimsby boss. He died in 1964 aged 81.

PRICE, John
Full-back
Born: *Aberystwyth, Wales*
Playing career: *Fordhouse Youth Club, Liverpool, Aston Villa, Walsall, Shrewsbury Town (1954-1959)*
Aberystwyth-born Price signed for Liverpool in October 1954 but figured only once in the first team at Anfield. He moved on to Villa and then Walsall but never made the grade and only ever represented the reserves. He retired in 1960 and became a teacher.

PRICE, Ken
Centre-forward
Born: *Ellesmere Port*
Playing career: *West Bromborough, Aston Villa, Tranmere Rovers (1959-1962)*
He began his youth career with West Bromborough and Aston Villa, never playing a senior game for either, before he turned out for Tranmere Rovers and Hartlepool United. He was appointed as player/manager of Spalding United in 1963 where he ended his career. His career was brief, with Price only recorded as having played eleven games for two clubs at senior level, scoring five goals. After he hung up his boots, he became a car salesman in Wolverhampton.

PRITCHARD, Roy
Full-back
Born: *Dawley, Telford*
Died: 1993
Playing career: *Dawley Council School, Dawley & District Schools, Wolverhampton Wanderers, Aston Villa, Notts County, Port Vale (1941-1960)*
The one-time Bevin Boy was such a distinguised performer for Wolves across his 223 League and Cup games that his name became attached in the 1990s to their Young Player of the Year award .Pritchard guested for Mansfield, Notts County, Swindon and Walsall during the war and, after Wolves, served Aston Villa, Notts County again, Port Vale and Wellington Town.He played 27 First Division matches in 1953-54, the season Wolves won the League Championship for the first time and added the FA Cup to his honours in 1949. Pritchard died in January, 1993, aged 67. His career at the Villa never got going and he only played three times in two and a half years at Villa Park. Pritchard died in 1993 aged 67.

RACHEL, Adam
Goalkeeper
Born: *Birmingham*
Playing career: *Aston Villa, Blackpool, Northwich Victoria (loan), Moor Green (1996-2011)*
Rachel started his professional football career as a trainee with Aston Villa, turning professional in August 1996. He played once for the claret and blue in the Premier League on Boxing Day 1998 when he came on as a substitute against Blackburn Rovers after Michael Oakes had been sent off. He is currently academy coach at Southern League Premier Division side Tamworth.

RALSTON, Andrew
Winger
Born: *1880* Died: 1950
Playing career: *Watford, Southend United, Tottenham Hotspur, Aston Villa (1915-1919)*
Ralston pursued a career in insurance in London and joined the London Caledonians FC, a team for Scottish exiles based in the capital. As a trainee he had also joined Villa but did not play a match for the first team. Ralston served as Honorary Secretary of London Caledonians and the Isthmian League. He also served on the Council of the Football Association where he represented the interests of the amateur game.

RAMSAY, George

Manager

Born: *Glasgow, Scotland* Died: 1935
Playing career: *Aston Villa (1874-1882)*
Ramsay became the first secretary and
manager of Aston Villa in the most
successful period of their history. His record
of six League Championships and six FA
Cups is second only to Arsène Wenger, who
has won seven FA Cups. Ramsay joined
Villa as player/coach almost by accident,
walking past a practice match in Aston Park
in 1876 when he was asked to make up
the numbers. He signed for Villa and soon
became captain. In 1880 Ramsay led Villa to
their first trophy – the Birmingham Senior
Cup – in but his influence wasn't restricted
to the pitch. He also negotiated the purchase
of Villa's new ground at Wellington Road,
Perry Barr. He became secretary/manager
in 1884 and then honorary advisor and
vice president. The Aston Villa team of
1899 that won First Division and Sheriff of
London Charity Shield (shared with Queen's
Park). The hugely successful team Ramsay
assembled at the end of the 19th Century.

REES, Tony

Forward

Born: *Merthyr Tydfil, Wales*
Playing career: *Aston Villa, Birmingham City, P
Barnsley, Grimsby Town, West Bromwich Albion,
Merthyr Tydfil (1980-1996)*

The Welshman had started out in the Aston
Villa youth system and was part of the 1980
FA Youth Cup winning side but left without
appearing for the first team. He went on
to play nearly 300 games in the Football
League, appeared in all four divisions,
and won one full cap for Wales. Rees was
dubbed the master of the back heel. After
retirement, he owned a youth hostel and ran
a leisure centre in Swansea.

REGIS, Cyrille

Striker

Born: *Maripasoula, French Guiana*
Died: January 2018
Playing career: *West Bromwich Albion, Coventry
City, Aston Villa, Wolverhampton Wanderers,
Wycombe Wanderers & Chester-City.*
He played in the Football/Premier League
between 1977-1996 as a striker. In that time
he made 610 appearances scoring 159 goals.
He played six times for England U21s and
five times for England between 1982-87. He
later coached at West Brom but for many
years and then worked as an agent with
Stellar Football. He was awarded the MBE
in 2008 and was one of the few footballers
who is regarded as a legend at two football
clubs - West Bromwich Albion & Coventry
City where he made over 200 appearances
for both clubs. He enjoyed golf and lived in
Birmingham until he suffered a heart attack
in January 2018 and died at the age of 59.

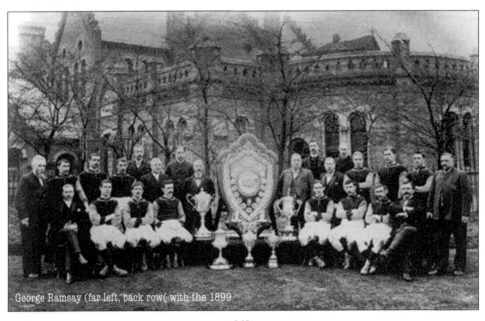

George Ramsay (far left, back row(with the 1899

REYNOLDS, Jack

Midfielder/Forward

Born: *Blackburn* Died: 1917

Playing career: *West Bromwich Albion, Droitwich Town, Aston Villa, Celtic, Southampton, Grafton F.C. (New Zealand), Stockport County (1884-1905)*

John 'Jack' Reynolds carved a unique niche in football folklore by playing full international matches for two countries – initially five times under a false identity for Ireland and then a further eight times for England after it was discovered he had been born in Blackburn. His goal against Wales in 1893 made him the only player to have scored both for and against England, a feat that can never be repeated under modern regulations. He became one of the highest-paid players of his generation and turned out for Villa before moving on to Celtic. He was a heavy gambler, drinker, frittering his money away. On retirement, Reynolds became a coal miner in Sheffield where his past caught with him and he died aged just 48 from heart failure

REO-COKER, Nigel

Midfielder

Born: *Southwark*

Playing career: *Wimbledon, West Ham United, Aston Villa, Bolton W, Ipswich Town, Vancouver Whitecaps FC, Chivas USA, Montreal Impact (1997-2015)*

A veteran journeyman player, Reo-Coker was born in London but lived his early years in Sierra Leone. He came through the youth system at Wimbledon, and had previously played for West Ham United before joining Villa for £8.5 million in July 2007 in the belief that European football was more likely with his new club. A regular starter for most of his stay and had notched up over 100 appearances before being allowed to leave at the end of his contract in 2011. He earned England caps at both Under 20 and Under 21 level, and proved a versatile utility man for his many clubs, capable of filling in at the back if needed. He captained both Aston Villa and West Ham and played in the 2006 FA Cup final. Reo - Coker is currently a free agent.

RICHARDSON, Kieran

Left winger/Left-back

Born: *Greenwich, London*

Playing career: *West Ham United, Manchester United, Sunderland, Fulham, Aston Villa (2001-2014)*

Nicknamed 'Lord Snooty' by a fanzine, Richardson looked set for a glittering career. both Manchester United and Sunderland paid big money for his signature. Roy Keane was his boss on Wearside and his subsequent role as assistant at Villa Park may have infuenced the decision to sign him for a two year stint at Villa. He has struggled to find a permanent employer ever since. Trials at several clubs including Granada in Spain have failed to generate a contract and he hasn't made a professional appearance since December 2016.

RICHARDSON, Kevin

Midfielder

Born: *Newcastle upon Tyne*
Playing career: *Montagu and North Fenham BC, Everton, Watford, Arsenal, Real Sociedad, Aston Villa, Coventry City, Southampton, Barnsley, Blackpool (loan), Blackpool (1978-2000)*

Richardson's biggest achievements at the club were leading the team to second place in the inaugural Premier League and holding aloft the Coca-Cola Cup after his man-of-the-match performance had inspired the 3-1 final triumph over Manchester United at Wembley. It was fitting that he should win a major honour in claret and blue, having helped both Everton and Arsenal to league titles earlier in his career. Richardson was an ever present for three and a half seasons before he was sold to Midlands rivals Coventry for £300,000 in 1995. Played once for England in 1994. After retirement, he took up coaching in the north east with Sunderland, Darlington and Newcastle. Richardson current works at St James Park as an academy coach.

RIDEOUT, Paul

Striker

Born: *Bournemouth*
Playing career: *Swindon Town, Aston Villa, Bari, Southampton, Notts County, Rangers, Everton, Qianwei Huangdao, Kansas City Wizards, Shenzhen Jianlibao, Tranmere Rovers (1980-2002)*

Bournemouth born striker, who spent two seasons at Southampton before losing his place to Iain Dowie. He eventually went on to play in China 1997-98 before moving to the United States in 1998 to play for the Kansas City Wizards from 1998-1999 and then had a spell in the Chinese league. After his career, Rideout returned to the United States and began coaching in the area for KCFC Alliance Soccer Club. He had obtained his USSF "B" license in January 1999 and is a permanent resident of the United States. Rideout scored 14 goals in 29 games during his time at Villa Park.

RIDGEWELL, Liam

Defender

Born: *Bexleyheath*
Playing career: *West Ham United, Aston Villa, Bournemouth (loan), Birmingham City, West Bromwich Albion, Portland Timbers, Wigan Athletic (loan), Brighton & Hove Albion (loan) (1999-2016)*

Ridgewell became the first man to transfer between the bitter derby rivals when he swapped claret and blue for St Andrew's in 2007. He was made Birmingham captain and went on to play more than 150 times for the Blues. At Villa, he was a member of the 2002 FA Youth Cup winning side and earned six caps for England U21s whilst at Villa. He moved on to another Midlands club, West Brom, then had a spell across the pond before returning to England. Ridgewell turned out for Wigan, Brighton and Hull. Having been let go by the Tigers, Ridgewell - now 35 - continues to ply his trade in League One with Southend United.

RILEY, Tom

Full-back

Born: *Blackburn* Died: 1939
Playing career: *St. Mary-ês, Chorley, Blackburn Rovers, Brentford, Aston Villa, Brentford, Southampton (1902-1907)*

Riley began his football career with Chorley in 1901 before joining hometown First Division club Blackburn Rovers in 1902. Although he made 18 appearances during 1903-04 he was a fringe player during his three seasons at Ewood Park, totalling 23 appearances for Rovers, before moving to Southern League Brentford in 1905. But late on in the 1905-06 season he was bought by First Division Aston Villa, where again he was a fringe player during the next two years, making 16 appearances before returning to Brentford in 1908. After a single season at Griffin Park he joined Southampton in 1909, but failed to make the first eleven at The Dell and subsequently retired from professional football. After he had hung up his boots, Riley worked as a bricklayer in Cheshire.

Liam Ridgewell

RIMMER, Jimmy

Goalkeeper

Born: *Southport, Lancashire*
Playing career: *Manchester U, Swansea C, Arsenal, Aston Villa, Swansea City, Luton Town (1967-1986).*

Lancashire born keeper who had already won a European Cup winner's medal with Manchester United and been named Arsenal's player of the season before arriving at Villa Park. He spent the next six seasons as first choice between the sticks and was a member of the team which won the First Division championship in 1981. His 7 minutes on the field before being injured in the European Cup final the following year was enough to earn him a second winner's medal. Now retired and living back in Swansea, Rimmer was described by the Birmingham Mail as: "probably the greatest goalkeeper Aston Villa Football Club have ever seen."

RIOCH, Bruce

Midfielder

Born: *Aldershot*
Playing career: *Luton Town, Aston Villa, Derby County, Everton, Derby County, Birmingham City, Sheffield United, Torquay United. (1964-1983).*

Bruce Rioch was the first English-born player to captain Scotland, which demonstrates the respect he commanded.

Signed for Villa from Luton Town by Tommy Docherty in 1969, Bruce steered Villa to the Third Division crown with a record points total in 1972. He is still revered by Villa fans, as was clearly evident when he attended the book launch of Encounters of the Third Kind - Aston Villa's Division 3 Odyssey. His managerial career included a season in charge of Arsenal in 1995-96. His other managerial jobs jobs have seen him appointed boss of Torquay, Seattle, Middlesbrough, Millwall, Bolton, Norwich, Wigan and Odense and Aalborg in Denmark.

RIOCH, Neil

Defender
Born: *Paddington, London*
Playing career: *Luton Town, Aston Villa, York City, Northampton Town, Plymouth Argyle (1968-1975)*

The younger brother of former Arsenal boss Bruce, is a successful businessman running Neil Rioch (Holdings) Ltd and also runs the Former Villa Players Association. He played as a defender in the Football League for Aston Villa, York City, Northampton Town and Plymouth Argyle, in the North American Soccer League for Toronto Metros and Portland Timbers. He was also on the books of Luton Town without making a league appearance. He was capped by the England national youth team in 1969.

ROBERTS, Bob

Goalkeeper
Born: *West Bromwich* Died: 1929
Playing career: *West Bromwich Strollers, WBA, Sunderland Albion, Aston Villa (1879-1893)*

He then moved to Aston Villa from West Bromwich Strollers (who were to become Albion) in April 1892, making four appearances, before hanging up his gloves. Won the FA Cup with West Brom in 1888. Also represented Birmingham FA, as well as Staffordshire FA and played three games for England. After retiring, he returned to the Newcastle area to continue his trade as a plasterer. Died in 1929.

ROBERTS, Ken

Winger
Born: *Wrexham, Wales*
Playing career: *Wrexham, Aston Villa (1951-1958)*

Roberts made his Football League debut in 1951 for Wrexham aged only 15 years, 158 days, his one and only appearance for the Welsh team. His was a record that stood for 57 years until it was broken by Reuben Noble - Lazarus in 2008. Roberts made 38 appearances and scored three goals for Villa, before he moved into management after retiring as a player. Secured promotion from Division Four with Chester, and reacher the League Cup semi finals in 1975. He later returned to the dugout as manager of Oswestry Town in 1983, spending 12 months in charge. He also coached at Wrexham and Roberts would later rejoin Chester as chief scout. He now lives in retirement in Oswestry with his wife Betty.

ROBERTS, Les

Inside-forward
Born: *Halesowen* Died: 1980
Playing career: *Aston Villa, Redditch, Bristol Rovers, Chesterfield, Sheffield Wed, Bristol Rovers, Bolton Wanderers, Swindon Town, Brentford, Manchester City, Exeter City, Crystal Palace (1920-1937)*

An inside forward, he is best remembered for his three years with Swindon Town, for whom he made 119 appearances and scored 35 goals. He started his career as an amateur at Villa and played for 18 different clubs across an expansive 16-year career. Having hung up his boots, he opened a chain of gyms in the Midlands area.

ROBERTSON, Thomas

Midfielder
Born: *1864* Died: 1924
Playing career: *Cowlairs, Aston Villa, Queen's Park,*

A Scottish midfielder, reported to be strong in the tackle and fleet of foot, who played for Cowlairs, Aston Villa, Queen's Park, St Bernard's and Scotland. He won four caps for his country and combined his three-year footballer with a job in a factory. After retiring as a player, Robertson was a football referee in both Scotland and north of the border, and became president of the Scottish Football League.

ROBINSON, Jack

Midfielder
Born: *Birmingham*
Playing career: *Aston Villa, Stoke, King's Heath Birmingham (1908-1912)*

Robinson began his career with Aston Villa before joining Stoke in 1911, although he never made a senior appearances for the club. He turned out eight times for the "Potters" before leaving to play amateur football with King's Heath Birmingham. Upon hanging up his boots, he returned to Stoke as a coach and later worked as a labourer. Died in 1923 after illness.

"DID YOU KNOW?"

"Billy Garraty became the top goalscorer in world football by scoring 27 goals in just 33 league games and a total of 30 goals in 39 league and cup games (1899–1900)."

ROBINSON, Phil

Midfielder
Born: *Stafford*
Playing career: *Aston Villa, Wolverhampton Wanderers, Notts County, Huddersfield Town, Chesterfield, Stoke City, Hereford United, (1985-2007)*
Robinson began his career as a Villa Park trainee and enjoyed relatively brief but productive spells at Wolves and Notts County before joining Huddersfield Town in 1992. During his last few years as a player, Robinson began training as a physiotherapist, and was released by Notts. County in June, 1998 to further his career in this profession, and he took up an appointment at Stoke City. After a spell at Hereford, Phil moved to manage Stafford Rangers. In 2008 he began working for Birmingham City's academy, and fulfilled the same role with Villa. Robinson currently works as international youth Scouting and Recruitment Manager at Manchester City.

ROBSON, John

Born: *Consett*
Died: 2004
Playing career: *Derby County, Aston Villa*
Robson joined Villa for £90,000 in 1972. He won the League Cup in 1975 and 1977 during his spell at Villa Park before his contract was cancelled after playing 176 matches in the claret and blue. Robson also won seven England under-23 international caps during his career as part of Brian Clough's legendary title-winning Derby County. The dependable centre-back, born in Consett, County Durham, only missed one match in the 1971-72 season when the Rams won their first of two championships in three years. But he was later displaced in the side and sold to Villa where he collected two League Cup trophies. He ran a newsagents after retiring and according to his son he was virtually penniless when he died after a battle with multiple sclerosis.

ROGERS, Kevin

Midfielder
Born: *Merthyr Tydfil, Wales*
Playing career: *Aston Villa, Birmingham City, Wrexham, Rhyl, Merthyr Tydfil (1979-1986)*
When Rogers left school in 1979, he joined Aston Villa as an apprentice, and turned professional two years later. Rogers was at the club in 1982 when they won the

European Cup but he was always on the fringes and never played a senior game for the first team. Having left Villa, he moved to derby rivals Birmingham City (nine games) and then onto Wrexham. Rogers - a box to box midfielder - played in the European Cup Winners' Cup for both Wrexham and Merthyr Tydfil and later managed his local part-time team Troedyrhiw.

ROOSE, Leigh

Goalkeeper
Born: *Holt, Wales* Died: 1916
Playing career: *Stoke, Everton, Sunderland, Celtic, Port Vale, Huddersfield Town, Aston Villa, Woolwich Arsenal (1895-1912)*
A celebrated amateur at a time when the game was played largely by professionals, Roose was renowned as one of the best players in his position in the Edwardian period. He kept goal for a number of League clubs - including Villa - and represented the Wales national team on 24 occasions. Roose served in the Royal Army Medical Corps in France and Gallipoli during the First World War in 1914. Died in 1916

ROSS, Ian

Defender
Born: *Glasgow, Scotland*
Playing career: *Liverpool, Aston Villa, Notts County, Northampton Town, Peterborough United, Wolves, Hereford United (1966-1982).*
He began his career at Liverpool before starring as captain for Aston Villa, for whom he played 175 times and scored three goals. He had joined from Sheffield Wednesday in 1972 for a fee of £60,000 and helped the club regain First Division status. A classy, solid and reliable player in his position and certainly a crowd pleaser. Ross later moved into coaching and was initially registered as player/coach at Wolves before accepting the offer of a role at his former club, Peterborough. He then widened his horizons in the same capacity in various countries abroad. Returning to England he took up roles as Assistant Manager at Hereford then as a manager in Iceland, before returning to these shores once again as Manager of Huddersfield and reserve team manager at Sunderland. Ross died in 2019 aged 72.

ROWAN, Brian
Full-back
Born: *Glasgow, Scotland*
Playing career: *Aston Villa, Toronto Metros, Watford, Morton, New York Cosmos (1969-1976)*

Active in Scotland, England, Canada and the United States, Rowan made nearly 100 appearances in a seven year career. His one and only Villa game must have put him in the shop window because even though they lost 3-0 at Watford in September 1969 he subsequently joined Watford, with the Glaswegian left-back going on to play for Toronto Metros and New York Cosmos. He remained in the USA following his retirement and became a clerk.

ROXBURGH, John
Winger
Born: *Granton, Scotland* **Died:** 1965
Playing career: *Leicester City, Aston Villa, Stoke, Sheffield United, Sheffield, (1920-1926)*

Roxborough wasa right winger who joined Villa in 1922. Capped eleven times by Scotland, he finished his career with Sheffield FC and Leicester Nomads. Later served on Leicester's board as a director.

RUTHERFORD, Joe
Goalkeeper
Born: *Fatfield* **Died:** 1994
Playing career: *Birtley Colliery, Southport, Aston Villa (1936-1952)*

County Durham born goalkeeper Rutherford played for Fatfield Juniors and after a spell with Blyth Spartans on trial in 1931 he played for Chester Moor Temperance, Ferryhill, Chester-le-Street and Birtley Colliery at amateur level. He combined his early football career with working in a quarry. He joined Southport in October 1936. Rutherford joined Aston Villa for £2,500 in February 1939 and played in 156 league and cup matches before he called it a day in 1951. During the Second World War, he played in several games as a guest, for Margate, playing one game in 1939–40, Solihull Town, Nottingham Forest, Lincoln City and Mansfield Town. Rutherford served in the war as a PT instructor and Company Sergeant Major in the Army. One week before Hitler declared war he was picked to play for England. A dream never realised as hostilities put paid to that. Died in 1994 aged 80.

SALIFOU, Moustapha
Midfielder
Born: *Lome, Togo*
Playing career: *AC Merlan, Rot-Weiss Oberhausen, Brest (loan), FC Wil, Aston Villa, 1. FC Saarbrucken, 1860 Rosenheim (1998-2014)*

Moustapha Salifou's name was sung despite the Togo international rarely making it off the Villa bench. He signed in 2007 after being offered a one-year deal on August 31 following a successful trial. Capped 65 times by Togo, Salifou left Villa in 2011 having played only four times. The midfielder now plays for Turkspor Augsburg in Germany's sixth tier and has also captained the side in the Landesliga Bayern Südwest.

SAMUEL, Jlloyd
Defender/Midfielder
Born: *San Fernando, Trinidad and Tobago*
Died: 2018
Playing career: *West Ham United, Charlton Athletic, Aston Villa, Gillingham (loan), Bolton Wanderers, Cardiff City (loan), Esteghlal, Paykan (1998-2015)*

Samuel grew up in London and started out with locally based Senrab alongside John Terry and Jermaine Defoe. Played for West Ham and Charlton at youth level before joining Aston Villa in 1998. He made a total of 198 appearances for Villa before moving to division rivals Bolton Wanderers in 2007, where he spent a further four years including a brief spell on loan at Championship Cardiff. Samuel spent the last four years of his professional career overseas in the Iran Pro League, representing Esteghlal and Paykan After returning to Blighty, he became player-manager of Cheshire-based amateur team Egerton. He died in a 2018 car crash at the age of 37.

SAUNDERS, Dean
Striker
Born: *Swansea, Wales*
Playing career: *Swansea City, Cardiff City, Brighton Oxford United, Derby County, Liverpool, Aston Villa, Galatasaray, Nottingham Forest, Sheffield United, Benfica, Bradford City (1982-2001)*

Saunders set a new British transfer record when signing for Liverpool from Derby. He was also, at the time, Villa's most expensive player at £2.5m. Reunited with former colleagues Steve Staunton and Ray Houghton at Villa, Saunders struck up a prolific partnership with Dalian Atkinson. Linking up with Dwight Yorke, he ended the inaugural Premier League season with 16 goals in 18 games as they finished runners up behind United. Saunders scored twice in the 1994 League Cup final to help end the claret and blue's 12-year wait for silverware. He played 75 times for Wales scoring 22 goals. Upon retirement, he took up jobs in coaching and management with Wrexham, Doncaster, Wolves, Crawley and Chesterfield. Saunders has also done punditry work. He was arrested and jailed for 10 weeks for drink driving and failing to provide a breath test in 2019 - although the sentence was later overturned on appeal.

SAWARD, Pat
Defender
Born: *Cobh, Ireland* Died: 2002
Playing career: *Millwall, Aston Villa, Huddersfield Town. (1951-1962).*

Saward was an imposing Ireland international who helped to take Aston Villa to victory in the 1957 FA Cup Final. He signed from Millwall for £7,000 in August 1955 and was already an Ireland international, winning his first cap against Luxembourg in 1953 - and, in all, he represented his country 18 times. He became Villa captain in the 1959-60 season, during which the club won the second division championship and reached the semi-final of the FA Cup, where they were defeated by Wolverhampton Wanderers.After leaving Villa in March 1961, he ended his playing career at Huddersfield Town and then joined the coaching staff of Coventry City. Went on to manage Brighton, in the mid 1970s he coached in Saudi Arabia and then set up a holiday home business in Minorca. Saward, died in September 20, 2002, aged 74.

SCHMEICHEL, Peter
Goalkeeper
Born: *Gladsaxe, Denmark*
Playing career: *Gladsaxe-Hero, Hvidovre, Brondby, Manchester United, Sporting CP, Aston Villa, Manchester City (1972-2003)*

Regarded as one of the greatest goalkeepers of all time, he is best remembered for his most successful years at United, whom he captained to victory in the 1999 UEFA Champions League Final to complete the Treble, and for winning UEFA Euro 1992 with Denmark. He scored ten goals during his career, including one for Villa, which made him the first keeper to score in the Premiership. Since retirement, he has had an acting career, worked as a pundit and appeared in charity matches. The Swede was awarded the MBE but also caused some controversy by appearing in a programme on Russian TV called the Schmeical Show.

SCIMECA, Riccardo
Defender
Born: *Leamington Spa*
Playing career: *Aston Villa, Nottingham Forest, Leicester City, West Bromwich Albion, Cardiff City (1993-2009)*

Scimeca, a versatile defender capable of playing anywhere across the back, rose through the ranks at Villa. Mainly plied his trade as a centre-back and was only ever a squad player at Villa. Scimeca left the club after four years in which he made 73 appearances, joining Nottingham Forest for £2.5m in 1999. Became Forest captain and moved on to Leicester, West Brom and Cardiff. Retired in 2009 and joined the vets team of his home town club Leamington. He's also turned out for the Villa Old Boys team and has been working at Solihull Moors in a role coaching the youth teams.

Peter Schmeical

SCOTT, Tony
Winger
Born: *Huntingdon, Cambridgeshire*
Playing career: *West Ham, Aston Villa, Torquay United, Bournemouth, Exeter City (1959-1974)*
A right winger, Scott played for West Ham, Aston Villa, Torquay United, Bournemouth and Exeter City. Scott joined Villa for £25,000 and went on to make 57 appearances and score five goals for the Midlanders until his departure in September 1967. He was forced to retire through injury in 1974 and went on to coach at former clubs Bournemouth and West Ham. He also worked on the ground staff of the east London club.

SCOTT-WALFORD, Frank
Goalkeeper
Born: *Birmingham* Died: 1935
Playing career: *Tottenham Hotspur, London Caledonians, Lincoln City, Small Heath, Aston Villa (-)*
Frank Scott-Walford was born in Perry Barr, Birmingham, around 1866, and trained as an engineer, giving his profession in the 1901 Census as a fitter. He went on to become Tottenham's first registered professional and also worked for them in an administrative capacity. Scott-Walford later played for London Caledonians, Lincoln, Small Heath (later Birmingham) and Aston Villa. After leaving Villa he appealed successfully to the Football Association for reinstatement as an amateur. His real aptitude, however, always lay in management and administration, and he is credited with the formation of the Enfield and District League. He was an experienced referee, officiating at a number of Southern League matches, and in September 1900 took charge of a benefit match between Spurs and Millwall. He also enjoyed cricket and cycling. Later managed Brighton, Coventry and Leeds United. In later life, Scott - Walford worked as a mechanical engineer. Died 1935.

SCULLION, David
Winger
Born: *Lurgan, Northern Ireland*
Playing career: *Portadown, Aston Villa, Glenavon, Dungannon Swifts, Glentoran, Derry City, Richmond, Coleriane, Glentoran F.C. (2000-2013)*
At Villa, he was part of the 2002 FA Youth Cup winning side, but was unable to break into the first team.

Scullion returned to his native Ireland and joined home town club Glenavon, before moving to Dungannon Swifts in 2003. Played for Glentoran, Derry, Richmond, Coleraine. A winger, Scullion is currently playing in the League of Ireland aged 35 for Larne - winning the league in the 2018/19 season - and has also played for the Northern Ireland Under 21 team. Scullion combines his football career with employment as a quantity surveyor in his native Lurgan, NI.

SEALEY, Les
Goalkeeper
Born: *Bethnal Green, London* Died: 2001
Playing career: *Coventry City, Luton Town, Plymouth Argyle, Manchester United, Aston Villa, Birmingham City, Blackpool, West Ham United, Leyton Orient, Bury (1976-2000)*
Sealey was first choice at Villa Park for much of the 1991/92 season but fell out of favour, lost his place to stalwart Nigel Spink and his time at the club was up. He played in the League Cup Final defeat to Aston Villa before being given a free transfer and moving to Blackpool. Sealey was appointed player-goalkeeper coach of West Ham United in 1999. He died of a heart attack in August 2001 aged 43.

SEWELL, Jack
Forward
Born: *Kells, Whitehaven* Died: 2016
Playing career: *Notts County, Sheffield Wednesday, Aston Villa, Hull City. (1946-1960).*
He played for several teams including Sheffield Wednesday, Notts County and Aston Villa. When he was transferred to Sheffield Wednesday from Notts County, for £34,500, he was the most expensive signing in English football. A quick, clever and incisive inside-forward, Sewell figured in the Villa team that won the 1957 FA Cup with victory over United at Wembley. 145 games for the club in total having signed for £20,000 under Eric Houghton in 1955. When Sewell captained the newly independent nation of Zambia in October 1964, he became one of the few footballers who have played for two different countries having also earned six caps for England. Later worked as a car salesman for Bristol Street Motors in Nottingham. Sewell died in 2016.

SHARP, Bertram

Full-back

Born: *Hereford* Died: 1949
Playing career: *Hereford Comrades, Hereford Town, Hereford Thistle, Aston Villa, Everton, Southampton, Kirkdale, Southport Central (1897-1904)*

A Southern League title winner with Southampton in 1900/1901, Sharp played as a full back and later became director of his former club Everton FC along with his brother Jack Sharp (see below). Sharp was also a good cricketer and in the summer of 1900 averaged over 40 for Herefordshire. He joined double-winning Villa in 1897 and went on to make only 22 appearances in two seasons for the club. In 1904, he became the landlord of a public house situated opposite Goodison Park.

SHARP, Jack

Outside-right

Born: *Hereford* Died: 1938
Playing career: *Aston Villa, Everton (1897-1910)*

A talented multi-sportsman who is most famous for his eleven-season playing career at Everton F.C. from 1899–1910. It saw him win two caps for his country, as well as being a cricketer for Lancashire County Cricket Club who played in three Test matches for the England cricket team in 1909. After being signed from Aston Villa Sharp went on to be a Championship runner-up on three occasions with Everton and scored in the 1907 FA Cup Final. He won the trophy the previous year. Along with his brother Bertram, he became an Everton director and also opened a sports shop in Whitechapel.

Gary Shaw

SHARPLES, John

Full-back

Born: *Wolverhampton* Died: 2001
Playing career: *Heath Town, Aston Villa, Walsall, Darlaston (1953-1964)*

He played for Aston Villa, Walsall and Darlaston and also turned out for the Army representative team. Played for the claret and blue initially as an amateur for six seasons. Played for Walsall in two spells with his time at Villa sandwiched in between. Upon retirement he worked in a warehouse making car parts.

SHAW, Gary

Striker

Born: *Birmingham*
Playing career: *Aston Villa, Blackpool, Walsall, Shrewsbury Town. (1978-1990)*

Shaw has the distinction of being the only Birmingham born player in Villa's League Championship and European Cup winning sides of 1981 and 1982. Named the PFA Young Player of the Year in 1981, Shaw suffered an injury two years later which undoubtedly hindered his progress. Later went over to Hong Kong where he worked as a sales executive and was head coach at the International school, then became a representative for Carlsberg and Tetley. He also worked for the Players Association ran an FA Soccer School. In recent years, Shaw has proved himself to be a popular after dinner speaker – find out more at: https://football-speakers.com/after-dinner-football-speakers/gary-shaw

SHELDON, Jackie

Winger

Born: *Clay Cross, Derbyshire* Died: 1955
Playing career: *Manchester United, Liverpool, Tottenham H, Aston Villa, Derby County (1913-1921)*

Sheldon was embroiled in the Good Friday match fixing scandal in 1915 and suspended for life – a suspension lifted after the war. He joined Villa but stayed only one season before moving to Derby. He was forced to retire early through injury and died in 1955.

"DID YOU KNOW?"

"Villa Park was the first English ground to host international football in three different centuries."

SHELTON, Gary
Midfielder
Born: *Nottingham*
Playing career: *Walsall, Aston Villa, Notts County (loan), Sheffield Wednesday, Oxford United, Bristol City, Rochdale (loan), Chester-City (1974-2000)*

He made an £80,000 switch to Villa Park in January 1978 but struggled to establish himself at the club. He was named assistant manager at Chester in 1995 but left the role in June 2000 shortly after they were relegated out of The Football League and took up a coaching role with West Brom. He also managed Bristol City and the Baggies.

SHOREY, Nicky
Left-back Defensive midfielder
Born: *Romford*
Playing career: *Leyton Orient, Reading, Aston Villa, West Bromwich Albion, Bristol City, Portsmouth, Pune City, Colchester United (1998-2016)*

Known as an attacking left-back with a cultured left foot, Shorey made his name with Reading where he helped them to promotion in his debut campaign. Shorey went on to make over 300 appearances for the club and was the first Reading player in over a century to earn an England cap when he made a debut against Brazil in 2007.

He joined Aston Villa in 2008, but was limited to fewer than 40 appearances over two seasons. Currently back at the Royals as head of Academy scouting, he also had a spell as manager of Wingate & Finchley.

SIDEBOTTOM, Geoff
Goalkeeper
Born: *Mapplewell, Yorkshire* Died: 2008
Playing career: *Mapplewell Village Youth, Wath Wanderers, Wolverhampton Wanderers, Aston Villa, Scunthorpe United, New York Generals, Brighton & Hove Albion (1954-1971)*

A former Wolves goalkeeper whose chance to shine was curtailed by the presence of the club's legendary stopper Bert Williams has died aged 71. Geoffrey Sidebottom went on to sign for West Midland neighbours Aston Villa, playing in the first-ever Football League Cup Final in 1961. He went on to make 88 appearances for the Claret and Blues up to January 1965 when he was transferred to Scunthorpe United, later assisting the New York Royal Generals after a move to the USA during the 1968-9 season, when he also coached the Columbia University side. Also played for Brighton&Hove Albion. He later worked in highway maintenance. Died in 2008.

Replica of the 1961 League Cup

SIDWELL, Steve
Central midfielder
Born: *Wandsworth*
Playing career: *Chipstead, Arsenal, Beveren (loan), Brighton & Hove Albion (loan), Reading, Chelsea, Aston Villa, Fulham, Stoke City, (1997-2016)*
A varied career saw Sidwell work under managers as different as Arsène Wenger and José Mourinho, . Also played for England at U21 level. A defensive midfield with a penchant for the spectacular, he captained Villa and played 64 times in two and a half years. Sidwell announced his retirement as a player in August 2018, taking up roles as an ambassador and youth development coach at his final club, Brighton & Hove Albion.

SIMMONS, David
Striker
Born: *Ryde, Isle of Wight* Died: 2007
Playing career: *Arsenal, Bournemouth, Aston Villa, Walsall, Colchester United, Cambridge United, Brentford, Cambridge United. (1965-1975).*
Simmons was a prolific goalscorer at youth level and his form was impressive enough to earn him a move to English giants Arsenal. Joined Villa for £15,000 in 1968 and scored at a ratio of one in two games despite only featuring sporadically. Retiring from the professional game through arthritis, he later played for several non-league clubs. Died in 2007.

SIMS, Nigel
Goalkeeper
Born: *Coton in the Elms*
Playing career: *Wolves, Aston Villa & Peterborough.*
A goalkeeper who played in the Football League between 1948-65. During his spell with Aston Villa between 1956-64 he played a total of 310 games, appearing in the 1957 FA Cup Final and three years later he won a 2nd Division winners medal. He was also in the Villa side that won the inaugural League Cup in 1961. At the end of his career he spent five years in Canada playing and coaching youngsters. He later ran a Wolverhampton timber firm and then worked in insurance. Finally he set up a wardrobe and bed parts business in South Wales.

SIMS, Steve
Central Defender
Born: *Lincoln*
Playing career: *Leicester C, Watford, Notts County, Watford, Aston Villa, Lincoln City (1975-1990)*
Sims started his career at Leicester City in 1975 and, after 3 seasons he was transferred to Watford for £175,000 and was the player of the season for 1980/81. Signed for Aston Villa from Watford and played 41 games between 1987 and 1989. After retirement, he spent two years managing an indoor football and cricket stadium before becoming Youth recruitment manager at Coventry City. Sims is now working for the Premier League where he monitors club academies.

Didier Six

SIX, Didier
Left winger
Born: *Lille, France*
Playing career: *Valenciennes, Lens, Marseille, Cercle Brugge, Strasbourg, VfB Stuttgart, Mulhouse, Aston Villa, Metz, Galatasaray, Stade Vallauris, ASPV Strasbourg, VfB Leipzig (1972-1992)*

He played as a winger and earned 52 caps for France. He played in the 1978 1982 World Cups, and was also part of the winning team at Euro 84. As a player he played across Europe in his native France, England, Germany, Turkey and Belgium. After retirement, he managed the national teams of Togo and Mauritius and was player/boss of Strasbourg in his homeland during his playing career. As of 2019, Six is currently the manager of Guinea.

SKEA, David
Inside-forward
Born: *Arbroath, Scotland* Died: 1950
Playing career: *Arbroath, Aston Villa, Dundee Thistle, Darwen, Bury, Leicester Fosse, Swindon Town, New Brompton, Cowes (1892-1898)*

Skea, an inside forward, started out in his native Scotland with hometown club Arbroath and latterly Dundee Thistle. A one game wonder for the claret and blue, he played in an FA Cup tie for Villa in 1892. Moved to Darwen and Bury in the Lancashire League but then made his breakthrough as top scorer in the Second Division for Leicester in the 1894/95 season. He spent two seasons at the club, making 45 League appearances and scoring 28 goals. After leaving Filbert Street, he played for Swindon Town and New Brompton of the Southern League. In retirement, he held a variety of manual labour jobs and also worked as a harbourmaster.

SLADE, Charlie
Midfielder
Born: *Bath, Somerset* Died: 1971
Playing career: *Aston Villa, Huddersfield Town, Middlesbrough, Darlington, Folkestone (1913-1927)*

Slade played three times for the first team before moving to Huddersfield Town in March 1914. He was a member of their 1922 FA Cup winning team, also playing as they beat Champions Liverpool in the Charity Shield a month later. Slade later became a scout for Crystal Palace and remained with the south London side until 1955.

SLATTER, Les
Winger
Born: *Reading, Berkshire*
Playing career: *Luton Town, Crusaders, Aston Villa, York City, Scarborough (1949-1955)*

Played as a winger in the Football League for Luton Town and York City, in non-League football for Mount Pleasant YC and Scarborough, in Northern Ireland for Crusaders (scoring 10 goals in his sole season), and was on the books of Aston Villa without making a league appearance. He was briefly a coach at hometown club Reading and later became an advisor for the professional players union.

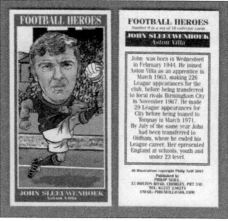

SLEEUWENHOEK, John
Centre-half
Born: *Wednesfield* Died: 1989
Playing career: *Aston Villa, Birmingham City, Torquay United, Oldham Athletic. (1961-1971).*

For a number of years, Sleeuwenhoek was a commanding centre-half with Villa having come through the Villa's youth system; a member of 'Mercer's Minors'. In the latter part of the 1960s it was often a case of he and goalkeeper Colin Withers keeping Villa away from severe defeats during the club's fight against relegation from the top-flight. He soon left for Birmingham City after Villa were relegated, but never settled there and drifted into obscurity after having gained England u-23 caps with Villa. Worked as a joiner at an Aldridge firm with his former Villa colleague, Alan Deakin. Sleeuwenhoek sadly died in Birmingham in July 1989 aged only 45. Sadly, this son of a Dutch wartime paratrooper died aged only 45.

SMALL, Bryan
Defender
Born: *Birmingham*
Playing career: *Aston Villa, Bolton Wanderers, Stoke City, Walsall (1990-2003)*
He began his career at Villa and went on to play 35 times for the club before defecting to local rivals Birmingham City on loan. Won the First Division with Bolton He also spent time out on loan at Luton Town, Bradford City and Bury. Following his release from Stoke, Small finished his playing career and then took up coaching at Walsall, Stourbridge and Halesowen. Represented Bolton and Villa in Masters Football.

SMART, Tommy
Full-back
Born: *Blackheath, Staffordshire* Died: 1968
Playing career: *Halesowen Town, Aston Villa, Brierley Hill Alliance (1920-1936)*
Smart moved to Aston Villa in January 1920 for a £300 transfer fee and quickly became a regular in the Villa defence, playing in the 1920 FA Cup Final win over Huddersfield Town (he also appeared in the 1924 Cup Final defeat to Newcastle). Earned five caps for England. After 14 seasons and having played his last game for Villa in March 1933, he retired in 1934 after 451 appearances. Only six players turned out more often for the claret and blue. He died in 1968.

SMITH, George
Half-back/Inside-forward
Born: *Preston* Died: 1908
Playing career: *Preston North End, Aston Villa, New Brompton, Blackburn Rovers , Plymouth Argyle, Southampton (1899-1908)*
Smith spent part of the 1901–02 season at Villa before moving to non-league New Brompton. Later joined Southampton where he ended his career before becoming a dockyard worker in the city.

SMITH, Gordon
Full-back
Born: *Partick, Scotland*
Playing career: *Rangers B.C., St Johnstone, Aston Villa, Tottenham Hotspur, Wolverhampton Wanderers, Pittsburgh Spirit (1972-1985)*
A former St Johnstone, Aston Villa, Tottenham Hotspur and Wolves player, he was signed by Villa for a then club record £80,000 fee in 1976.

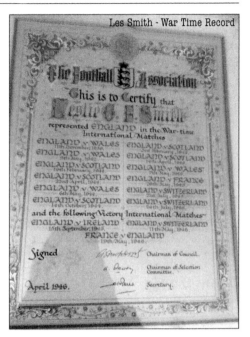

Les Smith - War Time Record

He had been recruited to succeed long-serving Charlie Aitken at left-back and he was an immediate success at Villa Park, supplying the cross from which Brian Little scored the winner in a 3-2, second-replay victory over Everton in the League Cup Final. He was to spend almost three seasons with the club, making just short of 100 appearances, before he was on the move again – to Tottenham Hotspur –for a fee of £150,000. Finished his playing career with Barnet. He later ran a company that sold and installed the special Champions League sponsors advertising for the big European games. Died aged 59 in his native Glasgow.

SMITH, Jay
Midfielder
Born: *London*
Playing career: *Aston Villa, Southend United, Notts County, Eastwood Town, Tamworth, AFC Telford United (loan), AFC Telford United (2001-2013)*
Smith started his professional football career with Villa. After a season, he was transferred to Southend United having never played for the first team at Villa Park. Despite a plethora of injuries including a broken ankle, dislocated shoulder and hamstring problems, he became a regular for Southend. Had an extensive career in the non league game and retired in 2013 having been let go by his last club AFC Telford.

SMITH, Les
Outside - left
Born: *Ealing* Died: 1995
Playing career: *Brentford, Aston Villa (1936-1954)*
In 1945, Smith signed for Aston Villa for a fee of £7,500, where he spent six seasons and became a crowd favourite. He won 15 War Time and Victory caps for England and remains the youngest player to have appeared in an FA Amateur Cup final. After his retirement, he went into management with Kidderminster Harriers, before becoming a scout for Wolves. The former winger owned a radio and TV shop in Aston, then lived in retirement in Lichfield until his death in 1995.

SMITH, Les
Outside-right
Born: *Halesowen, West Midlands* Died: 2008
Playing career: *Wolverhampton Wanderers, Aston Villa (1947-1960)*
A winger who was formerly with Wolves but it was only after moving to Villa Park that he finally established himself as a first team footballer. He played in the team to beat Manchester United in the 1957 FA Cup final and was a regular over the next two seasons, too. Was forced into retirement after suffering a ruptured Achilles tendon inf the 1958-59 campaign. He died in March 2008 at the age of 80.

SMITH, Stephen
Outside-left
Born: *Abbots Bromley* Died: 1935
Playing career: *Cannock Town, Rugeley, Hednesford Town, Aston Villa, Portsmouth (1893-1908)*
Steve Smith joined Aston Villa from Hednesford Town in 1893 and played in five League Championship winning teams and also won the FA Cup with Villa in 1895 (although he was not selected for the Cup Final of 1897 which sealed the League and FA Cup double), the same year he won his single England cap against Scotland. He made 187 appearances, scoring 42 goals, during Aston Villa's most dominant period in their history. In May 1901 after 8 seasons at Villa he joined Portsmouth and played 5 years for them. Died in 1935

SMYTH, David
Centre-forward
Born: *Clydebank, Scotland*
Playing career: *Maryhill, Petershill, Aston Villa, Newcastle United, Darlington (1935-1938)*
He was on the books of Aston Villa and Newcastle United without playing first-team football for either, although he did turn for the reserve and youth teams in the Birmingham Combination League. After retirement he became a railway signalman in his native Scotland.

Painting of Sunderland v. Aston Villa 1895

SOLANO, Nolberto

Midfielder
Born: *Callao, Peru*
Playing career: *Sporting Cristal, Deportivo Municipal, Sporting Cristal, Boca Juniors, Newcastle United, Aston Villa, Newcastle United, West Ham United, AEL, Universitario de Deportes, Leicester City, Hull City, Hartlepool United (1987-2012)*

He spent much of his playing career in the English Premier League and also played 95 times for Peru between 1994 and 2009. He is a popular figure in his native country, where he is seen as one of the most famous Peruvians, appearing on telephone cards and having his wedding televised live. After retirement - Solano played for eleven different clubs (including Villa, Newcastle, West Ham, Leicester and Hartlepool in England) - he became a manager. He went on to take charge of Universitaro, Jose Galvez and Internacional de Toronto. As of 2019, he is technical assistant to Ricardo Gareca with the Peru national team. The first player from his country to play in England and a self confessed "adopted Geordie", Solano was known as an excellent crosser with accurate set piece deliveries.

SORENSEN, Thomas

Goalkeeper
Born: *Fredericia, Denmark*
Playing career: *Errits√®, Assens, Odense BK, Vejle (loan), Svendborg (loan), Sunderland, Aston Villa, Stoke City, Melbourne City*

Sorensen signed for Villa in 2003 and soon established himself as first choice, with his ability as a shot stopper under both Martin O'Neill and David Leary keeping him ahead of Stefan Postma and Stuart Taylor. He only missed three games in his first four seasons at the club. But after he fell out with O'Neill, he was dropped, released and snapped up by Stoke. Sorensen enjoyed 12 unbroken years as Denmark's number one, having big gloves to fill as the successor to the legendary Peter Schmeichel. Since retiring, Sorensen has done some punditry and commentary work on TV.

SOUTHGATE, Gareth

Defender
Born: *Watford*
Playing career: *Crystal Palace, Aston Villa, Middlesbrough (1989-2006)*

Southgate began his career at Crystal Palace, playing initially at right-back and then in central midfield. He became captain and led the club to the 1993–94 First Division title. He moved to Aston Villa for a fee of £2.5 million, and won the League Cup in his first season at the club, a competition he would go on to win again with Middlesbrough. Southgate embarked on a managerial career after retirement, and is currently in charge of the England men having also managed the U21 team. He played 57 times for his country, playing in three major tournaments, and has also done punditry work. Southgate played more than 500 games at the top level and won the BBC Sports Personality Coach of the Year award in 2018.

Gareth Southgate

Nigel Spink

SPENCER, Howard
Full-backs
Born: *Edgbaston, Birmingham* Died: 1940
Playing career: *Aston Villa, Newcastle United, Millwall Athletic*

Often referred to as the "prince of full-backs" due to his sportsmanship, Spencer joined Aston Villa in 1892. He made his professional debut in October 1894 at the age of 18 and would go on to become a first-team regular for the club. In his 13 years as a senior player, he helped the side to three First Division championships and three FA Cup victories as well as earning six England caps. Following his retirement, Spencer became a successful coal merchant and joined Aston Villa's board of directors in 1909 and served as a director until 1936.

SPENCER, Ray
Wing-half
Born: *Kings Norton, Birmingham*
Playing career: *Aston Villa, Darlington, West Ham United, Torquay United, Bath City*

Ray Spencer joined Aston Villa as a junior, turning professional in June 1950. Despite remaining at Villa Park until March 1958, when he joined Darlington, he never made the Aston Villa first team. In retirement he lived in France.

SPIERS, Cyril
Goalkeeper
Born: *Witton* Died: 1967
Playing career: *Aston Villa, Tottenham Hotspur, Wolverhampton Wanderers (1920-1939)*

Spiers had first began his career with Aston Villa with whom he remained for seven years before transferring to Tottenham Hotspur. A leg injury virtually ended his career after taking his total of League appearances to 262. Following on from this, he became assistant manager to Major Frank Buckley whilst at Molineux, as well as having two spells as manager of Cardiff City and one each with Norwich City and Crystal Palace. Spiers died on 21 May 1967.

"DID YOU KNOW?"

"Charlie Aitken still holds the record for the most appearances Villa - 657 between 1959–1976."

SPINK, Nigel
Goalkeeper
Born: *Chelmsford*
Playing career: *Chelmsford City, Aston Villa, West Bromwich Albion, Millwall (1976-2001)*

He made his name at Aston Villa and also made one appearance for England at international level on the tour of Australia in 1983. He came on as an early substitute in the 1982 European Cup final. He also played in the Football League for West Bromwich Albion and Millwall, and at non-league level for Chelmsford City and Forest Green Rovers. Won the European Cup, European Super Cup and the League Cup in the claret and blue. After retiring as a player, Spink worked as a coach at West Bromwich Albion and then had a two-year spell as manager of Forest Green Rovers in the Conference National. Later started up his own courier business.

STAINROD, Simon
Striker
Born: *Sheffield*
Playing career: *Sheffield United, Oldham Athletic, QPR, Sheffield Wed, Aston Villa, Stoke C. (1975-1988).*

Stainrod joined Villa for £350,000 from Sheffield Wednesday and enjoyed a stunningly spectacular debut. The striker hit all four goals in a 4-1 win at Exeter in the League Cup to announce his arrival to the claret and blue faithful. Despite this explosive start, he struggled to ever nail down a place in the Villa team, moving on to Stoke after two years, 63 games and 16 goals for the club. Went on to play in France and Scotland before he managed Dundee and Ayr. Since retiring he has set up his own player agency company, Matchday Media.

STANDING, Michael
Midfielder
Born: *Shoreham-by-Sea*
Playing career: *Brighton & Hove Albion, Aston Villa, Bradford City, Walsall, Chesterfield, Bournemouth, Oxford United (1995-2012)*

Standing never played a game for Villa in four years but went on to play for Bradford City, Walsall, Chesterfield, Bournemouth, and Oxford. Since terminating his playing career, Standing has become an agent for former teammate and long-term friend Gareth Barry. He also played part-time for his hometown club, Shoreham FC.

R. STARLING
ASTON VILLA

STARLING, Ron
Inside-forward
Born: *Pelaw, Gateshead* Died: 1991
Playing career: *Hull City, Newcastle United, Sheffield Wednesday, Aston Villa. (1927-1946).*
Starling played for Hull, Newcastle, Sheffield Wednesday and Villa, for whom he made 88 appearances scoring eleven goals. He also earned two caps for England and won the FA Cup with Wednesday in 1935. Starling's skill, turn of pace and distribution earned him the moniker: "The Man with the Fluttering Feet." He was a key man in Villa's surge to Division One promotion in the 1937/38 season. After retirement he spent time as a coach with Nottingham Forest before retiring from football altogether, becoming a newsagent in Sheffield.

STAUNTON, Steve
Defender
Born: *Drogheda, Ireland*
Playing career: *Liverpool, Bradford City, Aston Villa, Crystal Palace, Coventry City, Walsall (1985-2005)*
He earned 102 caps for the Republic of Ireland national football team, captained his team to the knock-out stage of the 2002

FIFA World Cup and earned his place in the FIFA Century Club. Staunton enjoyed a distinguished club career with Aston Villa and Liverpool. After retiring, he served as Republic of Ireland national team coach prior to Giovanni Trapattoni but was sacked after 21 turbulent months in charge. He also spent five months as manager of Darlington in Football League Two. Staunton has since remained involved in football as a pundit and radio commentator.

STEPHENSON, Clem
Inside-forward
Born: *Seaton Delaval* Died: 1961
Playing career: *Aston V, Huddersfield T (1910-1929)*
Stephenson joined Aston Villa in March 1910 and soon made a name for himself. He was part of the side that beat Sunderland 1-0 to win the 1913 FA Cup at Crystal Palace. By the time official competition had been suspended at the end of the 1914/15 season, Stephenson had played 132 league and 13 FA Cup matches for Villa, scoring 55 goals. After serving in the Royal Navy during the First World War, Stephenson returned to football following the Armistice and was to win a second FA Cup in 1920 when Villa beat Herbert Chapman's Huddersfield Town 1-0 at Stamford Bridge. Played once for England in 1924. Stephenson finally retired in May 1929, when he was appointed Huddersfield Town manager. Going on to become the club's longest-serving boss, Stephenson held the role until he retired from the game completely in June 1942.

STEPHENSON, George
Inside - forward
Born: *New Delaval* Died: 1971
Playing career: *Aston Villa, Derby C, Sheffield W, Preston North End, Charlton Athletic (1927-1936)*
From November 1919 to November 1927 , George Stephenson played for Villa, but - initially a fringe player. Eventually establishing himself, he scored 22 goals in 95 appearances before moving on to Derby County in November 1927. Like his younger brother Clem, he was capped by England. After being forced to retire joined Charlton's backroom staff, becoming assistant manager in May 1938. He became Huddersfield Town's manager in August 1947 and stayed five seasons until leaving the post in March 1952 in a season that saw their relegation.

STEPHENSON, Jimmy

Outside-right
Born: *New Delaval* Died: 1958
Playing career: *New Delaval Villa, Aston Villa, Sunderland, Watford, QPR, Boston (1913-1931)*
He joined brother Clem at Aston Villa in May 1913. After making his debut the following year, Stephenson would make a further ten appearances during the 1914/15 season, scoring two goals. For a period while a professional footballer, he ran the Nascot Arms pub in Watford. Died in 1958.

STEVENTON, Edwin

Goalkeeper
Born: *Nantwich* Died: 1961
Playing career: *Walsall, Southampton, Aston Villa, Nantwich Victoria, Stoke, Nantwich Victoria, Wolverhampton Wanderers (1914-1922)*
Nantwich born keeper, Steventon never played a senior match for the club but did embark on an extensive lower and non league career in the game. He retired in 1940 after captaining Nantwich for 16 successive seasons, but completed 26 years as the club's secretary in 1947. The owner of a footwear business, he was also chairman of the Beam Heath trustees for many years.

STOBART, Barry

Forward
Born: *Doncaster* Died: 2013
Playing career: *Wolverhampton Wanderers, Manchester City, Aston Villa, Shrewsbury Town. (1959-1968).*

Stobart joined Aston Villa in November 1964 for £22,000. He remained at Villa for three years, making 53 League and cup appearances and scoring 20 goals before moving to Shrewsbury Town. Stobart then headed for South Africa where he played for Durban Spurs. Back in England he later managed Willenhall Town and returned to Wembley as a manager when they reached the FA Vase final in 1981, losing 3–2 to Whickham in extra time as a window cleaner in Sedgley near Wolverhampton having previously run a grocer's shop.

STONE, Steve

Winger
Born: *Gateshead*
Playing career: *Nottingham Forest, Aston Villa, Portsmouth, Leeds United (1989-2006)*
He managed to establish himself in the Nottingham Forest first team despite breaking his leg three times. Earned nine caps for England and played at Euro 96. He moved to Villa for £5.5 million in 1999, and came on at Wembley in the FA Cup final the following year. Having played 121 times for Villa, he moved on to Portsmouth and finished his career at Leeds. After he hung up his boots, Stone was named as Newcastle's assistant boss after a successful time coaching their academy. He later became first team coach and is currently manager of Burnley's Under 23 team.

STEVE STONE
NEWLY APPOINTED U23s' BOSS

STOTT, Harry

Outside-forward
Born: *North Shields* Died: 1955
Playing career: *Aston Villa, Brentford, Preston Colliery, Barnsley (1921-1927)*

Stott spent 1921-22 on the books at Aston Villa but failed to make the first eleven at Villa Park, moving to join Brentford in the close season of 1922. He made his Football League debut at Gillingham that August and made 24 appearances during the 1922-23 season, before joining non league Preston Colliery in the summer of 1923. He subsequently returned to the Football League spending 1927-28 at Barnsley, but again he failed to make a first team appearance during his spell at Oakwell. Later worked in a Durham colliery.

SUTTON, Chris

Striker
Born: *Nottingham*
Playing career: *Norwich City, Blackburn Rovers, Chelsea, Celtic, Birmingham City, Aston Villa (1991-2007)*

He played as a forward from 1991 to 2007 for Norwich City, Blackburn Rovers, Chelsea, Celtic, Birmingham City and Aston Villa. A physical target man up top, Sutton scored over 150 career goals in over 400 league appearances spanning 16 years in the English and Scottish Premier Leagues. It was whilst at Villa that Sutton was forced to retire through an eye injury sustained in a match against Manchester United. He was capped once by England. He was appointed as manager of Lincoln in 2009 but resigned after a year. Briefly came out of retirement to feature for non league Wroxham, and is now a pundit and commentator for BT Sport and Five Live.

SWAIN, Kenny

Full-back/midfielder/Striker
Born: *Birkenhead*
Playing career: *Chelsea, Aston Villa, Nottingham Forest, Portsmouth, West Bromwich Albion, Crewe Alexandra. (1973-1994).*

Swain's career is the tale of the man who quit teaching to sign for Chelsea, the glamour club of the 1970s, and then moved on to Aston Villa for £100,000 where - having converted from striker to a full-back role - he played his part in winning the First Division championship and the European Cup. Next, Kenny was signed by Brian Clough at Nottingham Forest, and he now paints an evocative personal picture of the most charismatic and controversial manager in English football history. Portsmouth and Crewe were the last clubs to figure in an illustrious career that saw him play more than 100 games for five different clubs. He later moved into management with Wigan, Grimsby and England's age group side. Today, Kenny has remained in the England set-up, heading up the FA's talent ID programme, and has helped develop players such as Michael Owen, Joe Cole and Danny Welbeck.

TALBOT, Alec

Centre-half
Born: *Cannock, Staffs* Died: 1975
Playing career: *Aston Villa, Bradford (1920-1930)*

A centre-half, he signed for First Division Aston Villa in April 1923, making his debut in an FA Cup tie in 1924 during the FA Cup run that saw them reach the Final at Wembley. On the fringes of the first team over the next four seasons, he broke into the first eleven on a regular basis in November 1928, and he was an ever present for the 1930-31 and 1931-32 seasons. Twice a losing FA Cup semi finalist in 1929 and 1934, when they lost to Portsmouth and Manchester City respectively, he was also a runner up in the League Championship on two occasions. In all he made 263 appearances for Villa, scoring seven goals for the club. In June 1935 he joined Second Division Bradford Park Avenue where he scored once in 6 appearances, before joining Brierley Hill Alliance in 1938 and Stourbridge in 1939, the Second World War then forcing his playing retirement. After the war Talbot started his own dairy business in Stourbridge.

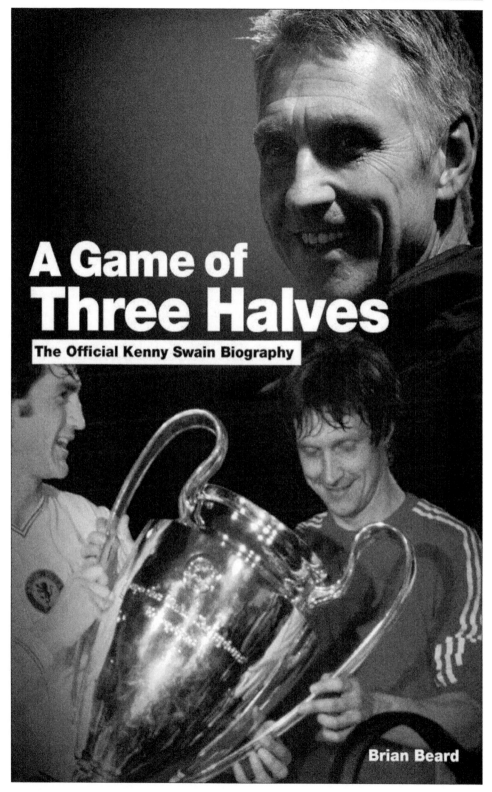

A Game of
Three Halves
The Official Kenny Swain Biography

Brian Beard

TARRANT, Neil

Forward
Born: *Darlington*
Playing career: *Darlington, Shamrock Rovers, Aston Villa, Ayr United, York City, Motherwell, Ross County, Boston Utd, Barrow (1996-2011)*

Tarrant would of course go in a similar rich vein of scoring form which resulted in him winning a move to English Premiership side Aston Villa. His time at Villa would however see the young, energetic striker struggle to break into the first team. Villa's manager at the time was John Gregory and Tarrant was competing for a starting place with the likes of Paul Merson, Dion Dublin and Gareth Southgate. As a result, he never made a first team appearance, and sometimes even missed out on a place on the reserve team bench. He was capped five times by the Scotland U21 team.

TATE, Joe

Left-half
Born: *Old Hill, Cradley Heath*
Died: 1973
Playing career: *Stourbridge Council School, Birch Coppice Primitives, Grainger's Lane Primitives, Round Oak Steel Works FC, (Brierley Hill), Cradley Heath, Aston Villa, Brierley Hill Alliance (1925-1935)*

Played cricket with Stourbridge CC of the Birmingham Cricket League, and represented Aston Villa at cricket too. Began his junior career playing with Round Oak Steelworks FC, and moved up into the Birmingham League with his local side, Cradley Heath FC in 1923, during which he was one of the juniors who represented Birmingham FC in 1925. Aston Villa FC signed Tate in April 1925 as an inside-left, moving into defence in 1927. His Villa Park career was marred by injury. He made just 180 league appearances and scored twice, before he joined Brierley Hill Alliance FC on 21 August 1935, playing alongside Tommy Smart once more. Tate was appointed as their player-manager on 12 August 1936. A broken neck in an FA Cup match against Moor Green FC ended his playing career in 1937 After war service in the Army, he returned to the tobacconist's shop he started before the conflict. He later worked as a PE teacher at the same school where his wife also worked. He earned three caps for England.

TAYLOR, Daryl

Midfielder
Born: *Birmingham*
Playing career: *Aston Villa, Walsall, Hereford United (loan), A.F.C. Bournemouth, Bury, Tamworth, Halifax Town, Kettering Town, Halesowen Town, Chippenham Town (1999-2010)*

Taylor, a mobile and strong midfield maestro, carved out a nomadic career in the lower echelons of the game. He began his career on the books at Villa but drifted away having never turned out for the senior team in five years at the club, despite being given a squad number. Taylor earned a reputation for moving from club to club, his longest stint being spent at Conference side Kettering between 2008 and 2010. Known for having "exceptional pace", Taylor is currently a free agent.

TAYLOR, Ian

Midfielder
Born: *Birmingham*
Playing career: *Port Vale, Sheffield Wednesday, Aston Villa, Derby County, Northampton Town (1992-2007)*

Won the League Cup with Villa in 1996 - scoring in the final - and also played in the 2000 FA Cup final. A boyhood fan of the claret and blue, he went on to make 250 appearances, scoring 30 goals as a midfielder. He was remembered by the Villa faithful as an adored prodigal son, known for his unstinting work rate, utterly committed approach and knack of popping up with important, match winning moments. Taylor retired at the end of the 06/07 season, and went into working for Aston Villa Television as a summariser. He now works for BBC Radio Derby and co-commentates on Derby County matches. He's also a club ambassador at Villa Park.

TAYLOR, Stuart

Goalkeeper

Born: *Romford*

Playing career: *Arsenal, Bristol Rovers (loan), Crystal Palace (loan), Peterborough United (loan), Leicester City (loan), Aston Villa, Cardiff City (loan), Manchester City, Reading, Yeovil Town (loan), Leeds United (1997-2015)*

Currently a free agent after being released by Southampton in 2018. Taylor began his career with Arsenal, winning the 2001–02 Premier League and 2002–03 FA Cup and representing England at under-16, under-18, under-20 and Under-21 level. He was second choice at Villa Park behind Thomas Sorensen and played only 12 times in four seasons at the club. Taylor has spent most of his career as a third-choice goalkeeper; he has made only 95 career appearances, played in just 10 games since a loan spell at Cardiff City ended in May 2009 and hasn't played at all since 2015. Has also been contracted with Man City, Reading, Yeovil , Leeds United and the Saints. On his time at Villa, where he was told he would play in cup matches or if Thomas Sorensen got injured, he said: "That never materialised. I kept being told I would play this game or that game, and I never did. You get your hopes up, and it's hard to take. Football is a cruel game. People tell you what they think you want to hear."

TEALE, Shaun

Defender

Born: *Southport*

Playing career: *AFC Bournemouth, Aston Villa, Tranmere Rovers, Preston North End, Sin Tao, Motherwell, Carlisle United, Southport, (1988-2004)*

He also played in the Football League for Bournemouth, Tranmere Rovers, Preston North End and Carlisle United, the Scottish Premier League for Motherwell. As well as having a spell in Hong Kong with Sing Tao he has played at a Non-league level for Weymouth, Southport, Burscough and Northwich Victoria before moving into management with the two latter clubs, as well as having a spell in charge of Chorley. Won the League Cup with Villa in 1994 before leaving the sport to run a restaurant business in Burscough. Twitter: https://twitter.com/shaunteale

TEMPLETON, Robert

Outside-right

Born: *Coylton, Ayrshire, Scotland* Died: 1919

Playing career: *Aston Villa, Newcastle United, Woolwich Arsenal, Celtic (1898-1915)*

He played as an outside right for six clubs both in England and across the border in his homeland. Earned eleven caps for Scotland and went on to manage Hibernian. His international debut would have been on 5 April 1902 against England, but the match was declared void after 26 spectators died during the first Ibrox disaster. Templeton himself died of a heart attack in 1919 aged 39. He also worked as a shop owner.

Shaun Teale

TEWKESBURY, Ken

Goalkeeper
Born: *Hove* Died: 1970
Playing career: *Aston Villa, Notts County, Aston Villa, Bradford Park Avenue, Walsall (1929-1939)*
Tewkesbury made 102 appearances in the Football League playing for Birmingham, Notts County, Villa, Bradford Park Avenue and Walsall. Before turning professional he won six caps for the England national amateur football team as a goalkeeper. Described as brilliantly unorthodox, he was signed by Villa in 1931 but only stayed for three months without appearing in the first team. After retirement, he worked in Birmingham's "Jewellery Quarter" before moving to Cornwall. Later became the first ever boss of Falmouth Town. His grand-daughter became an MP for Truro and Falmouth in 2010.

THOMAS, Martin

Goalkeeper
Born: *Senghenydd, Wales*
Playing career: *Bristol Rovers, Birmingham City, Aston Villa (loan), Cheltenham Town (1975-1995)*
Thomas is more closely associated with Villa's derby rivals Birmingham having played over 150 games for the Blues across a five year stint at St Andrew's. Former Welsh International goalkeeper had abrief loan stay at Villa Park but was not called into first team action. Having suffered a severe injury, Thomas dropped out of professional football and went to Cheltenham Town where he played for a further two seasons. After retiring as a player he became a coach, and has worked for various clubs and for the English Football Association.

THOMPSON, Alan

Midfielder
Born: *Newcastle upon Tyne*
Playing career: *Newcastle U, Bolton W, Aston Villa, Celtic, Leeds United, Hartlepool United (1991-2008)*
He made 550 appearances for six different clubs and was a "one cap wonder" for England against Sweden in 2004. He moved to Aston Villa from Bolton for £4.5m in 1998 and played 52 times for the club. A multiple league title winner with Celtic, he also played in the 2003 UEFA Cup final for the Bhoys. In 2008 he was appointed an academy coach at Newcastle United and then became first team coach at Celtic.

THOMPSON, Garry

Striker
Born: *Birmingham*
Playing career: *Coventry City, WBA, Sheffield Wednesday, Aston Villa, Watford, Crystal Palace, QPR, Cardiff City, Northampton Town (1977-1997)*
His peak years were earlier in his career with Coventry City, for whom he scored 49 goals in 158 appearances and West Bromwich Albion, for whom he was voted the club's 1984–85 Player of the Year. Thompson played 60 games for Villa in the late 1980's and finally hung up his boots at the end of the 1996–97 season. After retirement, he moved into coaching and management with Bristol Rovers, Brentford as caretaker boss and Hucknall Town as assistant manager to Kevin Wilson. A Villa supporter, he has worked in PR, as a driver and as a summariser for BBC West Midlands. Twitter: https://twitter.com/g11klt

THOMPSON, Tommy

Inside-forward
Born: *Fencehouses, Houghton-le-Spring* Died: 2015
Playing career: *Newcastle United, Aston Villa, Preston North End, Stoke City, Barrow (1947-1964)*
He moved to Aston Villa for £12,500 in 1950 from Newcastle and went on to play 165 times for the club, scoring 76 goals including three hat-tricks. Thompson was sold to Preston North End in August 1955 for £27,000 Won two full caps for England at senior international level, with his two appearances coming six years apart. After retirement he drifted out of the game and worked in the cotton trade. He died in September 2015 at the age of 86.

THOMSON, Bobby

Forward
Born: *Dundee, Scotland*
Playing career: *Albion Rovers, Airdrieonians, Wolverhampton Wanderers, Aston Villa, Birmingham City, Stockport County (1952-1970)*
Won Division Two in 1960 in claret and blue and then the inaugural League Cup a year later having signed for £8,000 in 1959. Also represented fierce local rivals Birmingham City with distinction, then after a brief spell with Stockport he moved into non league football with Bromsgrove. He spent nearly all of his entire career in the Midlands. Coached at Villa after his retirement as a player.

TILER, Brian
Central Defender
Born: *Rotherham* Died: 1990
Playing career: *Rotherham United, Aston Villa &*
Carlisle United.

It was from Yorkshire outfit Rotherham that he signed for Aston Villa and it was after his second season at Villa Park that the Villans were relegated to the Third Division (now League One) for the first, and only time in their history. He stayed at Villa long enough to help them regain their former status two years later. He managed 107 appearances for the Villans during which he netted three times before signing for his final Football League club, Carlisle United in October 1972. Tiler went to pay for Wigan and Portland Timbers - both of whom he later manager, as well as a spell in charge of the Zambia national team.Tiler later became managing director of AFC Bournemouth, but was killed in a car crash in Italy during the 1990 World Cup. His close friend and team manager Harry Redknapp was seriously injured but survived the accident.

TILER, Carl
Defender
Born: *Sheffield*
Playing career: *Barnsley, Nottingham Forest,*
Swindon Town, Aston Villa, Sheffield United, Everton,
Charlton A, Birmingham C, Portsmouth (1988-2003)

A willing and capable performer, Tiler was snapped up by Villa boss Brian Little for £750,000 in 1995. However, the 27-year-old became unsettled at Villa Park.

Andy Townsend

Tiler's chances of senior action were increasingly limited as youngster were chosen ahead of him. A big defender, he ruptured his hamstring on debut and did not return for over a year. He played 12 times for the club in total before embarking on a whistlestop tour of English football, taking in Sheffield United, Everton, Charlton, Portsmouth and Birmingham. Tiler - no relation to namesake Brian (above) - also earned 13 caps for the England U21 side. After retiring he was a coach and then drifted away from football to become a council worker in Hampshire.

TINDALL, Mike
Midfielder
Born: *Birmingham*
Playing career: *Aston Villa, Walsall, (1959-1969)*

No relation to his more famous rugby union namesake, Tindall was best known as a wing-half for Villa and playing for the famous claret and blue became his only ambition as a boy. Tindall, who enjoyed a 12-year spell with the Villans, owned two shops after retiring from football but then encountered serious personal problems when he tried his hand at being a publican. Tindall and his wife later went on to travel the world as missionaries.

TOWNSEND, Andy
Midfielder
Born: *Maidstone*
Playing career: *Southampton, Norwich City, Chelsea,*
Aston Villa, Middlesbrough, WBA (1980-2000)

Gave up his day job at the local council to join Southampton and become a full time professional. He has since worked as a pundit for ITV Sport and a radio presenter for Talksport. He is a football consultant for "Harlequin Property" where he helps set up soccer schools at their Caribbean resorts. The Republic of Ireland international (70 caps) would go on to become a favourite among the Villa faithful. Yet, despite a host of impressive performances in the Villa engine room, Townsend was unable to inspire the club to the title. They finished in a disappointing 10th place in 1993-94, followed by 18th, 4th and 5th in his other three seasons in a claret shirt. However, he was a part of the teams that won the League Cup in 1994 and 1996 against Man United and Leeds United respectively.

TRANTER, George
Midfielder
Born: *Stourbridge* Died: 1958
Playing career: *Aston Villa, Stourbridge (1906-1918)*
Tranter signed for Villa from non-league Stourbridge in 1906 and immediately established himself as a first team regular, helping win the League Championship in 1909-10, when he played 28 League games in the triumph, and to four League runners up positions in 1908, 1911, 1913 and 1914. He was described "as hard as nails, he never shirked a tackle, was totally committed, had an infallibly cool temperament and was a good passer of the ball, very rarely hoofing it downfield." He retired through injury and later owned a menswear clothing shop in Stourbridge.

TRAVERS, George
Forward
Born: *Birmingham* Died: 1946
Playing career: *Wolves, Birmingham, Aston Villa, QPR, Leicester Fosse, Barnsley, Manchester United, Swindon Town, Millwall, Norwich City (1904-1931)*
A much travelled inside forward, Travers began his career in the Birmingham League before moving to Wolves. Transferred to Villa in a part-exchange deal involving Jack Wilcox in December 1908. Finished his career in the Southern League having served in the Army and went on to work as an auctioneer in his home city of Birmingham. Died in 1946.

TREVIS, Derek
Midfielder
Born: *Birmingham* Died: 2000
Playing career: *Aston Villa, Colchester United, Walsall, Lincoln City, Stockport County, Philadelphia Atoms, Philadelphia Fury (1962-1978)*
Derek Trevis, who began his career with Aston Villa and was also captain of Walsall, also played for Lincoln City under former England manager Graham Taylor and gained his FA coaching badge there. A graduate in applied science, Trevis went to Philadelphia in 1971 as skipper and player-coach of the Philadelphia Atoms and helped them win the North American Soccer League championship. He later worked as a sales representative with a pharmaceutical company in America until he retired. Trevis had two toes amputated as a result of poor circulation in his feet. Died in 2000.

TULLY, Fred
Winger
Born: *St Pancras, London* Died: 1969
Playing career: *Aston Villa, Southampton (1926-1939)*
A winger of great enterprise, Tully appeared seven times for Villa in the 1927-1928 and 1928-1929 seasons but spent the next four seasons in the reserves before moving to the south coast to join Second Division Southampton in June 1933. Also played for Clapton Orient. After two seasons playing in east London, the onset of the Second World War brought about his retirement. He then joined his father's carpentry business before returning to Chaddleston Mental Hospital where he worked as an attendant.

TURNBULL, Fred
Central Defender
Born: *Wallsend*
Playing career: *Aston Villa & Halifax Town*
In August 1966 Turnbull came to Villa for a two-month trial. After impressing the scouts, he quickly became a first team regular. He went on loan to Halifax for seven games but otherwise spent his entire career in the claret and blue. A defender, Turnbull played in the 1971 League Cup final at Wembley as Villa lost 2-0. After 183 goals and three goals for the club, Turnbull was forced to retire through injury. He then held a number of jobs including insurance broker, car park attendant and in a shipyard in Wallsend.

TURNBULL, Lee
Forward
Born: *Stockton-on-Tees*
Playing career: *Middlesbrough, Aston Villa, Doncaster Rovers, Chesterfield, Doncaster Rovers, Wycombe Wanderers, Scunthorpe United (1985-2002)*
One of Graham Taylor's first signings in his Aston Villa overhaul, Turnbull was prised away from his hometown club Boro to sign for the claret and blue for £50,000. Turnbull, a highly rated striker, plied his trade at reserve and youth level for Villa and never made an appearance for the first team although he did feature on the bench. Having left Villa he had a nomadic existence in the lower leagues. Having retired, Turnbull moved into coaching. He managed non league Barrow between and went on to be appointed as assistant boss of Southport. Turnbull is currently works as head of recruitment at Scunthorpe United.

TURNER, Arthur

Inside right

Born: *Birmingham*

Playing career: *Aston Villa, Small Heath (1890-1891)*

Briefly on the books at Villa, he never played for the first team and instead crossed the city to turn out for hometown team Small Heath. Turner retired soon afterwards and took up a job in a paper mill. He died in 1902 aged only 35 after he contracted smallpox.

UNSWORTH, David

Centre-back/Left-back

Born: *Chorley, Lancashire*

Playing career: *Everton, West Ham United, Aston Villa, Portsmouth, Ipswich Town, Sheffield United, Wigan A, Burnley, Huddersfield Town (1991-2009)*

Initial success at Everton led to a move south to West Ham but his family failed to settle in the capital and he very quickly left the club to sign for Villa. With his family back in Merseyside, Unsworth soon concluded that the commute to and from Birmingham was too much and so after just over a month at Villa Park. Everton were willing to match the £3m that Villa had paid so he returned 'home' without having ever pulled on a Villa shirt. 'Rhino', as he was nicknamed by Everton fans, was eventually released by the club in 2004 and since his retirement five years later, he has had two spells as caretaker manager of both Preston and boyhood club Everton.

VALLANCE, Hugh

Centre-forward

Born: *Wolverhampton* Died: 1973

Playing career: *Aston Villa, QPR, Brighton and Hove Albion, Gillingham, Racing Club de Paris, Cork City, Evesham Town (1927-1935)*

The former guardsman from Wolverhampton played only in the reserves. He was to have a purple patch at Brighton but his contract on the south coast was cancelled in mysterious circumstances, and he ended up playing in the obscurity of the Birmingham League. He returned to professional football but gave up the game to focus on a career in the RAF. Vallance died in Birmingham in 1973.

VARCO, Percy

Forward

Born: *Fowey* Died: 1982

Playing career: *Torquay United, Aston Villa, QPR, Norwich City, Exeter City, Brighton (1924-1932)*

Varco was not a tall man - just 5ft 9 inches - but weighed in at 13 stones. His beefy, robust style was also backed up by an incredible eye for goal. The striker joined Villa for a fee of £200, scoring twice in 10 league games. Played for four more clubs before ending up in playing non-league football back in Devon. Varco was later elected Mayor of his hometown of Fowey and also worked in the fishing industry. Died in 1992.

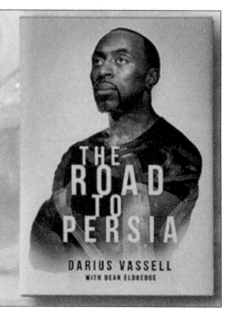

VASSELL, Darius

Striker/Winger
Born: *Birmingham*
Playing career: *Romulus, Aston Villa, Manchester City, Ankaragucu, Leicester City, (1996-2012)*

Vassell rose through the ranks at Villa Park, playing for every age group side before earning his shot in the first team with a debut in 1998. He played more than 150 games under three different managers for his boyhood team - John Gregory, Graham Taylor and David O'Leary. Vassell was allowed to live his dream, playing alongside idol Dion Dublin and banging them in on a regular basis at the Holte End. Held a unique record of not losing in 47 league games when he scored. Vassell earned 22 caps, scoring six times, and played at the 2002 World Cup and Euro 2004. His best qualities were considered to be his pace and agility, with many of his best performances seemingly coming in England colours. He also carved out a niche as a super sub. Since retiring - after spells with Manchester City, Ankaragucu in Turkey, Vassell has gone into coaching. He currently works as a youth coach at Wolves, and has set up his own sports agency, Inama Enterprises Ltd.

VOWDEN, Geoff

Forward
Born: *Barnsley*
Playing career: *Nottingham Forest, Birmingham City, Aston Villa. (1959-1973).*

The forward made history when becoming the first substitute ever to hit a hat-trick. Unfortunately it came in the blue of Birmingham rather the the claret and blue of Villa, but is still something that is unlikely to ever be surpassed. Then a 27-year-old striker of some repute, he plundered a treble as Blues beast Huddersfield at St Andrew's. He remained at St Andrew's until March 1971 when he joined Aston Villa for £12,500 and scored 11 times as they won the Third Division title. He moved on to New York Cosmos in 1974 before embarking on a coaching career in England and Saudi Arabia. Vowden had a spell as player/manager of Kettering in 1974/75.

WALKER, Billy

Striker
Born: *Wednesbury* Died: 1964
Playing career: *Aston Villa (1914-1933)*

Who is the greatest claret and blue star of all-time? What about the late, great Billy Walker? Walker had a massive impact and made his final appearance at Portsmouth having set a club record of 531 appearances - only beaten by Charlie Aitken in December 1973 - while his overall record of 244 goals still stands. Won the FA Cup in 1919/20 In 1920-21, he hit four goals against Arsenal on the opening day of the season - becoming the first Villa player to ever achieve this feat. Walker netted double figures for Villa in 12 consecutive seasons from 1919-20 - and also scored 12 league and cup hat-tricks. He scored nine goals in 18 England caps and went on to manage Sheffield Wednesday, Chelmsford and Nottingham Forest. He became only the second person to have played in and then managed an FA Cup winning team, leading the Owls to FA Cup success in 1934. Died 1964.

WALKER, Ray

Midfielder
Born: *North Shields*
Playing career: *Nottingham Boys, Aston Villa, Port Vale, Cambridge United (loan), Leek Town, Newcastle Town (1981-1994)*

Known as the 'Hoddle of the lower leagues'

Walker was a set-piece expert and briefly shot to fame with a stunning goal for Port Vale to knock Spurs out of the FA Cup. He had two spells for the Stoke club, having signed from Villa for £12,000 in 1986. Walker - a lovely passer of the ball - failed to establish himself at Villa Park and left after five years having only played 23 times. Walker represented England at youth level and went on to become a manager with Leek Town and non league Newcastle Town. He now works as Football in the Community officer at Crewe Alexandra.

WALKER, Richard
Forward
Born: *Birmingham*
Playing career: *Aston Villa, Blackpool, Northampton Town, Bristol Rovers, Burton Albion (1997-2012)*
Walker started his career at Villa in 1997 and made six Premier League appearances in claret and blue. He then had loan spells with Cambridge, Blackpool and Wycombe before an extensive career in the Football League and later in non league. Since 2012, he has lived in the south west and has continued his playing days as player/manager of Devon and Exeter League side Beer Albion.

WALLACE, Charlie
Winger
Born: *Sunderland* Died: 1970
Playing career: *Southwick, Crystal Palace, Aston Villa, Oldham Athletic (1905-1921)*
Wallace made 368 appearances for Villa, winning two FA Cups and the league title in 1909-10 but will go down in history as the first man to miss a penalty in an FA Cup final. He failed to score from the sport in the 1913 final against Sunderland but went on to get the winner to have the last laugh. A couple years later, World War I broke out. Wallace enlisted and was actually sent to the Western Front. He survived the war and returned to play help Villa to another FA Cup triumph in 1920. After that season, he was sold to Oldham Athletic for £1000. He played a few seasons for Oldham before retiring in 1923. Wallace was the recipient of three England caps during his career. Following his retirement from playing, Wallace became a youth team coach at Aston Villa and went on to work for the club in various capacities over the years. He passed away in 1970.

WALSH, Dave
Striker
Born: *1923* Died: 2016
Playing career: *West Bromwich Albion, Aston Villa, Walsall. (1946-1955).*
A nimble player with an eye for goal, Walsh was a prolific marksman in claret-and-blue, scoring 40 goals in 114 games after joining the club from neighbours West Brom for £25,000 in December 1950. Walsh began his career with Limerick United before joining Albion from Linfield in 1946. He scored 100 goals in 174 games for the Baggies. He was also an Irish international, playing for both the Republic and Northern Ireland, and was the last survivor of the team who famously became the first foreign side to beat England on home soil, at Goodison Park in 1949.

WALTERS, Mark
Midfielder/Winger
Born: *Birmingham*
Playing career: *Aston Villa, Rangers, Liverpool, Stoke City, Wolverhampton Wanderers, Southampton, Swindon Town, Bristol Rovers (1981-2002)*
He notably played for Liverpool, Rangers and Aston Villa, and later went on to play for Stoke City, Wolverhampton Wanderers, Southampton, Swindon Town and Bristol Rovers. He was a key man in Villa's promotion to the First Division in 1987/88, in all he played over 200 times for the club in a six year stay in the Midlands. He was capped once by England against New Zealand under Graham Taylor in 1991. After retiring, Walters went back to school and obtained teaching qualifications. He is currently Head of Languages at Aston Villa's academy and has since also played in the Sky Sports masters football competitions for Rangers.

WARBURTON, George
Forward
Born: *The Hague, Netherlands* Died: 1996
Playing career: *Morecambe, Aston Villa, Preston North End, Chester, Morecambe (1936-1939)*
Warburton was on the books at Villa for the 1936/37 and 1937/38 seasons. He never played a senior game for the first team and moved on to Fourth Division Chester. He stayed there for one year then linked up with his brother Joe at Morecambe. Ended his career in the non league game and then moved back to his native Netherlands where he worked in the tourism industry having hung up his boots.

WARD, Gavin
Goalkeeper
Born: *Sutton Coldfield*
Playing career: *Aston Villa, Shrewsbury Town, West Bromwich Albion, Cardiff City, Leicester City, Bradford City, Bolton Wanderers, Burnley, Stoke City, Walsall, Coventry City, Barnsley, Preston North End, Tranmere Rovers, Chester-City, Wrexham, Hednesford Town, Gainsborough Trinity (1987-2010)*
Played for 19 different clubs across a 26 year career, including notably in the Premier League for Leicester. He began his career with Villa before moving on to Shrewsbury Town. He failed to make an appearance for either club and left for West Bromwich Albion where he made his professional debut in a League Cup match against Bradford City. He is currently goalkeeping coach at QPR, a role he has held at Nottingham Forest. Ward was also assistant manager at non league Gainsborough Trinity from 2009/2011.

WARD, Joe
Striker
Born: *Glasgow, Scotland*
Playing career: *Clyde, Aston Villa, Hibernian, Dundee United, Ayr United, Stirling Albion, St Johnstone (1974-1987)*
Ward played three games for the Villans, returning to Scotland with Hibernian where he played a further nine times before joining Dundee United. Ward's time at Tannadice was equally short as he played only six times before moving to Ayr United. After nearly forty appearances, Ward moved on to Stirling Albion, before playing out his career with St Johnstone. After retirement he worked for the Scottish FA as an advisor.

WARING, Tom
Centre-forward
Born: *Birkenhead* Died: 1980
Playing career: *Tranmere Rovers, Aston Villa, Barnsley, Wolverhampton Wanderers, Tranmere Rovers, Accrington Stanley, (1926-1946)*
Just over six-feet tall he had everything a top striker needs. Height, speed, amazing strength – he was almost impossible to knock off the ball – and intelligence. As quick of thought as he was of foot, Waring was deadly in the box. Nicknamed "Pongo" after a famous cartoon of the time, Waring was one of Aston Villa's all-time great centre forwards. He was the first - and so far only - man to hit 50 goals in a single season for the claret and blue as he plundered a half century of strikes in the 1930/31 season. His 226 games for Villa yielded 167 goals including ten hat-tricks. Waring was also capped five times by England and scored four goals. He died in 1980 aged 74.

WARNER, Jimmy
Goalkeeper
Born: *Birmingham* Died: 1943
Playing career: *Milton, Aston Villa (1886-1894)*
The six seasons of goalkeeper Jimmy Warner's association with Villa between 1886 and 1892 were notable for the Cup finals - both between the Villa and local rivals West Bromwich Albion. In 1886-7 Villa were successful by 2 - 0, but in 1891-2 Albion had their revenge and caused a sensation throughout the football world by beating their more fancied rivals by 3 - 0.

It was that match and result which caused Jimmy Warner to cast aside Villa colours. Embittered by defeat, Villa partisans accused him of selling the Cup final. It was a cruel accusation which the slanderers lived to regret. Jimmy was made a broken-hearted man. After leaving Villa and football in general, he migrated to America and lived the remainder of his life in Pittsburgh, Pennsylvania and died there in 1943.

WARNOCK, Stephen
Full-back
Born: *Ormskirk*
Playing career: *Liverpool, Coventry City, Bradford City, Blackburn Rovers, Aston Villa, Bolton Wanderers, Leeds United, Derby County (1994-2016)*
Warnock played for Liverpool, Coventry City, Bradford City, Blackburn Rovers, Aston Villa, Bolton Wanderers, Leeds United, Derby County, Wigan Athletic and Burton Albion. He was capped twice by England and was part of the nation's squad at the 2010 FIFA World Cup. The left-back played for Villa in the 2010 League Cup final, when the claret and blue went down 2-1 to Man United. Since his retirement, Warnock has become a regular football pundit on radio and television, covering the Premier League, Champions League and EFL for the BBC, BT Sport, DAZN and Quest TV.

WATKINS, Walter
Centre-forward
Born: *Caersws, Wales* Died: 1942
Playing career: *Stoke, Aston Villa, Sunderland, Crystal Palace, Northampton Town (1894-1911)*
He joined Villa from Stoke under George Ramsay but played only six matches, scoring once for the club in a short lived Villa spell. Earned ten Wales caps between 1902 and 1908. Watkins went on to turn out for Southern League Crystal Palace, Northampton, Stoke again and Crewe in the Football League. After he retired from the game in 1911, Watkins worked in a garden centre and latterly in a factory during the war. He died in Stoke in 1962.

WATSON, Frank
Forward
Born: *Basford* Died: 1972
Playing career: *Aston Villa, Blackpool, Leeds United, Brentford, Southend U, Crewe A (1921-1931)*
Watson never progressed beyond Aston Villa's youth teams, but played at Football League level for Blackpool, Brentford and Crewe in the 1920s. Little seems to be known about his career. Despite the fact he was on the books of several different clubs, he is only recorded as having played for three of three of these, turning out ten times in total in as many years. Watson, a forward, died in Nottingham in 1973, aged 73.

Kennington Oval - home of the early FA Cup finals

WATSON, Steve
Defender/Midfielder
Born: *North Shields*
Playing career: *Newcastle United, Aston Villa, Everton, WBA, Sheffield Wednesday (1991-2009)*
A versatile player, Watson played over 500 games for Everton, Newcastle, Aston Villa and West Brom in a career spanning 19 years. He retired in 2009 after being released by Sheffield Wednesday. He joined the coaching staff at Huddersfield alongside former teammate Lee Clark before Watson was appointed as assistant manager at Birmingham. He briefly moved away from management to set up a coaching app known as ProSports and as a pundit for BT Sport. Watson has managed Gateshead and as of 2019 he's appointed as the boss of National League North side York City.

WEBB, Sid
Inside-forward
Born: *Coventry* Died: 1956
Playing career: *St Saviour's, Stourbridge, Aston Villa, Burton United, Wednesbury Old Athletic, Birmingham, Worcester City (1908-1914)*
Webb caught the eye of Villa's powers that be after impressing in the local amateur leagues for a number of clubs including Stourbridge, Burton united and Wednesbury. Although he spent a season at Villa Park, he only ever found himself in the reserves at Villa Park. Described as a rotund little schemer, Webb moved across the city to join the Blues of Birmingham. Unlike at Villa, Webb did actually play for the Blues albeit only three games. Webb returned to the non league scene in the city. After retirement, he stayed in the area and worked as a taxi driver in Tamworth. Webb died in 1956 aged 72.

WESTON, Tommy
Left-back
Born: *Halesowen* Died: 1952
Playing career: *Aston Villa, Stoke (1911-1923)*
Weston was born in Halesowen and played for several amateur sides including Old Hill Comrades, Coombs Wood and Stourbridge before joining First Division Aston Villa in 1911. He made his Football League debut against Manchester City in January 1912, and he soon established himself as first choice full back earning a reputation as a tough and uncompromising defender.

He helped Villa win the FA Cup in 1913 and again in 1920. in total, Weston made 179 appearances for the "Villans" in seven seasons losing four of them to the First World War, and he twice finished runners-up in the First Division with Villa in 1912-13 and 1913-14. He left Villa Park in the summer of 1922 and joined newly promoted Stoke where he only managed to play four matches in 1922-23 before deciding to retire. He served in the Army during WW1.

WHATELEY, Oliver
Inside-forward
Born: *Birmingham* Died: 1926
Playing career: *Aston Villa (1880-1888)*
Olly Whateley, as he used to be familiarly called, was a footballer of very pronounced ability and sometimes a good deal better than he was at others; but when he was at his best, Whateley was a very skilful and formidable forward indeed. Whateley earned two caps for England in 1883 and scored twice. Began with Gladstone Unity FC. He then moved to Aston Villa FC from July 1880 to May 1888. Villa won the FA Cup in his only season in charge but Whateley did not play in their run to the final or the final itself. Retired from football with cancer of the face. By vocation an artist, designer and draughtsman, and in 1911 underwent a severe operation. Nonetheless, although too old for military service, he served in Rouen, France, with the YMCA during the First World War. In the twenties, in poor health, he fell on hard times, and so strained were his circumstances that, in 1923, Aston Villa set up a fund to help him.

WHITEHOUSE, James
Goalkeeper
Born: *Birmingham* Died: 1934
Playing career: *Birmingham St George's Grimsby Town, Aston Villa, Bedminster, Grimsby Town, Manchester United, Manchester City, Third Lanark, Hull City, Southend United (1890-1907)*
A goalkeeper, Whitehouse began his football career with Albion Swifts in 1888 and played for Football Alliance side Birmingham St George's, but joined Grimsby Town at the end of the 1891/92 season. He became a regular in the first team, missing only two matches in 1893-94 and being an ever present for the following two seasons, making 131 appearances before a move

to Villa in July 1896 for a fee of £200. Whitehouse began his first season with Aston Villa as understudy to Tom Wilkes, but soon took over the goalkeeping gloves and ended up playing in 17 of the first 19 matches of the League season. He went on to play a key part as Aston Villa won the cup and were crowned champions, the first team to win The since Preston North End went undefeated throughout the 1888-89 season. He left for Grimsby having played in 40 matches across two years. After he hung up his boots, he returned to Grimsby as a coach and assistant manager.

WHITLEY, Jack
Goalkeeper
Born: *Seacombe* Died: 1955
Playing career: *Liscard YMCA, Darwen, Aston Villa, Everton, Stoke, Leeds City, Lincoln City, Chelsea (1899-1913)*
Whitley joined Aston Villa for £50 from Second Division Darwen in 1899 and went on to play eleven games over two seasons in the Midlands. Went on to play for Everton, Stoke, Leeds City and Lincoln City before finishing his career with Chelsea were he played over 100 games during a turbulent time in which the Blues were relegated and promoted again. He also played cricket for Yorkshire and Leeds CC. Having announced his retirement as a player, Whitley stayed on at Chelsea as a physio and trainer. Died in 1955.

Guy Whittingham
@guywhittingham

Former professional footballer & Manager/Coach. Currently FA Youth coach developer & Co-commentary summariser for BBC Radio Solent Sport.

WHITTINGHAM, Guy
Striker
Born: *Evesham*
Playing career: *Yeovil Town, Portsmouth, Aston Villa, Wolverhampton Wanderers, Sheffield Wednesday, Watford, Peterborough United, Oxford United, Wycombe Wanderers (1988-2001)*
He made over 450 appearances for a number of clubs, after leaving the British Army at the age of 25. Despite this relatively late start, he notched up over 100 Pompey goals and broke the club's all-time scoring record of 42 league goals in the 1992-3 season. He later went on to become player-manager of Newport, Isle of Wight, but left them when the club ran into financial difficulties. Whittingham also coached at Newbury and Eastleigh before joining the first-team coaching staff at Fratton Park. Served Pompey as both player and manager.
Twitter: https://twitter.com/guywhittingham

WHITTINGHAM, Peter
Midfielder
Born: *Nuneaton*
Playing career: *Aston Villa, Burnley (loan), Derby County (loan), Cardiff City (2003-2007)*
Whittingham is currently a free agent having most recently plied his trade for Blackburn. He was part of the Aston Villa team that won the FA Youth Cup in 2002, and a year later he made his Premier League debut. He was part of the Cardiff side to reach both domestic cup finals in 2008 and 2012. Played over 400 games for the Welsh side before he moved to Blackburn, his last club. Whittingham also played 17 times for the England U21 side.

WILCOX, Jack
Outside-right
Born: *Stourbridge* Died: 1940
Playing career: *Aston Villa, Birmingham, Southampton, Wellington Town (1906-1916)*
Wilcox joined Villa initially as an amateur, before he signed as a professional in 1907. He only played six games in the Football League for Aston Villa, before joining derby rivals Birmingham the following year. A winger who was known for his skill, Wilcox then moved to the the south coast with Southampton before he moved into the non league game with Wellington Town after one season at The Dell. He later went on to become a utility worker.

WILKES, Tom
Goalkeeper
Born: *Alcester* Died: 1921
Playing career: *Redditch Town, Aston Villa, Stoke (loan), Stoke (1894-1903)*
Wilkes joined Aston Villa in 1894 and immediately enshrined himself into club folklore as their ever-present custodian during Villa's Victorian era dominance. He was part of the side to win three League titles and two FA Cups but eventually fell out of favour but lost his place to Billy George. He had two spells at Stoke both loan and then permanent with another - albeit brief - spell back in claret and blue in between. He returned to Villa and played four more times for the first team in 1898-99 before joining Stoke permanently in the summer of 1899 after 77 appearances for Villa. Retired in 1903 and later owned the Wharf Tavern public house in Stoke.

WILLIAMS, Evan
Goalkeeper
Born: *Dumbarton*
Playing career: *Third Lanark, Wolves, Aston Villa, Celtic, Clyde, Stranraer*
More widely known for his time in Scotland during which time he helped Celtic to six successive league titles in a row. After months of pursuing the Wolves keeper, who was on loan at Aston Villa at the time, Jock Stein finally secured his signature in October 1969. He played 12 times under Tommy Docherty for the Villa. Despite his impressive performances for a variety of clubs, Williams never got a look in for Scotland at international level. Williams was also manager of Vale of Leven and Ardeer Thistle.

WILLIAMS, Gareth
Midfielder
Born: *Cowes, Isle of Wight*
Playing career: *Aston Villa, Barnsley, Bournemouth, Northampton Town, Hull City, (1985-2010)*
Played at amateur level on the south coast before he signed for Villa in 1988. In three years at the club, he only played 12 times but went on to enjoy a decent career with the likes of Northampton Town, Scarborough and Hull City in the lower echelons of the English game. Having retired as a player, Williams was appointed as joint manager of Derbyshire-based Matlock Town.

WILLIAMS, Jackie
Midfielder
Born: *Aberdare, Wales* Died: 1987
Playing career: *Llanelli, Huddersfield Town, Aston Villa, Ipswich Town, Wrexham (1932-1939)*
Williams played for five different clubs in England and his native Wales. Williams made 17 appearances for Villa scoring five goals in the 1935/36 season. He earned one cap for Wales in 1939, against France. He started his career with non-league Llanelli before signing for Huddersfield in 1932. He joined Villa three years later and also played for Ipswich before the outbreak of WW2. Went into coaching after retirement as a player. He died in 1987 in Wrexham aged 76.

WILLIAMS, Keith
Midfielder
Born: *Dudley*
Playing career: *Aston Villa, Northampton Town, Bournemouth, Colchester United (1973-1988)*
He joined Aston Villa on schoolboy terms before he signed as a professional in April 1975. He never progressed further than the club's youth teams however. Spent the bulk of his career with Northampton and AFC Bournemouth before he had one final year with Colchester United. Later turned out for several non league clubs including Salisbury and Poole Town. He later became a commissioner in the New Forest.

WILLIAMS, Lee
Midfielder
Born: *Birmingham*
Playing career: *Aston Villa, Shrewsbury Town (loan), Peterborough United, Shamrock Rovers, Mansfield Town, Cheltenham Town, Telford United (1991-2003)*
Williams was forced to give up playing after a freak eye injury suffered in training whilst at Cheltenham. He was on the books at Villa for three years but never played for the senior side. He played over 100 times for both Peterborough and Mansfield. After his retirement, Williams was appointed coach and then assistant boss to Paul Holleran at Walsall-based side Rushall Olympic.

"DID YOU KNOW?"

"Steve Staunton's 64 Republic of Ireland appearances means that he is Villa's most capped player."

WILSON, Bob

Goalkeeper
Born: *1943*
Playing career: *Aston Villa, Cardiff City, Bristol City, Exeter City. (1963-1975).*

Wilson began his career with Aston Villa as a youth player, signing a full contract in September 1961. He went on to make nine league appearances for the club before he was sold for £2,000 to Cardiff City in August 1964. In his first season at the club he helped the side to win the Welsh Cup and reach the quarter-finals of the European Cup Winners Cup. Finally, he decided to stay in Devon, having ended his career at Exeter City and worked for the Royal Mail based at Exeter St David's railway station

WILSON, Charlie

Inside-forward
Born: *Heeley, Sheffield Died: 1985*
Playing career: *WBA, Sheffield Wednesday, Grimsby Town, Aston Villa, Coventry City (1919-1937)*

Wilson had a long career as an inside forward without ever settling any any one club. Joined Villa from Grimsby in 1933 but never made a first team appearances for the club. Guested for Charlton and Aldershot during WW2, and also served as a policeman in Kidderminster. He retired in 1947 and later worked as a labourer.

WILSON, Joe

Outside-left
Born: *Birmingham Died: 1952*
Playing career: *Stoke (amateur), Walsall Town (amateur), Aston Villa (amateur), Walsall Town (amateur), West Bromwich Albion, Kidderminster Harriers, Birmingham St George's (1877-1892)*

Described as an intelligent, unobtrusive left-winger, Wilson represented several West Midlands sides with distinction. He rose to prominence with West Bromwich Albion, winning the FA Cup and scoring the club's first ever professional Football League goal. Wilson turned out for Walsall Swifts, twice, and Aston Unity for whom he also played cricket. He signed for Villa in 1886. Wilson retired from playing and then became a top level Football League referee and linesman, officiating in both divisions and also in the FA Cup. Wilson later worked as a goldsmith in Birmingham's Jewellery Quarter for 25 years prior to the Second World War. He died in Birmingham in 1952.

WILSON, Terry

Winger
Born: *Dunfermline, Scotland*
Playing career: *Aston Villa, Cowdenbeath, Arbroath, Hibernian, Dunfermline Athletic, Hamilton Academical, Dunfermline Athletic (1977-1983)*

His tender age undoubtedly proved a sticking point as he was only 16 during his time at Villa. Perhaps unsurprisingly, he never made the grade and quickly returned to his native Scotland without ever playing for the claret and blue. After he hung up his boots, Wilson remained actively involved in Scottish football as he worked as a scout for Arbroath and helped to coach schoolkids.

WILSON, Tommy

Forward
Born: *Preston Died: 1940*
Playing career: *Manchester United, Ashton-in-Makerfield, West Manchester, Ashton Town, Ashton North End, Oldham County, Swindon Town, Blackburn Rovers, Millwall Athletic, Queen's Park Rangers, Aston Villa, Bolton Wanderers, Leeds City*

A journeyman player for ten different clubs across 12 years. After the First World War had come to an end he took over as Rochdale chairman and combined the role with being manager until February 1923. Later became a publican back in his home county of Lancashire, this time in in Bolton.

WINDMILL, Jack

Half-back
Born: *Brierley Hill Died: 1927*
Playing career: *Aston Villa (1903-1910)*

He played initially for Halesowen Town before joining Aston Villa in 1903. Having become a regular, he played in - and won - the 1905 FA Cup with the club as Villa beat Newcastle in the final. Windmill, as with many footballers of the time, had employment away from football, in his case teaching. In total, the popular half-back had made 50 competitive senior appearances for Villa and scored one goal. Windmill saw active service in World War I in the Royal Warwickshire Regiment. He rose to the rank of Regimental Sergeant Major and gained the Military Cross and the Distinguished Conduct Medal for bravery. After the war he continued in the teaching profession and was appointed headmaster of Brook Street School in Wordsley in 1922.

WINTON, Doug
Full-back
Born: *Perth, Scotland* Died: 2006
Playing career: *Burnley, Aston Villa (1951-1964)*
A buccaneering full-back who eventually brought him to the attention of the Scottish selectors and he earned a B cap against England in 1957. Winton joined Aston Villa two years later and moved onto Rochdale, his last league club, in 1961, having played 37 times for the Midlands team. He played in the 1962 League Cup final for Dale. He retired in 1964 and continued to live in the north west, working as a coal merchant.

WITHE, Peter
Striker
Born: *Liverpool*
Playing career: *Wolverhampton Wanderers, Portland Timbers, Birmingham City, Nottingham Forest, Newcastle United, Aston Villa, Sheffield United, Huddersfield Town, Aston Villa (1970-1989)*
Scorer of the most famous goal in Aston Villa history with the winner against the might of Bayern Munich in the European Cup final of 1982. Capped eleven times by England and a much-travelled player, Withe had a spell in charge of Wimbledon before returning to Villa Park as Youth Development Director. He managed the national teams of Thailand and Indonesia before returning to his homeland in 2012. Had a spell as manager of Stockport Sports (formerly Woodley), and still lives in the Birmingham area. You can purchase a copy of his autobiography entitled 'All for the love of the game" at: 'https://www.peterwitheofficial.com/

WITHERS, Colin
Goalkeeper
Born: *Erdington, Birmingham*
Playing career: *West Bromwich Albion, Birmingham City, Aston Villa, Lincoln City (1956-1973)*
The Erdington-born goalkeeper, who had previously played for rivals Birmingham across the city, cost £18,000 when he joined Villa in November 1964. He made a total of 163 league and cup appearances for Villa. Withers played for England at youth level and also represented Go Ahead Eagles in the Netherlands. Withers served as player/manager of Midland League side Atherstone. In later life he took up a job as a player agent and briefly worked for the Football Association.

WOLLASTON, Arthur
Half-back
Born: *Shrewsbury* Died: 1933
Playing career: *Aston Villa (1888-1889)*
Wollaston played three league games and one FA Cup tie at left half during the first Football League season. Before and after his brief Villa spell he played at amateur level for Stafford Road and Chirk AAA in Wales. Wollaston played an important - albeit only fleeting - part in the ever Football League season for the Villa, playing four times as they finished runners up to Preston's Invincibles side. After he hung up his boots, he remained involved the game working for the Welsh FA and later in a steelworks. Wollaston, a half back during his career, died in Shrewsbury in 1933.

WOOD, Alf
Half-back
Born: *Smallthorne* Died: 1919
Playing career: *Stoke, Aston Villa, Derby County, Bradford Park Avenue (1891-1907)*
Interestingly, Wood - a half back by trade, was deployed in every position except as keeper during his four year spell at Villa. A versatile player, he quickly became a virtual ever present having signed for the club from Stoke in 1901. Villa finished league runners up to the Wednesday in 1902/03, and Wood left two years later having scored seven times in 111 games for the Villains. Also played for Derby and Bradford PA. In retirement, Wood went on to became a railway worker and also had a job as a museum curator.

WOODWARD, John
Forward
Born: *Stoke-on-Trent*
Playing career: *Stoke City, Aston Villa, Walsall, Port Vale, Scunthorpe United, Oostende (1964-1977)*
Woodward is one of an elite group of players to have featured and scored in all four divisions of the league system. Joining Villa for £300,000 from Stoke, he was brought in to replace the popular Tony Hateley who left for pastures new. He endured a turbulent time at Villa Park, with the club relegated and then twice languishing in the lower reaches of the Second Division. Woodward had three different Villa bosses, with Dick Taylor, and Tommys Cummings and Docherty all taking charge at various stages of his time at the club. Woodward scored seven goals in 26 league games for the club and in 1969 moved on again to Midlands rivals Walsall. He also played for Port Vale, Scunthorpe, Oostende in Belgium and Kidderminster Harriers where he later became a coach.

WOOSNAM, Phil
Striker
Born: *Caersws, Powys, Wales* Died: 2013
Playing career: *Manchester City, Leyton Orient, West Ham United, Aston Villa. (1952-1965).*
The cousin of golfer Ian Woosnam, he played for five clubs in England and one in the USA. Earned 17 caps for Wales and then coached and managed across the pond. Woosnam became coach at Atlanta Chiefs in 1968, and was named 'Coach of the Year' in 1968, going on to manager the United States national team the same year.

Woosnam was described as a "gifted, quick thinking striker with a pronounced intelligence and reading of the game." He later became managing director of the marketing arm of US Soccer, and helped bring the 1994 World Cup to the US. He was inducted into the US National Soccer Hall of Fame and the Georgia Soccer Hall of Fame in 1997. Woosnam died in 2013 at the age of 80.

WRIGHT, Alan
Defender
Born: *Ashton-under-Lyne, Lancashire*
Playing career: *Blackburn Rovers, Blackpool, Middlesbrough, Aston Villa, Derby County, Leeds United, Cardiff City, Doncaster Rovers, Nottingham Forest, Sheffield United (1989-2011)*
Small in size mighty in stature, Wright was nicknamed the mighty atom due to his diminutive size. The smallest player ever to have appeared in the Premier League at just 5ft 4, he had the heart of a lion and Villa quickly appreciated his unstinting efforts, work rate and commitment to the cause. He made 102 consecutive first-team starts in league and cup games, a record at the time. Wright won the League Cup with Villa in 1996 and, alongside Ugo Ehiogu, made the 1995-96 FA Premier League Team of the Year, proving that size counts for nothing! He is also remembered for one of the sport's strangest injuries when he developed RSI in his knee after straining to reach the accelerator of his Ferrari. After retirement he went into coaching and managed Northwich Victoria and Southport. Wright was capped twice by England U21.

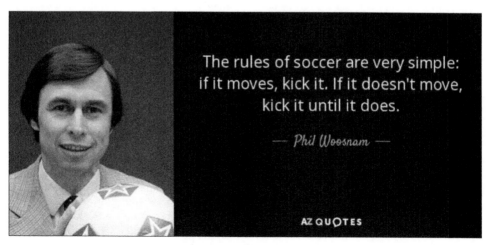

The rules of soccer are very simple: if it moves, kick it. If it doesn't move, kick it until it does.

— *Phil Woosnam* —

AZ QUOTES

WRIGHT, Edmund
Goalkeeper
Born: *Leytonstone* Died: 1978
Playing career: *Worcester City, High Wycombe, Aston Villa, Brentford (1919-1923)*
Wright played in the Football League for Brentford and Villa, but he turned out only twice for the latter before moving to west London. A goalkeeper, he later represented several teams at amateur level in the London area, before retiring in 1927. Having hung up his boots, he drifted out of the game to become a taxi driver. Wright was also a qualified engineer.

WRIGHT, Mick
Right-back
Born: *Ellesmere Port*
Playing career: *Aston Villa (1962-1973)*
Wright signed for Villa as an apprentice and went on to spend his entire decade-long career at Villa Park. A tough-tackling right back, he played over 300 games between 1963 and 1973, alongside the likes of Charlie Aitken, Vic Crowe, Ron Wylie, Harry Burrows and John Sleeuwenhoek. His career was brought to an untimely end by a knee injury in his prime, at just 27 years of age. After retirement, he stayed at Villa in a number of different roles including scout, board member and coach.

WYLIE, Ron
Right-half/Inside-forward
Born: *Glasgow, Scotland*
Playing career: *Notts County, Aston Villa, Birmingham City. (1951-1969).*
The inside-forward joined Villa from Notts County in 1958 and made 244 appearances for the club, scoring 27 goals, before moving across the city in the summer of 1965. But he was essentially a Villa man, later serving the club as assistant manager, reserve-team coach, scout and community liaison officer. He went on to play almost 150 games for Birmingham City before retiring aged 37. After he hung up his boots he joined the coaching staff at Villa before joining Coventry first as coach and then as assistant manager. Coached in Hong Kong and managed West Brom, before he was appointed boss of Villa's reserves, later working as a scout bet yet again returning as community liaison officer when he stayed until 2002.

YATES, Harry
Defender
Born: *Walsall* Died: 1932
Playing career: *Aston Villa, Walsall (1888-1898)*
A defensive wing-half known as "Tubby", he was a big, strong defender with considerable power. Yates played in 13 of Villa's 22 games during the inaugural Football League season of 1888/89 as they finished second behind the Invincibles of Preston. Weighing in at a hefty 14 stone, defender Yates only made one further appearance for the club. He retired in 1900, drifted out of football and went on to become a railway employee.

YATES, William
Forward
Born: *Birmingham* Died: 1957
Playing career: *Manchester United, Aston Villa, Brighton & Hove Albion, Heart of Midlothian*
Birmingham born, Yates was signed as an amateur by the Villa and played one match for the club in 1903 on a trial basis. A forward "with an eye for goal" Yates finished his career with Portsmouth and Coventry, playing over 100 games for each before hanging up his boots through injury. Yates went on to keep a pub in Coventry.

YORK, Richard
Winger
Born: *Birmingham* Died: 1969
Playing career: *Handsworth Royal, Birchfield Rangers, the RAF, Aston Villa, Port Vale, Brierley Hill Alliance (1915-1932)*
Born on the doorstep of Villa Park, 'Dicky' as he became affectionately known as, was capped three times for England as a schoolboy. At school, he captained the rugby and soccer teams, and was the fastest boy in the Birmingham schools at 220 and 440 yards, and also a fine long-jumper. Barely having survived a plane crash during the First World War (as an RAF pilot), he became the speediest winger in the land, and one of the most dangerous." He was Villa's regular right-winger until 1930 after beginning in the first team at right-half, behind Charlie Wallace, from whom he learnt some tricks of wing-play. He and Arthur Dorrell were Villa's two first-choice wing-men for the best part of ten years and both went on to play for Port Vale. After retirement York worked in the building trade

YORKE, Dwight
Forward /Midfielder
Born: *Trinidad and Tobago*
Playing career: *Aston Villa, Manchester United, Blackburn Rovers, Birmingham City, Sydney FC, Sunderland (1989-2009)*

The 'Smiling Assassin' joined United for £12.6 million in August 1998 and was a key player in United's Treble-winning season, forming a formidable partnership with Andy Cole. He was eventually sold to Blackburn Rovers at the end of that season for £2 million. Yorke was briefly made player assistant manager at Sunderland during the 2008-2009 season following Roy Keane's departure. Yorke was an integral part of the Villa team to win the League Cup in 1995/96. He is currently the sports ambassador for Trinidad and Tobago, and also appears as a pundit on Sky Sports.

YOUNG, Luke
Full-back
Born: *Harlow*
Playing career: *Tottenham Hotspur, Charlton A, Middlesbrough, Aston Villa, QPR (1997-2014)*

Unrelated to namesake Ashley, Luke Young comes from a talented football family (older brother Neil was also a professional footballer and younger sibling Jake was on the books at West Ham). Having made his England debut three years before,

Young was signed by then Villa manager Martin O'Neill in 2008 and went on to make 88 appearances across three seasons in the Midlands. In all, he played 379 career league games for five different clubs, with all but one of these in the Premier League. Capped seven times by his country, Young has stayed involved in football since retirement as a player. He is now an agent for player consultancy business Pitch Representation.

YOUNG, Willie
Winger
Born: *Glasgow, Scotland*
Playing career: *Arthurlie, Torquay United, Aston Villa, Manchester UnitedTorquay United (1978-)*

A Scottish born winger, Young signed for Villa in 1978 after turning out in the local amateur Midland League. He joined for a fee that was a record for a junior player at the time. Young, a tricky winger, went on to play four times for the Villa before he moved to Devon and Torquay for £10,000. Young was regarded as a player with potential but this promise was never fulfilled due to a plethora of injury problems, ultimately culminating in his early retirement from the game aged 31. After retirement, Young stayed in Devon where he drifted out of the game and worked as a tourism officer.

Dwight Yorke

Photo Credits

We are extremely grateful to the following for the use of their photographs, without which this book would be far less interesting.

We have made every effort to ensure that every image used complies with their own individual copyright requirements. However, please do let us know if we need to make any changes.

A list of the full details including links to the relevant photographers/sites can be found at www.where-are-they-now.co.uk/aston-villa-credits

Aitken - Charlie
By Jonesy702 at English Wikipedia,
Allback, Marcus Frankie Fouganthin
JuanPablo Angel Diego Valenzuela
Brookwood Military Cemetery:
Hobday Memorial
Atkinson, Dalian www.youtube.com
Atkinson, Ron Pontificake
Bakke, Erik commons.wikimedia
Bardsley, Phil commons.wikimedia
Baros, Milan commons.wikimedia
Barry, Gareth commons.wikimedia
Bartelt, Gustavo commons.wikimedia
Bent, Darren commons.wikimedia
Berger, Patrik commons.wikimedia
Bye, Habib commons.wikimedia
de Bilde, Gilles commons.wikimedia
Boateng, George commons.wikimedia
Bosnich, Mark PAPARAZZI
Bouma, Wilfred flickr.com naparazzi
Aston Villa old Stars footiebugs.com
Bremner, Des commons.wikimedia
Byfield, Darren commons.wikimedia
Calderwood, Colin
commons.wikimedia
Carew John flickr.com suetonius
Cole, Carlton Hilton1949
Cole, Joe Vladimir Mayorov
Collymore, Stan vimeo.com
Oulton, Frank
minghamhistory.co.uk
, Neil Rob Crane
, Ulises de la
bleanacional
r, Carlos empgomez
, Jim mmu.ac.uk
ley, Alan Egghead06

Cutler, Neil inky The Wingy
Delaney, Mark commons.wikimedia
Devey, Jack avcards.weebly.com
Draper, Mark Ben Sutherland
Dublin, Dion speakerscorner.co.uk
Ducat, Andy commons.wikimedia
Dunne, Richard Michael Kranewitter
Ehiogu, Ugo flickr.com bensutherland
Enckleman, Peter Jon Candy
Evans, Alun wolvesheroes.com
Fahey, Keith Struway
Farrelly, Gareth lawgazette.co.uk
Foster, Steve commons.wikimedia
Friedel, Brad Dagur Brynjólfsson
Ginola, David Georges Biard
Given, Shay thetelf
Gray, Andy Phil Guest
Graydon, Ray Oosoom
Grayson, Simon BradfordCityFC
Gregory, John Lm10ms7
Guzan, Brad defense.gov
Hadji, Mustapha flickr.com
Harewood, Marlon
Dagur Brynjólfsson
Heard, Pat Tommy Pinball
Heath, Adrian Asan'ny tena
Hendrie, Lee Picture Capital
Heskey, Emile Football.ua
Hitzlsperger, Thomas
mynewsdesk.com
Hughes, Aaron Nick
Hutton, Alan Ronnie Macdonald
James, David Gokulpoovlliyil
Jenas, Jermaine flickr.com irwandy
Johnsen, Ronnie Kjetil Ree
Kachloul, Hassan Jonesy702
Kapengwe, Emment
Times of Zambia Newspaper
Keane, Robbie Vladimir Maiorov
Keown, Martin Ronnie Macdonald
Kiraly, Gabor Ampfinger
Knight, Zat dalli58
Laursen, Martin Dagur Brynjólfsson
Lescott, Joleon Football.ua
Little, Brian Jonesy702
Massie, Alex
Lodge Heart of Midlothian
McAlinden, Bobby
mancinievents.co.uk
McClair, Brian Kjetil Ree
McGrath, Paul Jonesy702
McNaught, Ken Peter Lowe
Mellberg, Olaf Ricardo Alvarez
Morley, Tony Ben Sutherland
Mortimer, Dennis Ben Sutherland
Mwila, Freddie Ace72
Myhill, Boaz Gggrrr
Neilsen, Kent Lars Schmidt
Petrov, Stiliyan commons.wikimedia

Phillips, Kevin Egghead06
Pires, Robert Doha Stadium
Platt, David Egghead06
Romsey, George commons.wikimedia
Regis, Cyrille Ben Sutherland
Reo-Coker, Nigel
Dagur Brynjólfsson
Richardson, Kieran
flickr.com cfcunofficial
Liam Ridgewell commons.wikimedia
Rioch, Bruce Simon Wedege Petersen
Sorenson, Thomas vagueonthehow
Samuel Jlloyd Tasnim News Agency
Schmeichel, Peter mynewsdesk
Scimecia, Riccy Holdenbuckley
Solano, Nobby johnlew123
Southgate, Gareth Kirill Venediktov
Spink, Nigel Marcel Antonisse
Sutton, Chris Jonesy 702
Taylor, Ian Jonesy702
Taylor, Stuart dalli58
Townsend, Andy Marion O'Sullivan
Walters, Mark Jarle Vines
Yorke, Dwight
British High Commission
European Cup Reunion
commons.wikimedia
Ground (page 94) fitzyt
Wembley (page 157) Kolforn
Star (page 164) Brianboru100
Painting (page 183)
Thomas M. M. Hemy

Our Website

We hope that you enjoyed this book. If you like this topic, why not visit our website?

Not only will you be able to keep up to date with changes, you can leave your own comments, memories, or amusing stories.

www.where-are-they-now.co.uk

Printed in Great Britain
by Amazon